MARS
IUPITER
HICA AC HYDROGRAPHICA TABULA. à Pet. Kærio.
QUATUOR
ANNI TEM
PESTATES
VER
AESTAS
AUTUMNUS
HYEMS
NOVA ZEMLA
Oceanus
MEDITER RANEUM
Mare Arabicum
AFRICA
INDIA
MAR DI
MAGALLANICA
TERRA AUSTRALIS INCOGNITA
AMSTELODAMI
Excudebat
Ioannes Ianßonius
DIANÆ TEMPLUM
IUPITER OLYMPICUS
PHAROS

Before the First Fleet

Europeans in Australia 1606–1777

For my grandchildren,
Rohan, Christina, Gillian and Linda

Before the First Fleet

Europeans in Australia 1606–1777

John Kenny

Kangaroo Press

We little guess which deed a future year
May mark to mortals from our passing here.
John Masefield

(from *Early Days*,
courtesy Royal Western Australian
Historical Society)

Front cover

Left: Portrait of Abel Tasman, his wife and daughter by Jacob Gerritsz Cuyp, 1637. Oil on canvas. (Rex Nan Kivell Collection, NK3, National Library of Australia.)

Right: Oswald L. Brett, 'Heemskerck Shoals — Nanuku Reef, N.E. Fiji, 6 February 1643'. Oil on canvas, 1973. Tasman's ships, the *Heemskerck* and *Zeehaen*, sailed from Van Diemen's Land for Batavia, finding their way through these dangerous reefs near Fiji. (Courtesy of Mrs Douglas C. Fonda, Jnr.)

Back: Francois Jacobsz Visscher, 'General Map of Tasman's discoveries in 1642–3 and 1644', *c.* 1670. (Osterreichische Nationalbibliothek, Vienna.)

Back cover

This 'Sirenne', reportedly drawn from life after capture, was a marvel to the eighteenth-century seamen who swore that they saw her. The future scientific age provided proof of no such wonders. (From Louis Renard, *Histoire Naturelle des poissons, ecrivisses et crabes des Indes*, 1718; Mitchell Library, State Library of New South Wales.)

Endpapers

Jan Jansz and Pieter van den Keere, 'Nova Totius Terrarum Orbis Geographica ac Hydrographica Tabula', from *Atlantis Maioris Appendix* (Amsterdam, 1630). (Mitchell Library, State Library of New South Wales, ZM2 100/1639 ?/1.)

First published in 1995 by Kangaroo Press Pty Ltd
3 Whitehall Road Kenthurst NSW 2156 Australia
PO Box 6125 Dural Delivery Centre NSW 2158
Printed in Hong Kong through Colorcraft Limited

ISBN 0 86417 645 7

Contents

Acknowledgments

This book is my husband's. He researched it for four years, both here and in Britain, submitting finished chapters to historians, botanists, zoologists, anthropologists, archaeologists and hydrographers for checking. As a journalist, he had asked questions, sought answers and searched original records in his attempt to find what was known of this continent before the First Fleet.

He died in 1987 leaving the manuscript practically finished, but before choosing illustrations or writing the bibliography. These tasks I have tried to do as John would have wished.

On his behalf, I thank the people and institutions who helped so much.

In England: Mollie Gillen, Dr Judith Diment of the British Museum (Natural History); H.B. Carter, Angela Houstoun, Bridget Spiers, and the Rev. Tom Maidment, vicar of St. Leonard's, Heston, where Sir Joseph Banks is buried as he wished, beneath an unmarked slab in the aisle. The Hakluyt Society granted permission to reprint excerpts from Cook's Journals and the Public Record Office, Kew, allowed quotation. The British Library, the National Maritime Museum, the Captain Cook Birthplace Museum, Middlesbrough, and the Pannett Park Museum, Whitby, were all generous. Alecto Historical Editions also aided.

In Eire: E. Charles Nelson of the Botanic Gardens, Dublin, gave encouragement.

In the U.S.A.: the Australian marine artist, Oswald L. Brett, provided advice and offered freely of his illustrations.

In New Zealand: the Museum of New Zealand (Te Papa Tongarewa) through Eva Yocum, arranged for the Webber portrait of Cook to be lent. The Forest Service and Wildlife Service of New Zealand were helpful in answering questions.

In Australia: Dr Alan Frost gave invaluable aid. His generosity and time will be remembered. I am indebted to so many — to Geoffrey C. Ingleton, to Arthur Weller, chairman of the H.M. Bark Endeavour Foundation, to the Australasian Pioneers' Club and Dick Mackenzie, to the Royal Australian Historical Society and to John Bennett and Professor Brian Fletcher. Emeritus Professor Bernard Smith, Dr Peter Stanbury, Professor Sandy Yarwood, and D.J.G. Griffin, Director of the Australian Museum must have mention.

At the State Library of New South Wales, Russell Doust, Suzanne Mourot, Baiba Berzins, Di Rhodes, Jennifer Broomhead, Maree Jenner and Cheryl Evans gave assistance. Babette Pearson of the Australian Museum, Martin Terry and Jeffrey Mellefont of the Australian National Maritime Museum, Graeme Henderson, Jeremy Green and Patrick Baker of the Western Australian Maritime Museum, and Dianne Reilly of the La Trobe Library, State Library of Victoria were others who helped.

From the National Library of Australia in Canberra, Barbara Perry, Russell Farran, Corinne Collins and Sylvia Carr provided many illustrations and captions. Sonia Barron from the Art Collection, Parliament House, Canberra, was prompt with help.

Lastly, I thank family and friends, who stood by us. They include the late Vaughan Evans, the late Esther Corsellis, my sister Shirley Merchant, Rita and James Gibson, John Frizell, Barbara Sanders, Helen Lavender, Helen Clift, Sheila Cohen, Joyce Burnard, Joyce Bowden, Russell Nugent, Shirley McGlynn, Lynne Turner-Smith and Gillian Osborne. Some checked transparencies, some typed and some helped me check proofs.

The list could be endless but I end it now, apologising for any omissions. My gratitude.

Helen Kenny

Preface

The European exploration of the outer world from the fifteenth to the eighteenth centuries is of abiding interest.

As Europeans developed new ship-building techniques and new instruments to aid in navigation, they were able to break away from littorals and pioneer oceanic navigation. Thereby, they vastly increased geographical knowledge. Diaz's 1488 voyage to the Cape of Good Hope, was followed by Columbus's 1492 crossing of the Atlantic Ocean, which led to the discovery of the Americas. Then came da Gama's voyage to India in 1497–98; and Magellan's circumnavigation of 1515–19. Within the astonishingly short period of one hundred years, Europeans encompassed the world, coming to know its true circumference and the vastness of the Pacific Ocean, and developing a sea-route to the East.

These geographical and navigational achievements laid the basis for the integration of the non-European world into European systems of politics and commerce — that is, for the onset of a fully-fledged European imperialism, which saw Spain and Portugal gain control over much of the Americas and sections of Asia, followed by the Netherlands, Britain and France. Late twentieth-century studies have made abundantly clear the often brutal and deplorable consequences for indigenous people of this imperialism; but oppression and exploration do not constitute the whole story. As well as being oppressed by the newcomers, peoples in the Americas, Africa and Asia also dealt with them to mutual advantage, acquiring their technologies, sometimes their political systems, and — equally significantly — their knowledge of other ways and places.

The discovery of Australia was part of the Europeans' reconnaissance of the outer world, even if in the end the results were not those which had been hoped for. In the early Renaissance, theology and theoretical geography postulated a great southern continent, to provide a counter-balance to the land masses of the Northern Hemisphere, without which the Earth would crash to destruction beyond the sphere of the fixed stars. And analogy of latitudes and climates also suggested that this Terra Australis would be encrusted with minerals, covered with spices, and populated by numerous people having the useful arts and thus constituting a large mart for European goods.

As navigations progressively reduced the area in which the Terra Australis might lie, the real southern continent (Antarctica excepted) slowly took shape, to find a place on maps of the Southern Hemisphere. Called first the Land of Eendracht, then New Holland, then (in its eastern portion) New South Wales, in its nature and ambience this continent was quite other than that Europeans had expected and searched for. With many of its shorelines barren, lacking water and obvious attractions such as spices and minerals, and with its inhabitants exhibiting material culture and social structures so different from European norms as to suggest a primitivism hitherto little encountered, it seemed to offer nothing 'useful'.

However, if initially the discovery of Australia was the occasion of the expression of European preconceptions concerning nature and human-kind, it was also later the occasion for the manifestation of new views. For as the European scientific Enlightenment developed through the seventeenth into eighteenth centuries, so too did new ways of proceeding and recording.

In 1665–66, shortly after its inception, the Royal Society of London issued sets of instructions for the guidance of explorers and travellers, with the object of obtaining materials that would lead to the study of '*Nature* rather than *Books*, and from the Observations, made of the *Phaenomena* and Effects she presents, to compose such a History of Her, as may hereafter serve to build a Solid and Useful Philosophy upon'.

These instructions included the following points:

> 1. To observe the Declination of the *Compass*, or its Variation from the *Meridian* of the place, frequently; marking withal, the *Latitude* and *Longitude* of the place, wherever such Observation is made, as exactly as may be, and setting down the *Method*, by which they made them.
>
> 2. To carry *Dipping Needles* with them, and observe the Inclination of the Needle in like manner.
>
> 3. To remark carefully the Ebbings and Flowings of the Sea, in as many places as they can, together with all the Accidents, Ordinary and Extraordinary, of the Tides.
>
> 4. To make Plotts and Draughts of prospect of Coasts, Promontories, Islands and Ports, marking the Bearings and distances, as neer as they can.
>
> 5. To sound and marke the Depths of Coasts and Ports.
>
> 6. To take notice of the Nature of the Ground at the bottom of the Sea, in all Soundings whether it be Clay, Sand, Rock &c.
>
> 7. To keep a Register of all changes of Wind and Weather at all houres, by night and by day, shewing the point the Wind blows from, whether strong or weak; The Rains, Hail, Snow and the like, the precise times of their beginnings and continuance, especially *Hurricans* and *Spouts*; but above all to take exact care to observe the Trade-Winds...as near and exact as may be.
>
> 8. To observe and record all Extraordinary *Meteors*, Lightnings , Thunders, *Ignes fatui*, Comets, &c., marking still the places and times of their appearing, continuance, &c.
>
> 9. To carry with them good Scales, and Glasse-Violls of a pint or so, with very narrow mouths, which are to be fill'd with Sea-water in different degrees of *Latitude*, as often as they please, and the weight of the Vial full of water taken exactly at every time, and recorded, marking withall the degrees of *Latitude*, and the day of the Month: And that as well of water near the Top; as at a greater Depth.

Nor were travellers to confine themselves to natural phenomena. Robert Boyle, the first Secretary of the Society, further advised them to investigate the productions of lands, and the nature of the people who inhabited them:

> above the ignobler *Productions* of the earth, there must be a careful account given of the *Inhabitants* themselves, both *Natives* and *Strangers*, that have been long settled there: And in particular, their Stature, Shape, Colour, Features, Strength, Agility, Beauty (or want of it), Complexions, Hair, Dyet, Inclinations, and Customs that seem not due to Education. As to their Women (besides the other things) may be observed their Fruitfulness or Barrenness; their hard or easy Labour, &c. And both in Women and Men must be taken notice if what diseases they are subject to, and, in these whether there be any symptome, or any other Circumstance, that is unusual and remarkable.

One consequence of this approach was the development of scientific navigation, as exemplified by Cook's use of lunar tables to calculate longitude on his first voyage, and on his second, chronometers — a development paralleled by a previously unknown accuracy in charting.

Another was a new way of interpreting natural phenomena. As explorers and travellers attended to such injunctions, a large body of knowledge about oceanography, geography, products, natural history and peoples accumulated. By the early eighteenth century, scientists were seeking to systematise this knowledge. The most significant contribution to this massive task came from the work of the great Swedish naturalist Carl

Linnaeus, who in the 1730s produced his botanical system of classification. Developed with the express purpose of reducing the botanical world to order, Linnaeus' system (or a variation thereof) was soon being applied to zoology. Simultaneously, the bases of modern geology were laid, with the recognition of stratification, and the investigation of fossils.

'Natural Philosophers' also applied this systematising instinct to the study of human beings. As knowledge of peoples very different in their social organisations and moreover who lived in the far reaches of the world accumulated, so too did these proto-scientists classify them. By the later eighteenth century, these had arrived at a paradigm of social development. Humankind, they held, exhibited four fundamental stages of civilization:

1. the hunter/gatherer stage, where people roamed nomadically in search of food, lived in small family units and, sharing much property in common, possessed only rudimentary tools and utensils;

2. the pastoral stage, in which people lived in one locality and kept domestic animals, and, pursuing 'cottage' industries such as cheese-making, spinning and weaving, began to acquire significant individual property;

3. the agricultural stage, in which families expanded their domestic economies to encompass their farm and, trading its productions, further increased their private property; and

4. the manufacturing or commercial stage, when urban centres emerged, and nations traded their goods beyond their borders.

Expansion of class, educational, political and religious structures went hand in hand with progress from one of these stages to the next — so that the apogee of 'civilisation' was a Western European nation exhibiting a 'rational' religion, a mixed (i.e., partly democratic) form of government, an international economy, and a love of literature and the arts.

Slanted as it was to find all other nations inferior to European ones, such a paradigm nonetheless did offer the potential to view non-European cultures to some extent in their own terms. Between Dampier's observation that the Australian Aborigines were 'the miserablest People in the World...setting aside their Humane Shape, they differ but little from Brutes', and Cook's that:

> From what I have said of the Natives of New-Holland they may appear to some to be the most wretched people upon Earth, but in reality they are far more happier than we Europeans; being wholy unacquainted not only with the superfluous but the necessary Conveniences so much sought after in Europe, they are happy in not knowing the use of them...

...there lies the watershed of Enlightenment thought: and with Cook we have what is in its sensitivities recognisably a modern outlook.

The European reconnaissance of Australia from 1606 to 1777, then, is inextricably bound up with these marked changes in habits of exploring and recording, and in outlook. It is with this reconnaissance that John Kenny's *Before the First Fleet* is concerned. Rather than indulge in unresolvable speculation, Kenny keeps to what can authentically be known. Accordingly, he wisely does not notice the possibility of Portuguese or Spanish contact with the Australian continent in the sixteenth century: the evidence for such contact is still too obscure or uncertain for us to believe confidently in it. On the other hand, he does attend to the visits by French navigators in the eighteenth century. This focus is one of the study's strengths, for despite all the histories of the beginnings of European Australia, we are still too little aware of just how much the French also went in search of the southern continent, and with what results.

Before the First Fleet has other virtues. For the first time, it brings together the original descriptions, charts, views and drawings and paintings of this phase of European discovery; and to these it adds modern understandings of what fauna and flora the explorers saw. Accordingly, it offers materials to those interested variously in geography, botany, biology, anthropology and culture contact. This work should prove a rich mine for those interested in Australia's past.

Readers will see at once that Kenny has put this work together from what is essentially a European perspective. The nature of the surviving records makes this inevitable. Still, in having this stance, the study nonetheless acknowledges that there were two cultures in contact about Australian shores; and it provides some valuable materials for our understanding of Aboriginal life before the advent of Europeans.

Having generous help from experts in various fields (which he acknowledges freely), John Kenny worked on *Before the First Fleet* for four years, but unfortunately died before he was able to complete it. His family and Kangaroo Press have thought it deserving of publication. In a few places, it has not proven possible to locate the source of quotations. If informed of them the publisher will see that due acknowledgement is given in any subsequent edition. It may also be that some of Kenny's details are now superseded; again any corrections will be gratefully received. Otherwise, the work is as accurate as conscientious editing has been able to make it.

John Kenny had an abiding interest in Australian History. *Before the First Fleet* is a striking remembrance of that interest.

Alan Frost
School of History
La Trobe University
July 1994

Introduction

This is a digest of what Europeans knew of the continent now called Australia and its indigenous people before the First Fleet arrived in 1788 to establish a British penal settlement. As well as reporting explorers' discoveries of coastlines, the digest records what they thought of the country, their experiences with the Aborigines and with the hitherto unknown animals and plants that they saw.

Europeans knew Australia from the beginning of the seventeenth century but scorned it as barren for almost 200 years. They were to learn it was the fifth and smallest continent and the largest island; the driest continent; that its mountains and rivers were the smallest.

European exploration of Australia in this period exhibits two main phases — that of the Dutch and English on the northern, western and south-eastern coasts, mostly in the first half of the seventeenth century; and that of the English and French, mainly on the eastern and southern coasts in the second half of the eighteenth century. The explorers recorded what they learnt in a mass of information, in the journals, ships' logs, charts and reports to employers or governments that sent them there. This digest follows the chronological and geographical phases. It is further divided according to topics (e.g. ethnography, zoology, botany). Accordingly, it presents materials of interest to people working in various disciplines.

The sources of major quotations are given in the text and listed in these references. Those of minor ones are listed in the bibliography. In the commentary, distances, whether on land or at sea are given in kilometres; all should be regarded as approximate. Older measures have been retained in quotations.

Conversion table

1 mile = 1.61 kilometres
1 nautical mile = 1 minute of latitude at the earth's centre = 1.852 kilometres
1 league = 3 miles = 4.83 kilometres
1 Dutch 'mile' = 4.47 English miles
1 kilometre = 0.621 miles
1 fathom = 6 feet = 1.828 metres

Part I: Patterns of Exploration

1

The Dutch and English Period, 1606–1756

Whether or not various Asian peoples visited Australia in its pre-historic period, only the ancestors of the Aborigines permanently settled it. Whether there was a single migration, or there were several migrations, remains a matter of debate.

The Europeans long believed that a fifth continent existed in the Southern Hemisphere to balance the northern continents. This belief was given currency in the late thirteenth and early fourteenth centuries by the accounts of Marco Polo, the Venetian traveller. He told of a country to the south of Asia with its own king, of an extensive and rich province with considerable trade and abundant food. Cartographers made maps in the sixteenth century showing Terra Australis Incognita (the unknown Southland) extending across the southern oceans from below the Cape of Good Hope, the southern extremity of Africa, to Cape Horn, the southern extremity of America, and as far north as New Guinea. One map showed Marco Polo's 'Beach the golden province' south of Java (now part of Indonesia). Gradually, translators and paraphrasers changed Marco Polo's Locae, a country he named to the south of India to Locach, Boeach and, finally, Beach, which led Europeans to search for beaches of gold.

For centuries, dreaming of spices, precious metals and trade, Europeans explored the southern oceans for the Terra Australis. The Portuguese and Spaniards came to the near north of what is now called Australia early in the sixteenth century, the Dutch later. The Dutch were the first to know the real Terra Australis, early in the seventeenth century. The British came to know it in the second half of the eighteenth century. Neither found it to be the continent they sought. Although James Cook, the English explorer, in three voyages, disproved the existence of a southern continent where Europeans thought it should be above Antarctica, Australia was not accepted as the Great Southland until early in the nineteenth century. Indeed, Europeans did not choose to settle it for 182 years. (By contrast, the Spaniards, seeking and getting treasure, conquered Mexico, and the rich empire of the Aztecs, within 30 years of Columbus's discovery of America in 1492.)

The Dutch began to establish themselves in the East Indies in the last years of the sixteenth century. Then, in 1602, amalgamating a number of older ones, merchants formed a new company to trade there. This was the Verenidge Nederlandsche Geoctroyeerde Oostindische Compagnie (United Netherlands Chartered East Indian Company) or VOC. Progessively, this company gained control of spice production in the eastern islands of the Indonesian archipelago, and it became the foremost naval and commercial power in the region. The autocratic directors in the Netherlands were known as the Heren XVII (Seventeen Gentlemen). For nearly two centuries the VOC had the functions of a government in the East Indies, with a Governor-General assisted by a Council of India; a navy of 40 warships, an army of 10 000 soldiers; the right to make war, enter into treaties, make colonies and coin money. It was the directors' policy to put people

Title page from Gerard and Cornelis de Jode's *Specvlvm Orbis Terrae 1597.* In the right-hand lower corner is a strange beast — which is perhaps a marsupial with twins in the pouch. (British Library.)

The VOC symbol and the Prince Flag appear in this illustration by Geoffrey C. Ingleton for *Heemskerck Shoals*, the poem by Robert D. FitzGerald, published by the Mountainside Press in 1949. (Mitchell Library, State Library of New Wales.)

under the dominance of the 'High and Majestic States of the United Netherlands'. Foreigners had to go to them cap in hand. Inferiors addressed superiors with utmost deference, such as 'Most Noble, Wise, Provident and Very Discreet Gentlemen'; as 'High Mightinesses'; or as 'Lords and Masters'. They signed themselves as 'Your Worships' Servant to Command'.

So great was the VOC's concern with trade and profits that merchant sailors and explorers' ships had supercargos (merchants) in their complements, who had more authority than skippers. The Dutch had initiated the modern managerial practice of administration by committees or councils. It applied in their ships, the supercargos presiding; councils made all major decisions, including changes of ships' courses. The VOC told explorers' landing parties to 'return with something commercial'; overlong voyages of curiosity were disliked; time was money; they wanted quick returns.

The VOC had an armada of 200 merchant-men, known as East Indiamen, traversing the Atlantic Ocean to the south, crossing east through the Indian Ocean to the East Indies and beyond. For much of its history, the company earned annual dividends ranging from never less than 12 per cent up to 60 per cent. However, after two centuries it had run its course. Among other reasons, corruption, mismanagement and Britain's ascendancy had reduced it to bankruptcy by the end of the eighteenth century. The Netherlands government took over its assets and affairs.

In 1606, Dutch and Spanish ships approached northern Australia from the east and the west. These voyages led to the first known European sighting of the fifth continent, and brought it into history.

The VOC had organised its first exploratory expedition from Bantam in Western Java, then their headquarters in the East Indies. William Jansz, as

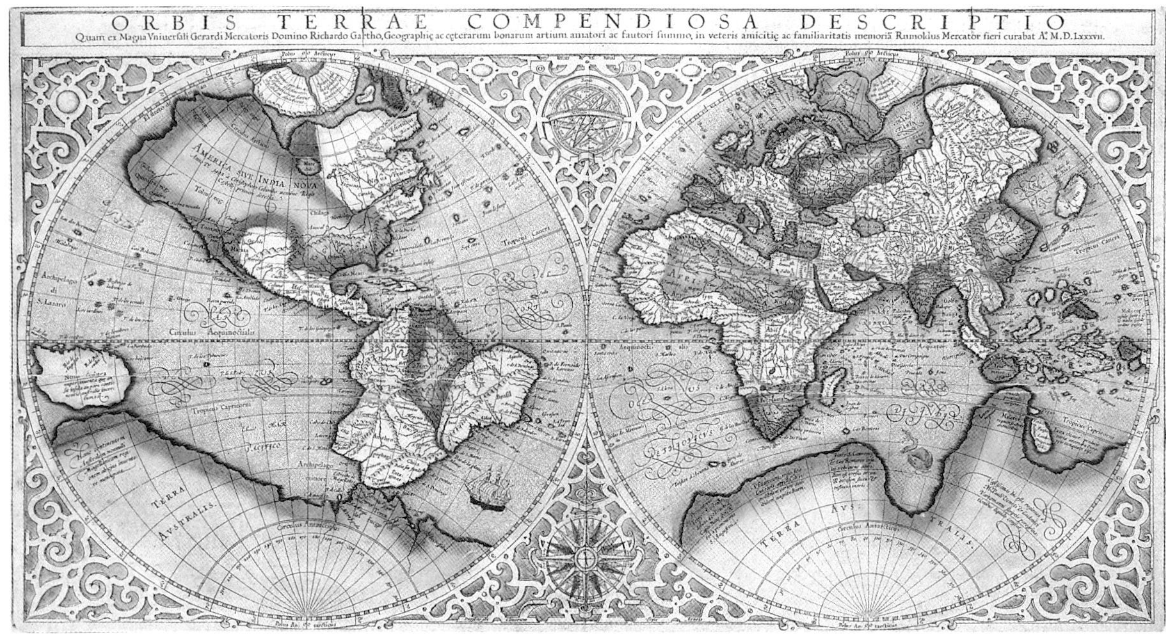

Gerard Mercator, 'Orbis Terrae Compendiosa Descriptio', from *Atlas sive Cosmographicae* (Duisburg, 1587). Mercator, a Flemish geographer, introduced new principles of map projection. This famous map is an example. (Mitchell Library, State Library of New South Wales.)

skipper, and Jan Lodewijksz, as supercargo in the *Duyfken* (Little Dove), were searching for gold expected to be found 'in abundance' in the beaches of the Isla del Oro, a Spanish name for northern New Guinea, which the Portuguese discovered in 1526–27. Jansz discovered and coasted southern New Guinea and, without realising that it was separate, sighted the north-eastern coast of Australia, probably in March, on the western side of Cape York Peninsula.

The sighting was in the vicinity of Pennefather River, fewer than 185 kilometres south of Cape York. Jansz anchored a few miles farther down the coast at the northern side of Albatross Bay, the port of today's Weipa bauxite deposits. At a prominence about 380 kilometres south of Cape York Jansz turned back, naming it Cape Keer-Weer (Turnagain). On the way to Cape York he anchored at Port Musgrave, north of Albatross Bay, for water. There, Aborigines fatally speared a crewman at the Wenlock River. Jansz drew the first chart of the Australian coast and islands, coral reefs and openings along

'The Duyfhen in the Gulf of Carpentaria' was published in the *Picturesque Atlas of Australasia* in 1886. (Mitchell Library, State Library of New South Wales.)

the western side of Torres Strait, between Australia and New Guinea. Although he did not see a strait he suspected one was there.

The Spaniards came from Peru to search for the Southland. Their commander, Pedro Fernández de Quirós, thought that he discovered it in April 1606 when he found what is now Vanuatu, which he called Austrialia del Espíritu Santo (Austrialia of the Holy Ghost; later New Hebrides) in honour of King Philip of the House of Hapsburg of Austria.

One of Quirós' captains, Luis Váez de Torres, of the *San Pedrico* (St Peter), became separated from him and sailed for Manila in the Philippines. He explored the southern coast of New Guinea and in October steered west through 200 kilometres of shallows, reefs and islands between Cape York and New Guinea, to find that a strait existed between the Coral and Arafura Seas. Torres was in Australian waters almost a month and perhaps landed on islands within sight of the mainland. His chart of the ship's track is lost, so which of the channels he sailed through is not known. He then went around the western extremity of New Guinea to Manila.

The Spanish authorities made no immediate use of Torres' discoveries, but filed his charts out of the sight of other nations' mariners who might have made use of them. Subsequently, six VOC explorers looked for an opening to the Pacific but the enigma of the western approach — its contrary winds and tides — baffled them; so that VOC maps showed Australia and New Guinea as connected until the late eighteenth century.

While the Spaniards had no further role in discoveries near Australia, the Dutch did. In 1610 Hendrik Brouwer, later a VOC Governor-General, suggested that the company's ships take what he thought would be a better and faster outward route from Holland to the Indies. Previously, ships had sailed north-east from the Cape of Good Hope and through the equatorial doldrums; the ravages of scurvy, resulting from improper diets on this long voyage, took heavy toll of crew. Brouwer's suggested route was due east from the Cape for almost 5300 kilometres in the favourable westerly winds of the Roaring Forties, then north with south-easterlies 2400 kilometres to the Indies. Sailing late in 1610 to test the feasibility of his ideas, Brouwer reached the East Indies in six months, about half the usual time. The VOC adopted the route formally in 1616.

As it was then impossible to calculate longitude at sea precisely, this route had the potential to bring captains who delayed turning north to the west coast

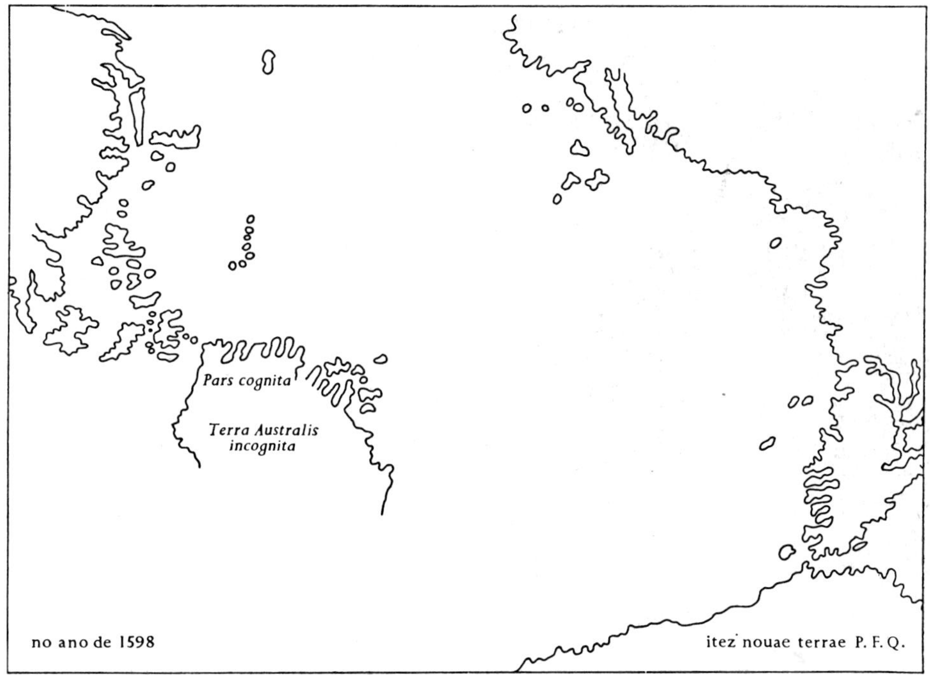

Fernando Quirós. Redrawn chart of the Pacific Ocean, 1598. (Courtesy Dr C. Jack-Hinton.)

Hendrik Brouwer, engraving after M. Balen, 1726. (Australian National Maritime Museum.)

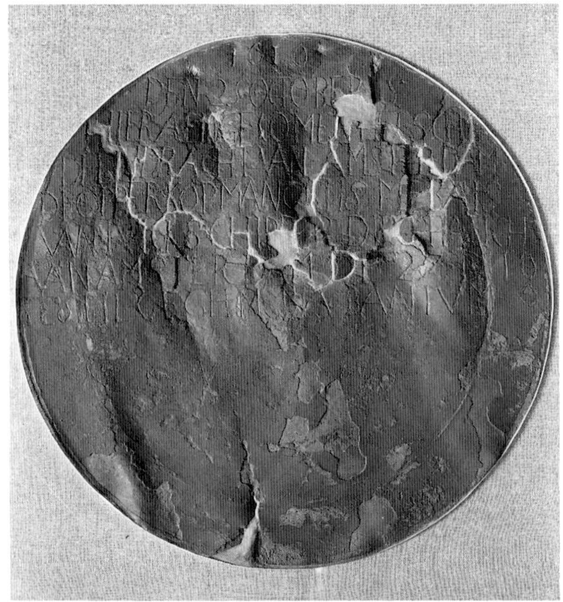

Dirck Hartochsz, pewter plate (1616). (Rijksmuseum, Amsterdam.)

of Australia. The first recorded instance occurred later, in 1616. As well as being a landmark, the coast soon became a hazard to navigation, as the VOC learnt from five shipwrecks. Merchantmen came across the Indian Ocean to landfalls ranging from Cape Leeuwin, at the south-western extremity, to places almost halfway up the western coast. They knew it as a vast, new land but did not know it was a continent.

The next 28 years, from 1616 to 1644, was the great period of Dutch discoveries of the western, northern and southern coasts of Australia. Twenty-one merchantmen made haphazard landfall — by accidents of navigation and charting; by ships overshooting the turning point to the north, being blown off course, stranded or wrecked; or by ships searching for wrecks. Their discoveries extended over 3200 kilometres of coast from Nuyts Archipelago in the Great Australian Bight on the South Australia coast to Port Walcott, now Cossack, the port for Roebourne on the north-western coast of Western Australia. In general, the discoverers showed little curiosity about the uninviting landscapes they observed; their concern was getting to port.

The Dutch discoverers identified and charted but did not explore five regions on the southern, western and north-western coasts over twelve years. They named them after people and ships. Many of the ships were named after Dutch communities.

1616: **Eendracht** (Unity, a ship) **Land** in the region of Shark Bay. Dirck Hartochsz, the skipper, was the first European to see and land on the western coast at an island, which bears his name, at the entrance to Shark Bay.

1619: **Edel Land** in the region of Swan River; after supercargo Jacob d'Edel, of the merchantmen *Dordrecht* and *Amsterdam* (cities' names).

Top right: Ptolemaic world map from *Cosmographia* (Ulm, 1482), showing the supposed continent spanning the Southern Hemisphere. (British Library, London.)

Right: Abraham Ortelius, 'Typvs Orbis Terrarvm', from *Theatrvm Orbis Terrarvm* (Antwerp, 1570). In this map the imagined southern continent swept upwards towards the equator, its north-western coast being marked with names such as Maletyr, Lvcach and Beach. (Reproduced with permission from the Nan Kivell Collection, National Library of Australia.)

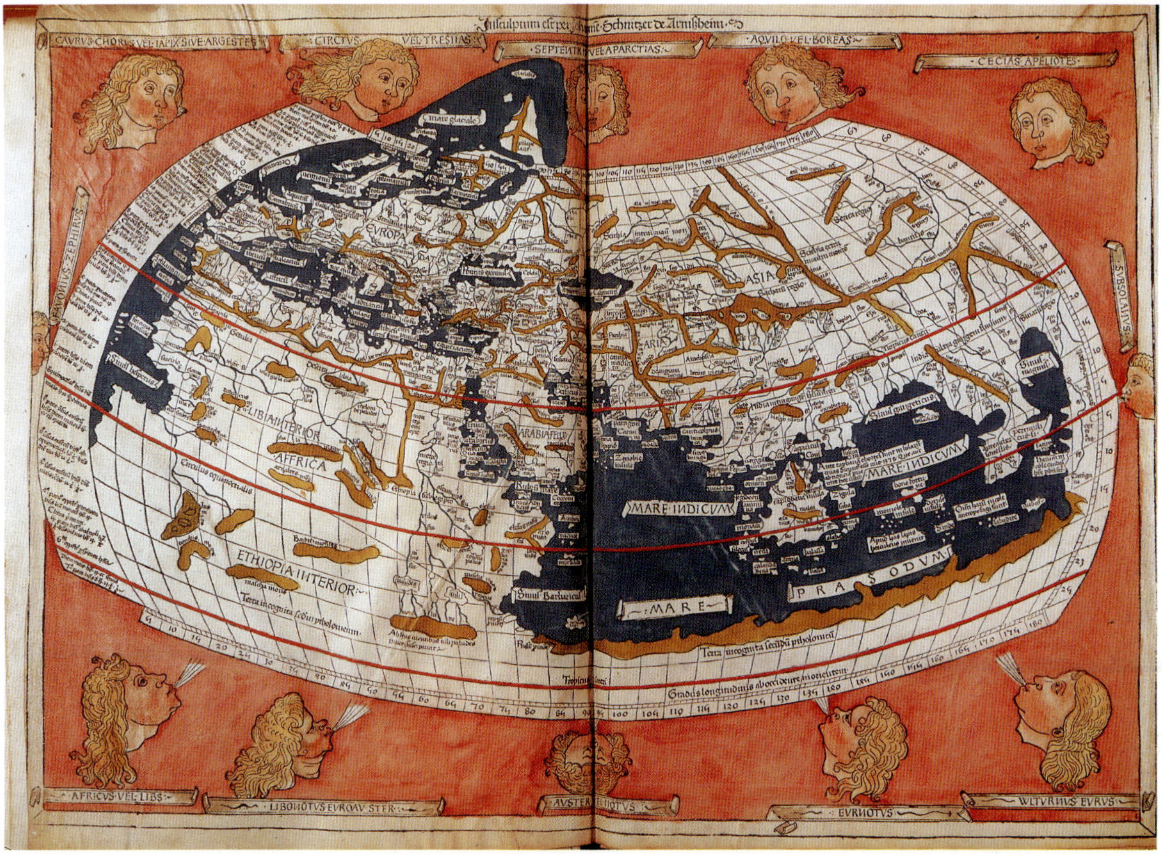
CAVRVS CHORVS VEL IAPIX SIVE ARGESTES
CIRCIVS VEL TRESIAS
SEPTENTRIO VEL APARCTIAS
AQVILO VEL BOREAS
CECIAS APELIOTES
FAVONIVS ZEPHIRVS
SVBSOLANVS
EVROPA
ASIA
LIBIA INTERIOR
AFRICA
ETHIOPIA INTERIOR
ARABIA FELIX
MARE INDICVM
MARE PRASODVM
AFRICVS VEL LIBS
LIBONOTVS EVROAVSTER
AVSTER NOTVS
EVRNOTVS
VVLTVRNVS EVRVS

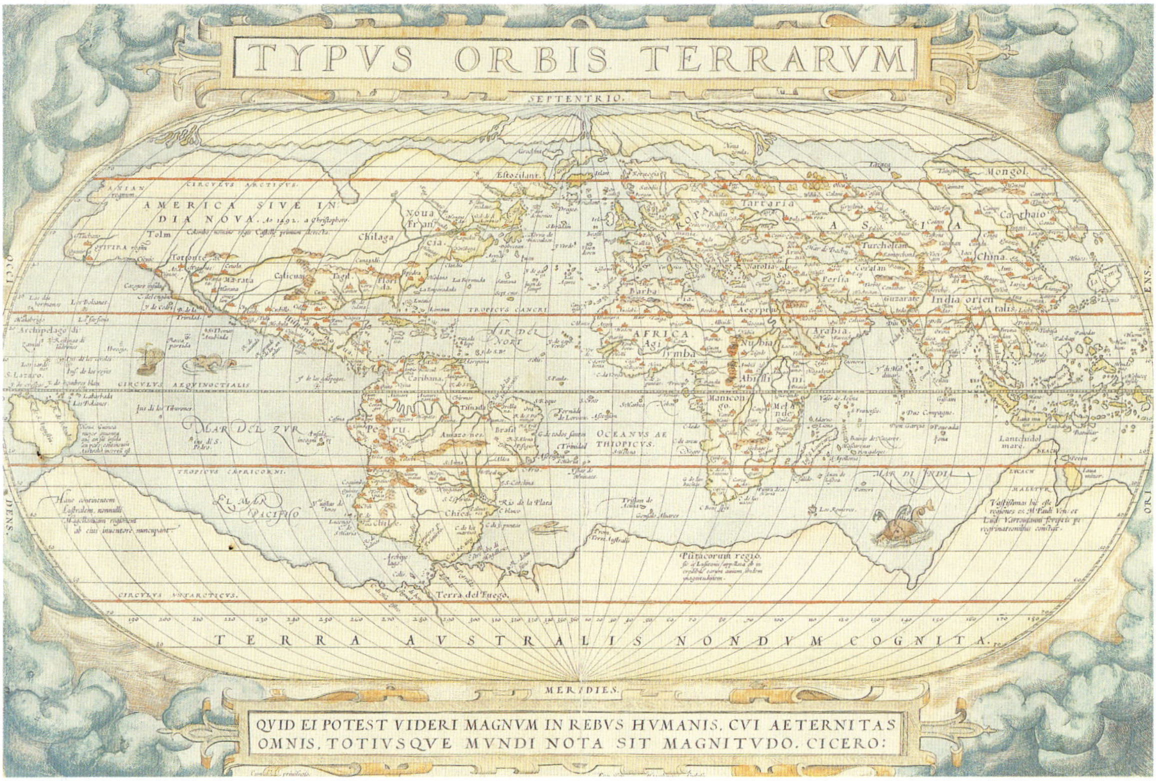
TYPVS ORBIS TERRARVM
SEPTENTRIO.
AMERICA SIVE INDIA NOVA
Tartaria
ASIA
Mongol
China
Persia
Arabia
India orientalis
AFRICA
TROPICVS CANCRI
CIRCVLVS AEQVINOCTIALIS
MAR DEL ZVR
OCEANVS AETHIOPICVS
TROPICVS CAPRICORNI
MAR DI INDIA
Terra del Fuego
CIRCVLVS ANTARCTICVS
TERRA AVSTRALIS NONDVM COGNITA.
MERIDIES.
QVID EI POTEST VIDERI MAGNVM IN REBVS HVMANIS, CVI AETERNITAS
OMNIS, TOTIVSQVE MVNDI NOTA SIT MAGNITVDO. CICERO:

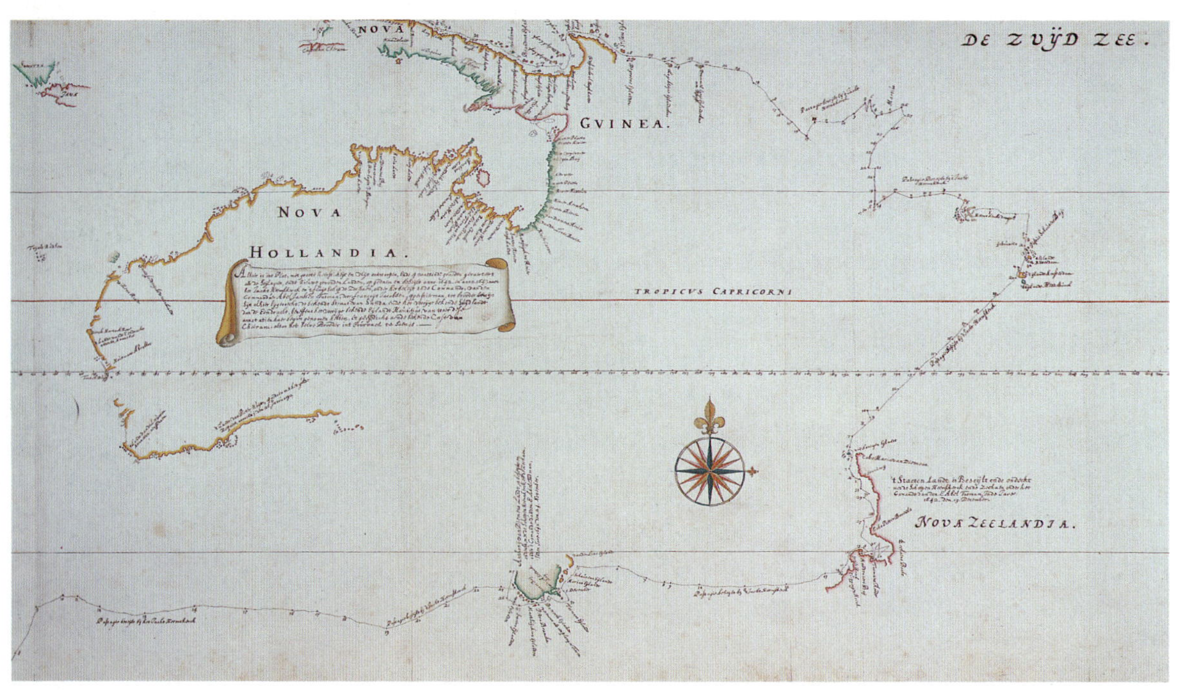

DE ZUYD ZEE.
NOVA
GUINEA.
NOVA
HOLLANDIA.
TROPICUS CAPRICORNI
NOVÆ ZEELANDIA.

INDIA quæ ORIENTALIS dicitur, ET INSVLÆ ADIACENTES.
PERSIÆ PARS
INDIA INTRA GANGEM
INDOSTAN
INDIA EXTRA GANGEM
SIAM
CAMBODIA
OCEANVS CHINENSIS.
INSVLÆ PHILIPPINÆ.
MINDANAO
BORNEO
CELEBES
Archipelago de S. Lazaro.
MARE INDICVM.
JAPON
D. LAVRENTIO REAL

1622: **Leeuwin** (Lioness) **Land** in the region of Cape Leeuwin. The skipper's name is not known.

1627: **Pieter Nuyts Land**, the western part of the southern coast. Nuyts was a member of the Council of India and passenger in the *Gulden Zeepard* (Golden Seahorse). Matthew Flinders, the renowned hydrographer and first circumnavigator of the continent, named Nuyts Archipelago in the Great Australian Bight in 1802.

Anonymous, Chart of the *Arnhem*'s discoveries (1623) from the *Van der Hem atlas*. (Osterreichische Nationalbibliothek, Vienna.)

Top left: Francois Jacobsz Visscher, 'General Map of Tasman's discoveries in 1642–43 and 1644', *c.* 1670. (Osterreichische Nationalbibliothek, Vienna.)

Left: Willem Jansz Blaeu, 'India quae Orientalis dicitur et Insvlae Adjacentes', from *Novus Atlas*, Amsterdam, 1635. (Dixson Library, State Library of New South Wales.)

1628: **De Witt's Land** in the region of Roebourne on the north-western coast; Gerrit Frederikszoon de Witt was skipper of the *Vyagen* (a commune's name).

On the other hand, all the discoveries on the northern coast and in Tasmania, and most of those on the north-western coast, came as the result of deliberate exploration. Altogether, explorers traversed these coasts for more than twelve months. The more active Governors-General were curious about the northern coast and the Great Southland to the south and between 1623 and 1756 organised six expeditions. However, the explorers made significant discoveries only in the first 21 years. They named four regions but did not give a name to Cape York because they thought it was part of New Guinea.

1623: **Arnhem Land** (a commune's name), which remains the name of the north-eastern part of the Northern Territory. Willem van Coolsteerdt was skipper of the *Arnhem*.

1636: **Van Diemen's Land**, the northern part of the Northern Territory; named after Anthoonij van Diemen, the most expansionist of Governors-General (1636–45). Pieter Pieterszoon was supercargo and commander of the ship *Cleen* (new) *Amsterdam*. The name is not now on maps.

1642: **Van Diemen's Land** (now Tasmania). Abel Tasman was the VOC's foremost navigator; he had two ships with him, *Heemskerck* (a commune's name) and *Zeehaen* (Sea Cock). Tasman rewarded the crewmen who first saw Tasmania with three pieces of eight (three Spanish dollars, each dollar consisting of eight reals) and a can of *arrack* (a potent spirit made in the East from fermented juices of coco and other palms). Tasman wrote in his journal:

> This land the first land in the South Sea that we have encountered is still known to no European people, so we have given this land the name of Anthoonij van Diemen's land in Honour of the Hon. the Governor General, our high superior, who sent us out to make this discovery, the Islands lying around it as many as are known to us we have named after the Hon. Councillors of India, as can be perceived by the chart which is made of them. (Sharp, 73)

Tasman charted 560 kilometres of coast from Macquarie Harbour on the western coast to St

'Seventeenth Century Dutch Naval Vessel...The Small War Yacht, *Heemskerck* showing the bow in detail', by Geoffrey C. Ingleton. From *Heemskerck Shoals* by Robert D. FitzGerald, The Mountainside Press, 1949. (Mitchell Library, State Library of New South Wales.)

'Seventeenth Century Dutch Naval Vessel...' The *Zeehaen*, companion ship on Abel Tasman's voyage of 1642. Illustration by Geoffrey C. Ingleton from *Heemskerck Shoals*, by Robert D. FitzGerald, The Mountainside Press, 1949. (Mitchell Library, State Library of New South Wales.)

Patrick's Head beyond Freycinet Peninsula on the eastern coast, having spent ten days there.

In 1644 New Holland displaced Eendracht Land as the VOC's main name for the continent. The VOC originally gave this name to Tasman's discoveries in 1644 from Melville and Bathurst Islands, off the Northern Territory, to Point Cloates, south of North West Cape, Western Australia. The continent became widely known by that name until the name Australia displaced it in the nineteenth century.

By 1623 the VOC was well-enough established to organise a second expedition to northern Australia. The directors had an inkling of Torres' passage through the strait, which, if found, would offer a new and shorter route to the Pacific and South America. Jan Carstensz in the *Pera* (a commune's name) and his subordinate, Van Coolsteerdt, in the *Arnhem*, tried to find Torres Strait and explored to the south of New Guinea, to the Gulf of Carpentaria and Cape York. Carstensz could find only shallows in the strait on the western side, which he described as a 'drooge bocht' (shallow bight). He traversed the eastern coast of the gulf a little further south than Jansz but not did go as far as the gulf's base. Van Coolsteerdt discovered Arnhem Land, the western side of the gulf, on the voyage home to the Indies.

Not knowing of the gulf's base, the VOC wondered what was between Cape York on the east and Arnhem Land on the west — channels or passages to the Southern Ocean, west to Eendracht Land or east to the Pacific Ocean. In 1636 van Diemen sent Gerrit Thomaszoon Pool in the *Cleen Amsterdam* and *Wesel* to resume the search for Torres Strait and follow the coast of the Gulf from where

Carstenz left off westward to Eendracht Land. This expedition reached the southern coast of New Guinea, where Pool and others were killed. It did not thereafter get further eastward than Arnhem Land.

Van Diemen deferred the Gulf question and broadened his horizons, to contemplate the Great Southland's lying in the unknown Pacific Ocean in the latitudes of the 'gold and silver-rich provinces of Peru, Chile, Monomotapa or Soffala'; and in 1642 mounted an expedition to discover it. Van Diemen gave the command of this expedition to Abel Janszoon Tasman, who sailed from Batavia (now Jakarta) with two ships, the *Zeehaen* and the *Heemskerck* in August. Tasman first crossed the Indian Ocean west to Mauritius, then made a great sweep eastwards between 40°S and 50°S latitude. This meant that he went too far south to see the Australian mainland. However, he did discover Tasmania, which he named Van Diemen's Land. Turning north, Tasman rounded Tasman Peninsula to North Bay, where he stayed for four days. On 5 December he sailed east into the Pacific, to discover New Zealand, Tonga and Fiji, returning along the northern coast of New Guinea to Batavia. Thus Tasman circumnavigated Australia without seeing it. By doing so, however, he established the continent's southern and eastern limits and showed it was separate from any Great Southland to the south and the east. What he found, neither trade nor treasure, was of no value to the VOC, which querulously considered him not to have explored thoroughly enough.

Anthoonij (Antonio) van Diemen, engraving after M. Balen, 1726. (Australian National Maritime Museum.)

Tasman's instructions had allowed him alternatives. He chose to follow an easterly course and turn northward in the longitude of the Solomon Islands. An imponderable of history is the consequences that could have followed a choice to sail no further eastward than the islands of St Peter and St Francis in Nuyts Archipelago in the Great Australian Bight. Then he would have turned northward to follow the coast eastward to see whether it joined the known western side of Cape York or was separated from it by channels or if a passage existed from the Indian Ocean to the South Sea to provide a shorter route to Chile.

Van Diemen wanted to send a more persistent explorer than Tasman to search for a passage to South America but the Heren XVII would not agree. The VOC gave no more thought to ideas which might have led to discovery of the eastern coast. Van Diemen returned to the enigmas of Torres Strait and a passage through the Gulf of Carpentaria to the south.

Van Diemen sent Tasman off again in 1644 in three ships — the *Zeemeeuw* (Seagull), *Limmen* (Lime) and *Bracq* (a type of dog). If Tasman was able to sail through Torres Strait he was to follow the eastern coast of Southland to Van Diemen's Land, then to the islands of St Peter and St Francis in the Great Australian Bight and complete the circumnavigation of the continent from the opposite direction of that of 1642. Torres Strait baffled Tasman as much as it had others, so he turned to explore the northern and western coasts. He proved the Gulf of

Carpentaria existed by traversing and charting a continuous coast from Cape York to Point Cloates on the west, a distance of more than 4185 kilometres and 640 kilometres — more than Cook was to chart on the eastern coast in 1770. His main discoveries were the coast westward from Gilbert River, Groote Eylandt, Crocodile Islands, the western extremity of Coburg Peninsula, Van Diemen Gulf and westward of Melville Island to Port Hedland. He also confirmed that the Southland was a continent and not, as some cartographers speculated, a series of islands.

Despite Tasman's convincing evidence that Cape York and Arnhem Land were connected, the notion of a divided continent persisted into the beginning of the nineteenth century. William Dampier, the Englishman who was on the western coast in 1688 and 1699 and knew of Tasman's discoveries, had a hydrographer's suspicion that the size of the tides on the north-western coast — the greatest in the continent — might mean a passage existed in the south into 'the great S[outh] Sea Eastward' (Dampier, 1906, 433).

Tasman is commemorated in the names of Tasmania (since 1855) and of the Tasman Sea (since 1890). The State Library of New South Wales has, in its Mitchell Library, a map known as the Tasman Map, which is one of its treasures. With Tasman's assistance, VOC cartographers composed a map of discoveries up to his time, practically all the coast from Cape York westward and south to Nuyts Archipelago, a distance of 7200 kilometres. This map hypothetically completed the continent with a line following the unknown part of it along the curve of the bight to Tasmania and then connecting Tasmania to the continent with a line which bulged on the eastern coast to correspond with the known bulge on the western coast. It connected Cape York with

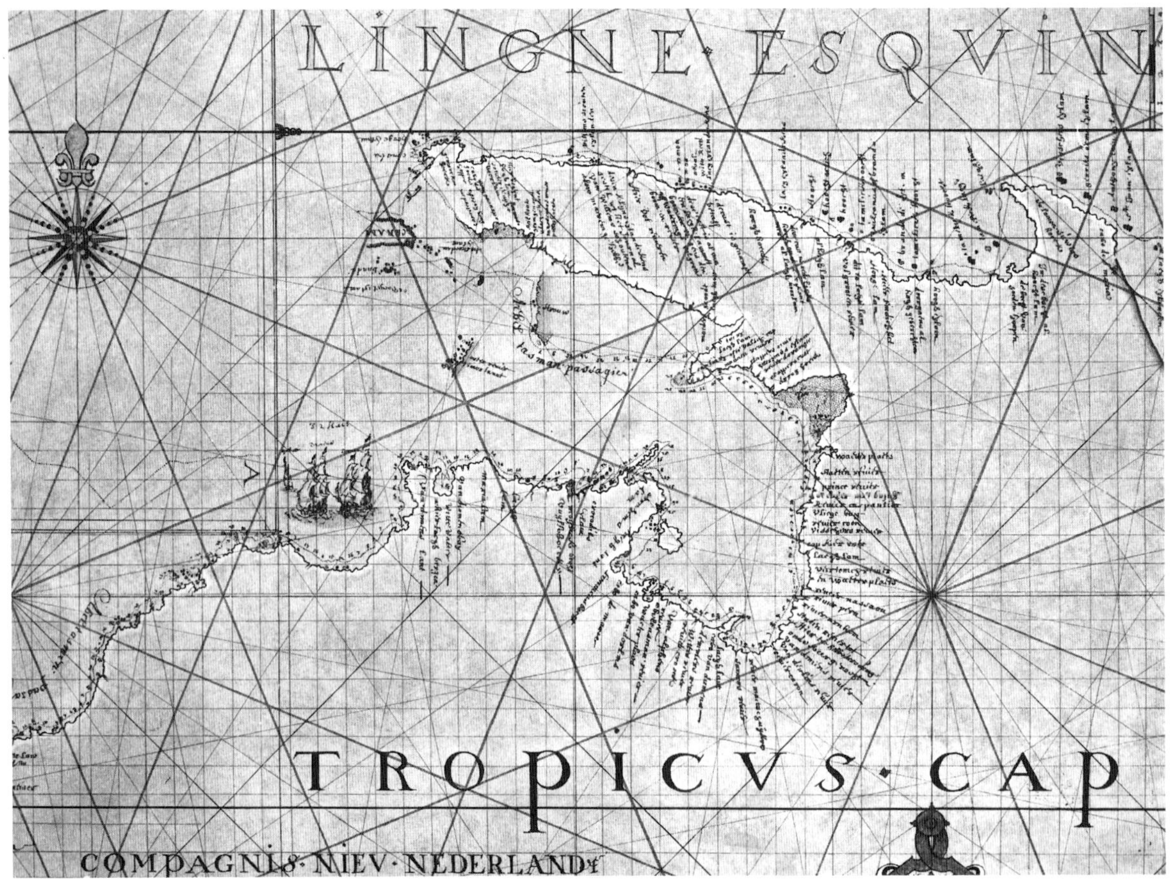

Anonymous, 'Tasman's 1644 route along the northern coasts of Australia, from the 'Tasman' map (*c.* 1695)'. (Mitchell Library, State Library of New South Wales.)

Herman Moll, 'Capt Dampier's New Voyage to New Holland &c in 1699', from William Dampier, *A Voyage to New Holland*, London, 1729. (British Library, London.)

New Ireland. The eastern coast bulged much farther than it actually does but the concept of the cartographers' imagination was acceptably like the continent. Prince Roland, of Paris, who bought the map in 1891, expressed a wish that it should eventually come to Australia and it did in 1933. A superb marble mosaic of the map measuring 4 x 5.5 metres, is in the floor of the vestibule of the library.

Tasman's achievements were memorialised in the mid-seventeenth century in marble and copper mosaics of the eastern and western hemispheres of the globe set in the floor of the central hall of the Amsterdam City Hall (built 1648–50, now destroyed). The eastern hemisphere, 623 centimetres in diameter, included Australia as Nova Hollandia. The depiction of the continent was similar to that of the Tasman Map, except on the eastern coast, where the coastline is almost vertical from Tasmania to New Guinea and 'Terra Espiritu Santo' (New Hebrides) is shown as part of it.

Tasman's two expeditions effectively ended the short period of VOC discoveries of the Australian continent. These discoveries evoked none of the exhilaration of the Spanish discovery of the Americas. Nothing was forthcoming from the explorers — no profit or promise of it, no passage to the Pacific, only reports of 'the most arid and barren region that could be found anywhere on earth'. The VOC's interest became desultory. The Heren XVII wrote: 'We do not expect great things of the continuation of such explorations [for gold and silver], which more and more burden the company's resources...The gold- and silver-mines that will best serve the Company's turn, have already been found, which we deem to be our trade over the whole of India' (Heeres, p. xvi).

Towards the end of the seventeenth century three exceptional events occurred on the western coast. The first Englishman to land on the continent, William Dampier (1652–1715), was there in 1688 and again in 1699; and Willem de Vlamingh, a VOC mariner, discovered the Swan River, the site of Perth, in 1697.

Was ever a seafarer of so many parts as Dampier? Certainly not in the Dutch period. He was variously a merchant seaman, naval officer, navigator, hydrographer, sugar planter in Jamaica, timber trader in Central America, buccaneer taking part in the sacking of ports and ships, showman (of a Filipino slave as the Tattooed Prince in England), naturalist, travel writer and a consummate confidence man. He was a buccaneer on the north-western coast in 1688 in the *Cygnet*, which was eluding pursuers. This was the first English ship to make a landfall in Australia and to be refitted here, though how long Dampier spent on the coast is uncertain. One source gives the stay at Karrakatta Bay as five weeks, another as nine.

A book Dampier published in 1697, *A New Voyage Around the World*, included about 2500 words of his observations in Australia. It made him a celebrity. He got influential patrons by dedicating the book to Charles Montagu, then Chancellor of the Exchequer and later Lord Halifax. Both patrons were associated with overseas commercial ventures and, as perhaps the only Englishman who had voyaged across the Pacific, Dampier was widely consulted about the South Seas. Possibly on Montagu's recommendation, the Lord High Admiral invited Dampier to take a geographic and scientific exploration to the South Seas, with particular attention to what might be to the south-east of the Dutch East Indies, which was New Holland. One of his inducements to his patrons was New Holland's likelihood of containing gold. His instructions read in part:

> ...but there is no larger Tract of Land hitherto undiscovered than Terra Australis (if that vast space surrounding the South Pole, and extend so far into the warmer Climate be a continued Land, as a great deal of it is known to be) so 'tis reasonable to conceive that so great a part of the world is not without very valuable commodities to encourage the Discovery.. an attempt upon the unknown tracts of that part of the world has this to recommend it, that none of our European neighbours can think themselves injured thereby: nor shall we need to interfere with any of them even in the passage thither [the VOC had taken possession of Van Diemen's Land but not of any part of the continent].

The Admiralty gave Dampier the rank of captain, although he had never been in the Navy, a ship, the *Roebuck*, and virtually a free hand. The Royal Society gave him no specific instructions. He had talked of going to the Pacific by way of Cape Horn, which might have led him to discover the eastern coast of Australia but he disliked cold weather so much that he avoided the cape and approached Australia from the west.

Setting out at the beginning of 1699, Dampier reached the western coast at the end of July. He landed at Shark Bay, which he named, in the vicinity of Dirk Hartog's landfall 84 years earlier. He traversed about 1600 kilometres of coast to the north, landing at Lagrange Bay, south of Broome, and at Rosemary Island, which he named. Dampier was on the coast for five weeks and might have stayed longer had he been able to get water, which was of more concern to him than discoveries. He obviously had not thought of taking possession of territory in New Holland. In contrast to the VOC's

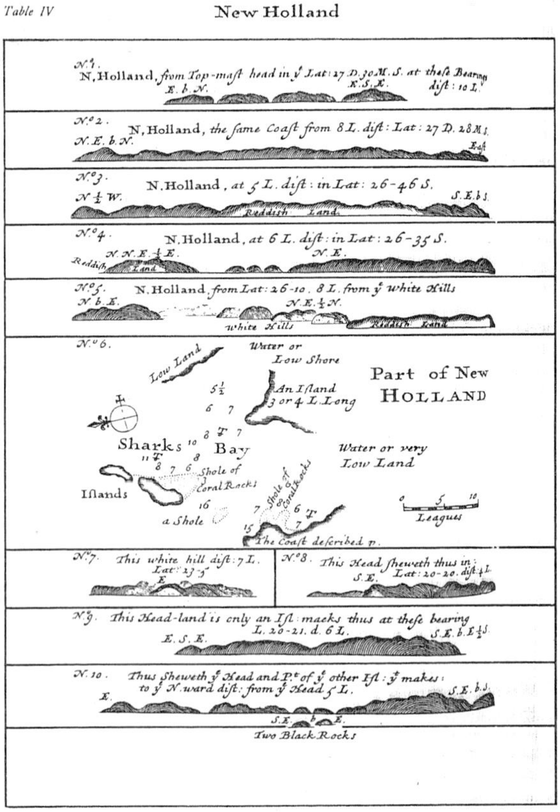

Anonymous, 'Map of Shark Bay, and coastal profiles (1699)', from William Dampier, *A Voyage to New Holland*, London, 1729.

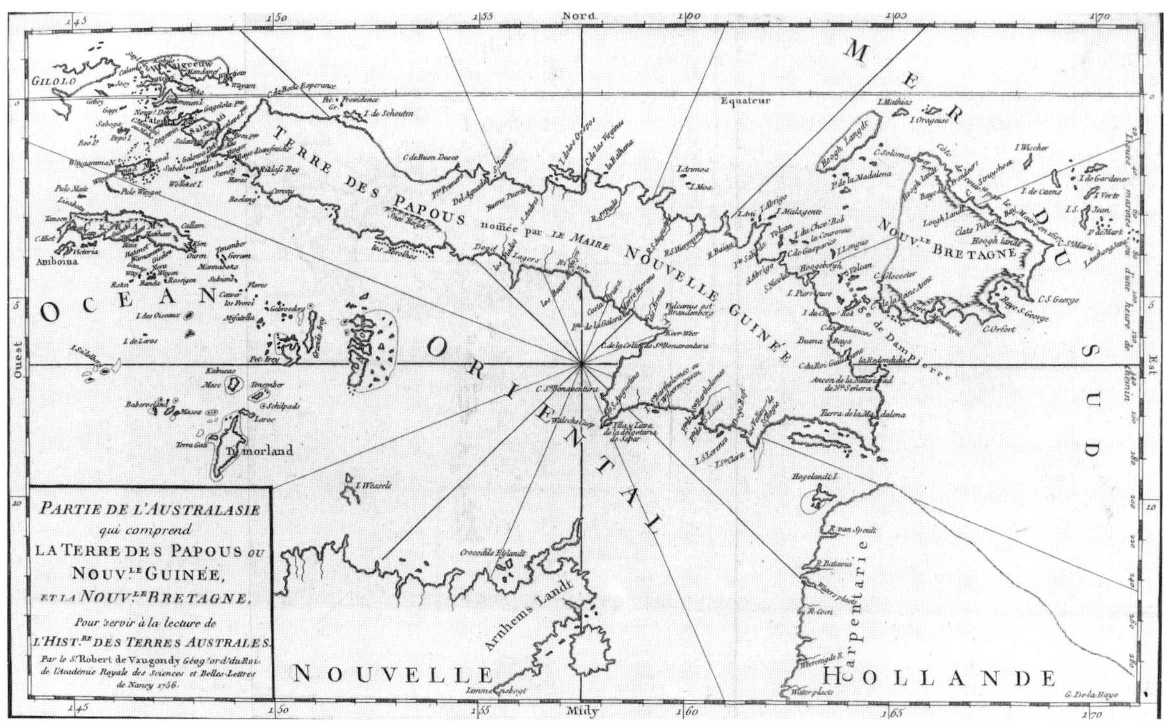

Robert de Vaugondy, 'Partie de l'Australasie', from Charles de Brosses, *Histoire des navigations aux terres australes*, Paris, 1756. (British Library, London.)

instructions to its explorers and those Cook had 70 years later, Dampier's were vague. He was told to discover 'such things' as might tend to the good of the nation and not to annoy the King's subjects or allies.

Dampier added little to what was known of the geography of Australia, which remained virtually unchanged from Tasman's time to 1770. However, he wrote the first naturalist's description of the Aborigines and of the country's flora and fauna, for the earlier observations of the Dutch had been meagre. In 1703 he published another bestseller, *A Voyage to New Holland*, which was dedicated to the Earl of Pembroke, president of the Privy Council. About a quarter of it dealt with Australia, the remainder with Brazil, Timor and New Guinea.

The book stirred English interest in discovery and inspired fables about New Holland. Jonathan Swift (1667–1745), the Anglican dean and satirist, used them in two of his books. In *A Tale of a Tub* (1704), a sectarian satire, he wrote: 'The first undertaking of lord Peter [the Pope] was to purchase a large continent (purgatory) lately said to have been discovered in Terra Australis incognita. This tract of land he bought at a very great pennyworth from the discoverers themselves'. Swift also prophesied the penal settlement in Australia 84 years later:

> The author...has at last thought of a project which will tend to the great benefit of all mankind and produce a handsome revenue to the author. He intends to print by subscription, in 96 volumes in folio, an exact description of Terra Australis incognita, collected with great care and pains from 999 learned and pious authors of undoubted veracity. The whole work, illustrated with maps and cuts agreeable to the subject, and done by the best masters, will cost but one guinea each volume to subscribers...This work will be of great use for all men, and necessary for all families, because it contains exact accounts of all the provinces, colonies, and mansions of that spacious country, where, by a general doom, all transgressors of the law are to be transported; and every one having this work may choose out the fittest and

> best place for himself, there being enough for all, so as every one shall be fully satisfied.

In his better known satire, *Travels into Several Remote Nations of the World by Lemuel Gulliver* (1726), Swift employed the literary device of identifying Dampier as Gulliver's cousin. His work was probably also influenced by a fantastic proposal for a Dutch colony in the area which was made in 1717, by Jean Pierre Purry. Purry claimed that the climate was the best in the world and the only opposition to be feared was from fortified towns on the mainland and from giants, which Tasman had thought might exist in Tasmania. Obviously no Europeans had ever set foot in this part of Australia: they had only seen it from the sea, and considered it desolate. Swift had a map of southern Australia, from Tasmania to Cape Leeuwin, as it was then known, showing real and imaginary islands.

Dampier's 1699 voyage was a fiasco. He had had no experience as a commander; his leaky old ship foundered on the way home; he was court-martialled to answer charges made by an officer of the ship, found guilty, deprived of his previous three years' pay and declared unfit as a commander. Such was his personality that within a year the Lord High Admiral ushered him to an audience with Queen Anne on his imminent departure on a privateering expedition of two ships to the Pacific during the war of the Spanish succession.

After Dampier, the VOC had brief revivals of interest in exploration on the northern coast in 1705 and 1756, but the expeditions produced few significant results.

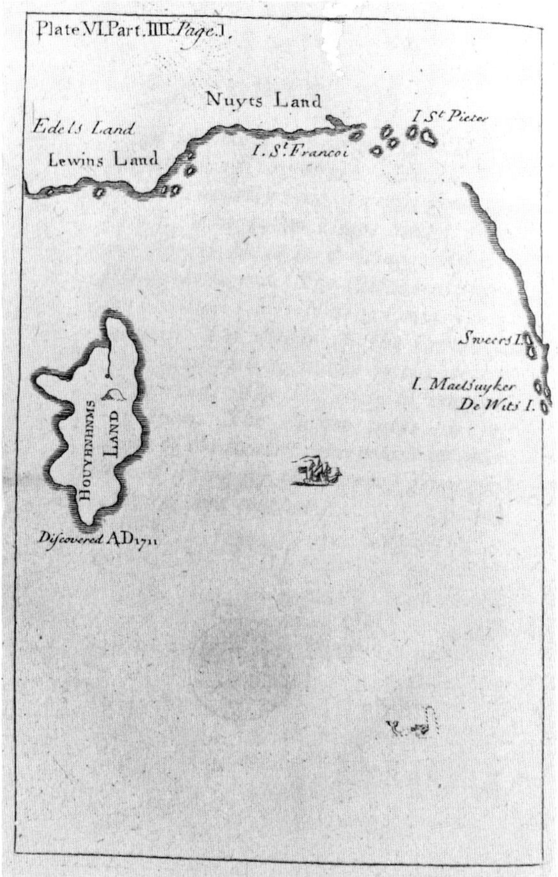

Anonymous, 'Map of Houyhnhnms' Land', from Jonathan Swift, *Gulliver's Travels*, London, 1726. Swift set his imagined land near the real land of New Holland, where Dutch explorers had charted and named the coast. (British Library, London.)

2

Perilous and Uninviting Coasts

In its many voyages to the East, the VOC experienced heavy losses of lives and ships. The wastage of European sailors from disease was severe in the tropics, both afloat and ashore. Between a quarter and a third of those who left Holland for the Indies did not return. Ships were months on the voyage of more than c. 20 000 kilometres from Europe to Batavia and scurvy took a heavy toll of lives. Those antiscorbutic vegetables and fruits that were taken aboard were soon eaten or rotted in the tropics. Without them a healthy, well-nourished body's reserves of vitamin C lasted between 68 to 90 days; then symptoms of scurvy appeared. Mariners knew that fresh fruit and vegetables prevented scurvy, and conversely that the staple sea diet of salted meats and fish gave rise to it. As well, ships never had enough men. Captains had to take what they could get. A Governor-General complained in 1629: 'How often we have been troubled in Asia with having so many Frenchmen and Englishmen...which we hope and trust Your worships will obviate in future by providing us with good, trusty Netherlands' hearts.'

These ships were known as East Indiamen. They were broad-beamed, and varied in length from 30 to 50 metres — less than that of the new Manly ferries in Sydney Harbour (70.4 m). Usually, they had three masts and ornately carved high poops, figureheads and bow beaks. They were significantly larger than explorers' ships. Their cargoes consisted of trade goods, chests of silver guilders or reales of eight for purchases and other treasure on outward voyages; cargoes mainly of spices on homeward voyages. Complements had up to a total of 350 seamen, passengers, and soldiers bound for VOC garrison service. Some had as many as 40 guns; and they sailed in fleets for protection against pirates.

The foods they carried for their passengers and crew were mainly salted or dried meats, fish and biscuits. Water stored in casks became foul and could be replenished only from rain. Usually they carried some small boats, which could accommodate only a fraction of the complement, so that the loss of life in shipwreck was high. In this period, the greatest danger of shipwreck came from skippers' inability to determine longitude reliably and therefore to know, when crossing the Indian Ocean, when to turn north for the East Indies. A Governor-General who commanded a fleet on the way to Batavia complained to VOC managers that they came on breakers on the west Australian coast when charts showed them 550 kilometres off it. North from Perth the coast was particularly hazardous, with offshore reefs, a not readily discernible low-lying shore and, for castaways, a most inhospitable countryside.

One English ship and at least four VOC East Indiamen were wrecked on the west coast in little more than 100 years from 1622 to 1727. Most of nearly 1100 people who were in the ships drowned or became castaways and died of starvation on offshore islands or the mainland; 202 survivors reached Batavia in open-boat voyages of from one to eight months, others in rescue ships. Five confirmed wrecks were found between 200 to 300 years later on the west coast in the 1950s and 1960s. The stories of their discoveries were sometimes as extraordinary as the stories of the wrecks were bizarre:

1622: *Tryall*

The first English sighting of Australia was made from the *Tryall* at Point Cloates, south of North West Cape. It was sailing to the East Indies on the VOC's supposedly secret route from the Cape of Good Hope. when it ran onto what became known as Tryal Rocks, in the vicinity of the Monte Bello Islands and Barrow Island (now an oilfield), about 80 kilometres west of Cape Preston, north-west coast. Forty-six of the complement of 139 saved themselves — 36 in the long boat, ten in the skiff — leaving 92 to 'God's mercy'. The longboat got water and birds for food at the nearby Monte Bello Islands, where Britain was to detonate a nuclear device in 1952. After a month at sea, both boats reached Batavia within a week of each other.

This wreck, and the fortuitous escapes of VOC ships, caused the company to assign two ships to chart the west coast but a rescue operation diverted them from the task. Only in 1697 was the coast carefully charted, by Willem de Vlamingh, who examined more than 1300 kilometres of it between the Swan River and Exmouth Gulf. In 1969 skindivers found a wreck thought to be the *Tryall*, complete with cannon, anchors, ballast stones and small artefacts.

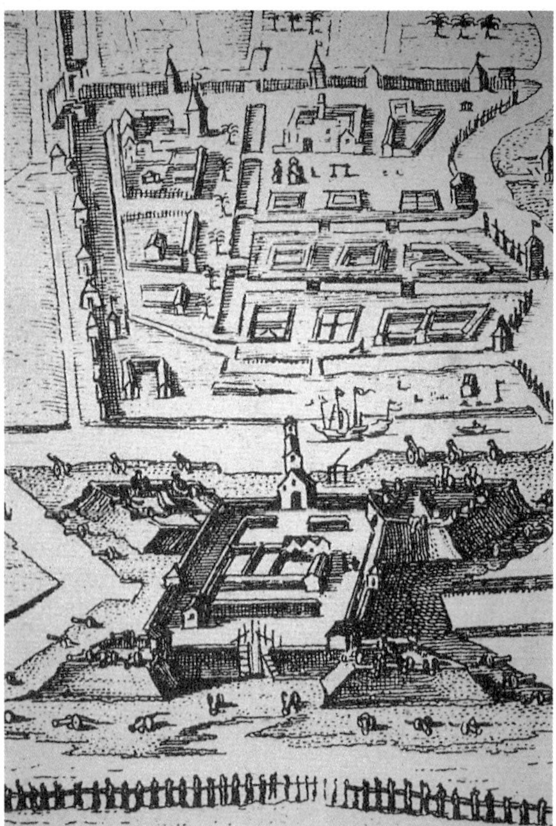

Batavia in 1629. Pieter van den Broecke's journal shows Batavia Castle in 1629 with scaffolding around the water port. (Photo by Patrick Baker, Western Australian Maritime Museum.)

1629: *Batavia*

The *Batavia* was the first of two shipwrecks on Houtman Abrolhos, three groups of islands about 64 kilometres west of Geraldton, on Australia's central west coast. It was wrecked at Beacon Island in the Wallabi group. Of the complement of 268, 40 drowned in the wreck and 74 eventually reached Batavia. The story is one of the most bizarre in Australian history. The chief was the merchant François Pelsaert. After the wreck, he took 47 others in the boats to the East Indies to seek help. These reached Batavia in a month.

Meanwhile, the other castaways established camps on three islands. On one, the supercargo Jeronimus Cornelisz led a gang that seized control, with plans to capture the rescue ship from Batavia. These men treated the women as their sexual slaves, and murdered 125 men on two of the islands who would not join them. The people on the third island resisted the mutineers.

Pelsaert returned little more than three months after the ship was wrecked and succeeded in capturing the conspirators. He tried, tortured (by Dutch law a person could be sentenced to death only on his own confession), and hanged some of them, and took the others, except two considered less guilty, with the loyalists to Batavia. He marooned the two excepted on the mainland, giving them guns, food and beads, bells and mirrors for trade with the Aborigines. Pelsaert told them to learn what they could about the country. Wouter Loos and Jan Pelgrom de By were the first Europeans to live on the continent. The VOC later told mariners to look out for them but none found them. Fifteen years later Tasman was again instructed to do so, and also to look for a chest containing 8000 Rix-dollars (silver coins of value varying from 253 *d.* to 456 *d.* — Pelsaert had recovered most of the remainder of the treasure) but he did not sail as far south as the wreck.

Although Pelsaert was a brother-in-law of Hendrik

Great stones in *Batavia*'s cargo were prefabricated to form part of Batavia Castle. They went down in the wreck and lay for centuries beneath the sea. Archaeologists of the Western Australian Maritime Museum have pieced them together into archway and portico. (Photo by Patrick Baker, Western Australian Maritime Museum.)

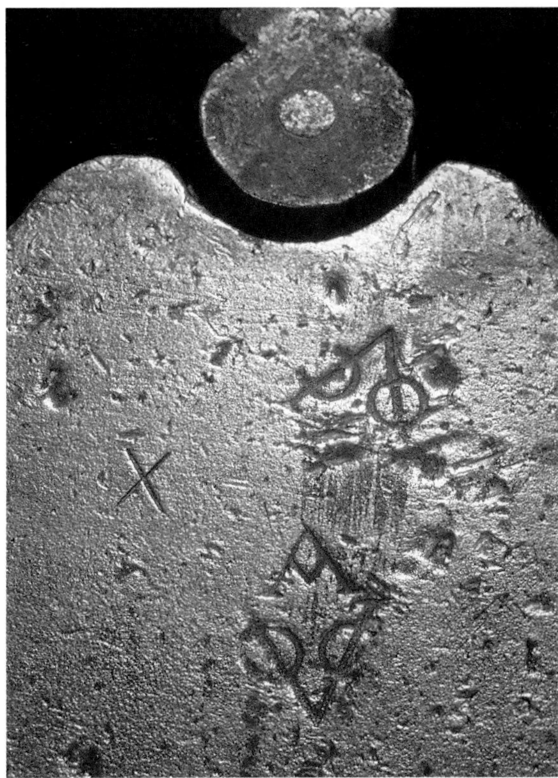

Detail of *Batavia*'s astrolabe (instrument for measuring the altitude of the sun and stars). (Photo by Patrick Baker, Western Australian Maritime Museum.)

Brouwer, a former Governor-General, the VOC never forgave him for leaving the ship leaderless. The Heren XVII considered that the single women on the ship had caused friction amongst the officers and were the cause of the disaster.

In 1963, on the 334th anniversary of the wreck, a lobster fisherman led skindivers to its site, having seen an anchor there. Of the VOC shipwrecks, the *Batavia* has yielded the most relics: stones cut and prepared for the portico of a building in Batavia; part of the port side of the ship; navigation equipment; silverware and ceramics. One of the largest and most distinguished of all the gems which were in the ship is now in the royal coin cabinet at The Hague. It is a cameo carved in AD 312–15, supposedly for the Roman emperor Constantine, and was on its way to the Mogul emperor at Agra, India.

Neck gorget (throat-protecting piece of armour) from the *Batavia*. This is a cast of the gorget. (Australian National Maritime Museum.)

1656: *Vergulde Draeck* (Gilt Dragon)

This ship was wrecked on a reef five kilometres off Ledge Point, 100 kilometres north of Perth. Only 75 of a complement of 193 got ashore. The skipper stayed with the ship and sent seven of the crew in

f. 2
nº. 2
f. 8

Opposite and above: The Dutch ship *Batavia*, bound for the city of that name, struck a reef off the Western Australian coast on 4 June 1629. Shipwreck, mutiny and murder followed. Then came retribution. These seventeenth-century engravings tell the story. (From *The Voyage of the Batavia*, the journal of François Pelsaert, 1647, Hordern House, Australian National Maritime Museum.)

an open boat to Batavia, which they reached 40 days later. The VOC organised five ship searches for the castaways but were unable to find any. Two of the searching ships lost 21 crewmen. Eleven went into the bush and did not return. Fourteen who were marooned by the ship in error set out in the boat they had for Java and arrived there in three weeks. They took three months to walk to civilisation and only four survived. A marine salvage contractor and a foremost underwater explorer, Ellis Alfred (Alan) Robinson, claimed he and others found the wreck in 1957 — which would be the first underwater discovery of one of the VOC's wrecks. He lost the location but rediscovered it in 1963. As a source of relics, the *Vergulde Draeck* ranks next to the *Batavia*.

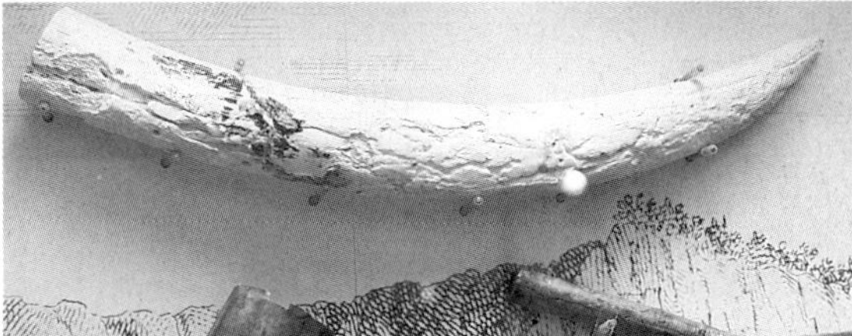

Elephant's tusk from the *Vergulde Draeck* (*Gilt Dragon*) wreck of 1656. (Australian National Maritime Museum.)

1712: *Zuytdorp* (a commune's name)

The VOC had no idea where this ship was lost and did not look for it. A stockman found wreckage in 1927 on the shore at the foot of cliffs north of Geraldton. This included a carved wooden figure of a woman, which had been a decorative support for a window in the ship's stern, and glass bottles. Coins found on the cliff tops showed that some of the crew had camped there. The *Zuytdorp* left Holland with a complement of 286, of whom 100 died on the way to the Cape of Good Hope. The

Model of *Zuytdorp* with VOC flag. (Photo by Patrick Baker, Western Australian Maritime Museum.)

number of crew replacements obtained is not known. Relics from here included brass cannon, coins and a ship's bell.

1727: *Zeewijk* (a commune's name)
This ship was wrecked on Half Moon Reef near Gun Island in the Pelsaert group of Houtman Abrolhos. Of the complement of 112, 96 made a camp on the island. Twelve of the crew set out in the long boat for Batavia but were never heard of again. The castaways built a sloop from salvage — the first ship built in Australia, named *Sloepie* (Little Sloop) — and ten months after the wreck reached Batavia. Two sodomites in the crew, who would not admit their offence, even under torture, were marooned on separate islands. A naval surveyor in 1840 found relics in the castaways' campsite, including a cannon. Guano miners found bottles and cooking pots in 1890. In the 1950s another naval officer found more cannon, six guns and pieces of iron. The wreck site was found in 1968.

The discovery of the VOC's wrecks set in motion a bizarre series of events involving the Commonwealth, Western Australian and Netherlands governments and Alan Robinson, who claimed to have found 97 wrecks and reported 25. In 1964 the Western Australian parliament legislated to place shipwrecks under the protection of the Western Australian Museum. It seized Robinson's treasure of coins and artefacts and excluded him from the wreck of the *Vergulde Draeck*. As the Netherlands government claimed rights to shipwrecks of the former VOC below tide-mark anywhere, a committee of two Australians and two Dutchmen was appointed in 1970 to allot relics to the Rijksmuseum, Amsterdam, to the Western Australian Museum and (later) to the National Maritime Museum at Darling Harbour, Sydney.

In 1976 Robinson claimed salvage rights to the wreck of the *Vergulde Draeck* in the High Court of Australia on the grounds that the Western Australian 1964 Act and the later legislation relating to wrecks were beyond the state's powers. After the court action began, the Commonwealth enacted the *Historic Shipwrecks Act*, which partly superseded the Western Australian legislation and gave stronger safeguards from vandals for wrecks and for the Netherlands' interests. This Act delegated powers to the Western Australian Museum to enable it to continue its conservation of shipwrecks. In 1977 the High Court declared invalid the Western Australian legislation excluding Robinson from the wreck and ruled that he was entitled to salvage and/or compensation but did not stipulate an amount. Finders of shipwrecks in Australian waters may now claim rewards.

Robinson wrote an embittered account of his experiences in 1980, titled *In Australia Treasure Is not for the Finder*. A leather-bound edition of the book contained a piece of eight coin in its cover. As well as litigation with governments, Robinson, with his common-law wife, was before the courts on a charge of conspiring to murder his former common-law wife. In 1983, early in the morning of the day a jury was to give its verdict, he hanged himself in his cell. The judge had directed the jury that if it acquitted one defendant in the conspiracy it must acquit the other. The jury first gave its verdict acquitting his wife without knowing that Robinson had committed suicide. Up to that time, Robinson had received neither salvage nor compensation from the *Vergulde Draeck*.

With the striking exception of William Dampier, the Dutch had the western and northern coasts to themselves for nearly 200 years, until the beginning of the nineteenth century. However, the dry, uninviting countryside, the lack of fresh water, and the absence of items of commercial interest discouraged them from making practical use of it for supplies of any kind or settlements.

Extended journals by four early VOC explorers survive — Carstensz, Delft and Gonzal on the northern coast and Tasman on the Tasmanian coast — as well as those by people on de Vlamingh's later expedition. These mostly record impressions of the country.

While explorers also had instructions to take note of the animals and plants they saw and ate, they and commercial skippers made scant reference to them. They could not readily communicate with the Aborigines, and so obtained little knowledge of indigenous food resources, which were extensive. (For example, Ms Sara J. Meagher has established that Aborigines in the south-west of Western Australia utilised at least 43 animals — 13 mammals, four birds, 10 reptiles, 13 fish, three insects — and 38 plants.) The VOC's instructions to Carstensz for his 1623 expedition to the north coast, for example, read in part:

> you will have to discover and survey all capes, forelands, bights, lands, islands, rocks, reefs, sandbanks, depths, shallows, roads, winds, currents and all that appertains to the same, so as to be able to map out and duly mark everything in its true latitude, longitude, bearings and conformation. You will moreover go ashore in various places and diligently examine the coast in order to ascertain whether or no it is inhabited, the nature of the land and the people, their towns and inhabited villages, the divisions of their kingdoms, their religion and policy, their wars, their rivers, the shape of their vessels, their fisheries, commodities and manufactures, but specifically to inform yourselves what minerals, such as gold, silver, tin, iron, lead, and copper, what precious stones, pearls, vegetables, animals and fruits, these lands yield and produce.
>
> To all which particulars and whatever else may be worth noting, you will pay diligent attention, keeping a careful record or daily journal of the same, that we may get full information of all your doings and experiences and the Company may obtain due and perfect knowledge of the situation and natural features of these regions, in return for the heavy expenses to which she is put by this expedition.
>
> According to the written statements of Jan Huygen, and the opinion of sundry other persons, certain parts of this South-land are likely to yield gold, a point into which you will inquire as carefully as possible.
>
> For the purpose of making a trial we have given orders for various articles to be put on board your ships, such as iron-mongery, cloths, coast-stuffs [i.e. items from Coromandel] and linens; which you will show and try to dispose of to such natives as you may meet with, always diligently noting what articles are found to be most in demand, what quantities might be disposed of, and what might be obtained in exchange for them; we furthermore hand you samples of gold, silver, copper, iron, lead and pearls. That you may inquire whether these articles are known to the natives, and might be obtained therein in considerable quantity...
>
> You will diligently inquire whether it yields anywhere sandel-wood, nutmegs, cloves or other spices; likewise whether it has any good harbours and fertile tracts, where it would be possible to establish settlements. (Heeres, 19–21)

The instructions given to Tasman for his 1642 voyage read:

> It is known that up to a hundred and fifty years ago, only about a third part of the globe (divided into Europe, Asia, and Africa) had been known, and that the kings of Castile and Portugal (Ferdinand Catholicus and don Emanuel) have caused the unknown part of the earth usually named America or new world, (and by the cosmographers divided into North and South America) to be discovered by the very famous Sea-heroes Christopher Columbus and Americus Vesputius (to their undying glory), as also about the same time, the unexplored Coasts and

islands of Africa, and East India were first sailed to by the renowned Vasco da Gama and other Portuguese captains. What inestimable riches, profitable trading, useful exchanges, fine dominions, great might and powers, the said kings have brought to their kingdoms and crowns by this discovering and its sequel, and also untold heathens have come to the salutary light of the Christian religion, is also well known to the experienced, and deemed most highly laudable by all knowledgeable men, appropriately served other European princes as an example for the discovery of many Northern lands.

Nevertheless up till now there has not been any serious attempt by any Christian kings, princes, or republics opportunely to discover the remaining unknown part of the globe (that situated in the south, and probably almost as large, as is the old or new world), although it is to be judged for good reasons, many attractive and fruitful lands are located therein, as being in the cold, temperate and hot zones, where necessarily there must be many inhabited places in the pleasant climate and attractive sky, and because in many lands, situated to north of the equinoctial (in the latitude of 15 to 40 degrees), many rich mines and other treasures are found, so it is beyond doubt, similar fruitful and rich lands are also situated south of the Equator, as the gold and silver-rich provinces of Peru, Chile, Monomotapa or Soffala (all situated south of the Equator) show and indicate as clear examples, thus it is certainly to be hoped, that the outlay and trouble, which must be incurred in the discovery of so large a part of the world, can be recompensed with certain fruits of gain and undying fame.

This being then so, and since no European Colony is situated more conveniently for this very evident discovering, than the town Batavia (like a middle point of the known and unknown Oriental India). (Tasman, 30–1)

The journal of Jansz, the discoverer of Australia in 1606, is lost, but a reference to the country he saw was included in the instructions to Abel Tasman in 1644:

It being only ascertained that vast regions were for the greater part uncultivated, and certain parts inhabited by savage, cruel, black barbarians who slew some of our sailors, so that no information was obtained touching the exact lie of the country and regarding the commodities obtainable and in demand there; our men having by want of provisions and other necessaries, been compelled to return and give up the discovery they had begun, only registering in their chart with the name of *Cape Keer-weer*, the extreme point of the discovered land in 13¾ degrees Southern Latitude. (Heeres, 6)

It is not known whether Jansz was describing New Guinea or Australia because he thought they were one country. Natives killed ten of his crew. Aborigines are known to have killed one of them; Papuans probably slew the others.

The journal of Dirk Hartog, the first European to land on the west coast in 1616, is also lost and nothing is known of references he may have made to the country. The first known comment on the continent was written in 1619 by Frederik de Houtman, a merchant, commander of a fleet of merchantmen on the west coast: 'We resolved to use our utmost endeavours to obtain some knowledge of this coast, which seemed to be a very good land, but could find no spot for conveniently landing owing to the surf and the heavy seas' (Heeres, 15). Jacob Dedel, a Councillor of India who was with the fleet, wrote: 'Eendracht Landt showed as red, muddy coast, which according to the surmizes of some of us might not unlikely prove to be gold bearing' (Heeres, 16).

Gold, of course, was what the VOC desired above all else. The directors associated the Southland with Marco Polo's beach of gold, reported to be south of Java, so much so that Houtman wrote they 'suddenly came upon the Southland of Beach' (Heeres, 14). After Hartog's landing the VOC told mariners to watch out for the beach of gold.

The first extended description of the north coast was made in 1623 by the explorer, Carstensz. He was in the Gulf of Carpentaria for a month: 'it was flat, fine countryside with few trees, and a good soil for planting and sowing, but so far as we could observe utterly destitute of fresh water' (Heeres, 36).

Portrait of William Dampier by W.C.T. Dobson. Oil on canvas. (Rex Nan Kivell Collection, National Library of Australia.)

Batavia Castle in the 1630s. This 1634 engraving is from Vingboom's *Atlas.* In 1619 the Dutch East India Company — the VOC — established its headquarters at Batavia (now Jakarta) in Java, setting up a great centre for shipping and trade. (Photo by Patrick Baker, Western Australian Maritime Museum.)

The earliest known shipwreck in Australian waters, was that of the English ship, *Trial,* (sometimes spelt *Tryall*) in 1622. The wreck was discovered in 1969. Here, fathoms down, is pictured the *Trial*'s anchor. (Photo by Patrick Baker, Western Australian Maritime Museum.)

Carstensz revised his opinion after traversing the west coast of Cape York Peninsula from Weipa to Normanton:

> a barren and arid tract, without any fruit trees, and producing nothing fit for the use of man; it is low-lying and flat without hills or mountains; in many places overgrown with bushweed and it has not much fresh water, and what little there is, has to be collected in pits dug for the purpose; there is an utter absence of bays or inlets, with the exception of a few bights not sheltered from the sea-wind; it extends mainly N. by E. and S. by W., with shallows all along the coast, with a clayey and sandy bottom; it has numerous salt rivers extending into the interior... [The natives] are utterly unacquainted with gold, silver, tin, iron, lead and copper, nor do they know anything about nutmegs, cloves and pepper, all of which spices we repeatedly showed them without their evincing any signs of recognizing or valuing the same; from all of which together with the rest of our observations it may be safely concluded that they are poor and abject wretches, caring mainly for bits of iron and strings of beads. (Heeres, 41–2)

The first known description of the west coast from experience ashore came from François Pelsaert, who was wrecked in 1629:

> in the morning [16 June] we continued our exploration in order to find out whether there were more water-pits in the mountains, but our search was fruitless, for it seemed not to have rained there for a long time past. And we found no traces of running water, the higher ground being again very barren and unpromising, without any trees, shrubs or grass, but with plenty of high ant-hillls in all directions. These ant-hills consisted of earth thrown up, and from afar somewhat resembled huts for the abode of men.
>
> We also found such multitudes of flies here, which perched on our mouths and crept into our eyes, that we could not keep them off our persons. (Heeres, 57)

The few other comments that the VOC explorers and mariners made on the continent were no different. Only one ship traversed the south coast, which was described as desolate. Willem de Vlamingh in 1696–97 was on the west coast for seven weeks, following it from the Swan River to Exmouth Gulf, and making a dozen or more landings. De Vlamingh discovered the best country to be found in the period of Dutch exploration. This was the Swan River area at the northern end of the south-west corner of the continent, which with the south-east corner and the east coast were the well-watered areas.

Even so, he said that the Swan River area had nothing to offer. Yet 131 years later it enraptured an Englishman, Captain James Stirling, as a spot 'so eligible for settlement that it cannot long remain unoccupied'. The explanation of this difference in response might be that de Vlamingh was there in mid-summer with flies and heat, but not, as he reported, with vermin. He might have had a better impression had he been there in winter. Of what he saw of the continent, his report said: 'in this part of the South-land...they have diligently skirted, surveyed and observed, they have found little beyond an arid, barren and wild land, both near the shore and so far as they have been inland' (Heeres, 84).

A journal kept on one of de Vlamingh's ships, the *Nijptang* (Little Nipper) describes the privations of a shore party north of Perth in the vicinity of Red Bluff:

> The 25th [January 1697] early in the morning I went shore with our under-steersman and another nine of our crew, as well as de Vlamingh's commander of the soldiers [Christiaan Climmerson], third mate [Jonas Marsman] and thirty-one soldiers. Having come to the beach, we found many oysters and started at once out on our march but sometimes had to rest through fatigue caused by the heat of the sun and the heavy going through thick scrub, until we came to the mountain range, where we camped. But if the march had been hard, the greatest grief struck us now, for finding no water, we thought we would perish from thirst. We could see our ships clearly from here and wished a thousand times to be back on board. Meanwhile, the commander of the soldiers had descended with another two men and brought back a report, with a cheerful face when he

returned, that he had found fresh water as well as a hut and footprints eighteen inches long, about an hour's march from our camp. Whereupon it was resolved to march there even though it began to grow dark, which was not done without great trouble because of the scrub and nightfall. Having arrived at the watering place, we found it to be a large hole but the water slightly brackish. We camped by it and having properly posted guards all the time passed the night as well as we could.

> The 26th [January] in the morning before sunrise we started marching again and arrived at the said hut after a while, around which we found a great many eggshells, but those eighteen-inch footprints changed into ordinary ones. We also passed this night on shore, camped again by the waterhole mentioned, although having split up, finding either humans or animals, there being nothing but scrub. (Schilder, 158)

Fifteen days later: 'Encountered thunder and lightning and the first South Land rain. Went ashore again in the evening and camped in a very bad spot, altogether wild and barren' (Schilder, 160).

Nicolaas Witsen drew his own conclusions from reports he received and conversations with members of the expedition:

> This land seems to reach as far as Van Diemen's Land, which I deem to be the westernmost point of Hollandia Nova, to which opinion the consideration makes one incline that the soil appears to have the same quality as also in vegetation, fruits and trees, a great change being noticeable on the opposite side of the sea or gulf which stretches out between this land and Zeelandia Nova, the people in Zeelandia Nova having a different colour and appearance, and the land differs in its fruits and vegetation. (Schilder, 219)

In other references Witsen wrote of there being 'fine forest at thirty-one degrees, and pleasant trees, but little population close to the sea: for which the reason is perhaps that there is a lack of drinking water there'. De Vlamingh left the west coast with a salute of guns 'to farewell the miserable South Land' (Schilder, 219, 161).

The only substantial area of Australia not disparaged by the Dutch explorers was Tasmania, although Tasman described it in 1642 without enthusiasm. What he saw was on the south-east coast, about 60 kilometres from Hobart:

> On 2 [December] in the morning early sent the chief pilot Francoijs Jacobszn...to an Inlet...to find out what commodities (as of fresh water, refreshments, timber and other things) might be there. About 3 hours before nightfall our boats came back, bringing various types of greens (which they had seen growing in plenty) some not unlike a certain green which grows at the Cabo de bona Esperance [Cape of Good Hope] and is suitable to use as vegetables another being long and salty, which has not a bad likeness to sea parsley...They had found high, yet level land with greens (unplanted being forthcoming from God in nature) fruit-bearing timber in abundance, and a running water place many empty valleys; which water was running down very good but rather difficult to get, so that no more than a bowl could be scooped ... The land is widely provided with trees, which stand so, that men may pass through everywhere, and see far from them, so that on land always, one could get sight of the people or wild animals, being unimpeded from thick dense forest or thicket, which on land should give freedom to exploring. (Sharp, 75–6)

The VOC was disappointed with the results of its explorations. The explorers had excuses: they were sailors, not bushmen, in 'heat, thirst, scrub — a bad desolate land with sand dunes'. Carstensz was spirited in his defence:

> that in all places where we landed, we have treated the blacks or savages with especial kindness, offering them pieces of iron, strings of beads and pieces of cloth, hoping by so doing to get their friendship and be allowed to penetrate to some considerable distance landinward, that we might be able to give a full account and description of the same; but in spite of all our kindness and our fair semblance the blacks received us as enemies everywhere, so that in most places our landings were attended with great peril; on this account and for various

> other reasons afterwards to be mentioned, we have not been able to learn anything about the population of Nova Guinea, and the nature of its inhabitants and its soil; nor did we get any information touching its towns and villages, about the division of the land, the religion of the natives, their policy, wars, rivers, vessels, or fisheries; what commodities they have, what manufactures, what minerals whether gold, silver, tin, iron, lead, copper or quicksilver. In the first place, in making further landings we should have been troubled by the rainy season, which might have seriously interfered with the use of our muskets, whereas it does no harm to the weapons of the savages; secondly, we should first have been obliged to seek practicable paths or roads of which we knew nothing; thirdly, we might easily have been surrounded by the crowds of blacks, and been cut off from the boats, which would entail serious peril to the sailors with whom we always effected the landings, and who are imperfectly versed in the use of muskets; if on the contrary we had had well-drilled and experienced soldiers (the men best fitted to undertake such expeditions), we might have done a good deal of useful work; still, in spite of all these difficulties and obstacles, we have shunned neither hard work, trouble, nor peril, to make a thorough examination of everything with the means at our disposal, and to do whatever our good name and our honour demanded. (Heeres, 41)

Although the members of the VOC council at Batavia acknowledged Tasman's abilities, they were also disappointed with the results of his voyages. Van Diemen reproved Tasman for not investigating the nature of the lands he discovered in his 1642 voyage and leaving this to a more inquisitive successor. Tasman's journal of his 1644 explorations is lost, so his opinions of the north and north-west coast are not known, but the VOC's comments on his report were scathing:

> they secured nothing advantageous, but only poor naked beach-runners, without riches, or any noteworthy fruits, very poor, and at many places bad natured men...What now is on and in said Southland, remains unknown, as the navigators have done nothing but sail along the coast, and who shall investigate what the lands give must walk therein and through, for which these agents say there was not enough opportunity, in which there may be something. Meanwhile, this great and still unknown Southland has been gone round by the aforesaid Tasman in two voyages and is reckoned to contain in it 8000 miles of land as the charts drawn thereof, which we send to Your Worships, make known. That such great land lying in various climes...shall have nothing of profit to find is scarcely acceptable. (Sharp, 87–8)

Poor Tasman! He was expected to be away only five or six months, despite the VOC's hopes that he might find a way to Van Diemen's Land. Part of the trouble was that the VOC looked for quick returns. But the company also placed an emphasis on preserving ships, so explorers proceeded more cautiously than they otherwise might have done.

The VOC gave its explorers instructions to take possession of countries — for example:

> To all such places which you shall touch at, you will give appropriate names as in each instance the case shall seem to require, choosing for the same either the names of the United Provinces or of the towns situated therein, or of any other appelations that you may deem fitting and worthy. Of all which places, lands and islands, the commanders and officers of these yachts by orders and pursuant to the commission of the Worshipful Governor-General Jan Pieterszoon Coen, sent out to India by their High Mightinesses the States-General of the United Netherlands, and by the Lords Managers of the General Chartered United East India Company...will, by solemn declaration signed by the ships' council, take, formal possession, and in sign thereof, bodies, erect a stone column in such places as shall be taken possession of; the said column recording in bold, legible characters the year, the month, the day of the week and the date, the persons by whom and the hour of the day when such possession has been taken on behalf of the States-General above mentioned. You will likewise endeavour to enter into friendly relations and make covenants with all such kings and natives as you shall happen to fall in with, and try to prevail

upon them to place themselves under the protection of the State of the United Netherlands, of which convenants and alliances you will likewise cause proper documents to be drawn up and signed.

All such lands, islands, etc. as you shall take possession of in the fashion aforesaid, you will duly mark in the chart in these true latitudes, longitudes and bearings, together with the names newly conferred on the same.

In virtue of the oath of allegience which each of you generally and personally has sworn to the Lords State-General, to this Princely Highness and the Lords Managers, none of you shall be allowed to retain for his private use or to abstract any written documents, journals, drawings or observations touching on this present expedition, but every one of you shall be bound on his return hither, faithfully to deliver up the same without exception. (Heeres, 20)

Such instructions were broadened for Tasman's 1642 voyage:

> All the mainland and islands which [you] shall discover, visit and land on, you must take in possession for the High and Mighty Lords States General as Sovereign of the united provinces, which in uninhabited lands, or which have no lord can be secured by the setting up of a stone as a memorial, or planting of our prince flag, for true possession, since such lands rightly belong to the finder and taker. But in populated lands, or which have undoubtedly lords, the consent of the people or king shall be necessary in the taking of occupation and possession, which is to be fittingly achieved by amicable influence with the presenting of a small tree planted in a little earth, the joint setting up of a stone, or the placing of the prince-flag in memory of their voluntary submission, or subjection, all of which you shall completely record in your journal, with naming of the persons who shall be present, so as to be able in future times to serve our republic. (Tasman, 39)

In reality these instructions were only sparingly followed. Two explorers and a merchantman skipper, Hartog, left signs of their presence. Carstensz seems not to have, perhaps because he believed Cape York to be part of New Guinea. Tasman alone took formal possession, of Van Diemen's Land. He wrote:

> we went with the said boats, including the Chief pilot Francoijs Jacobszn, the Skipper Gerrit Janszn, Isaac Gilsemans supercargo of the *Zeehaen*, the subcargo Abraham Coomans, and our senior Carpenter Pieter Jacobszn to the south-east side of the bay [Blackman's Bay], having with us a stake with the Company's mark cut in it, and the prince flag [of Prince Frederick Henry, Stadholder or governor of the States General] to set up there, so that later people may perceive, we have been here and taken the said Land (in possession and ownership)...We could not approach the land without danger of the vessel being smashed to pieces; we bade the said carpenter swim alone with the stake and the prince flag to land and remained with the boat lying in the wind: we made him erect in the earth the stake and the flag above...and the said carpenter having swum back through the surf to the boat, these things being carried out, we rowed back leaving for posterity and the inhabitants of this land (none of whom showed themselves, although we surmise some were not far away and were with watching eyes on our goings-on) the above things as a memorial. (Sharp, 77–8)

Tasman identified the spot by what he said were four easily recognisable trees.

Evidently the VOC mariners' inability to parley with Aborigines or find a chief among them discouraged them from taking possession of parts of the continent — as well, of course, as the country's unattractive appearance. On the way home from exploring the Gulf of Carpentaria Carstensz fulfilled instructions to take possession of the Aru Islands in the Arafura Sea, between the Northern Territory and western New Guinea. The islands were no great prize, but he was able to communicate with the people, who were of mixed Papuan blood. By contrast with the simple mark he left in the Gulf, Carstensz wrote:

> [We] anchored opposite the native village of Woodgier on the second of the northmost islands of the Aroe group, where they received

a friendly welcome. The same day concluded with the Aroe chiefs a TREATY under which they accepted Dutch protection. A high column was erected bearing the inscription: In the year 1623, on the 1st of February, there came here to Aroe the Yachts *Pera* and *Arnhem*. Commander Jan Carstensz, Koopleiden (traders) Jan Bruwel and Pieeter Lingtes, Skippers Jan Sluijs, Dirck Meliksz, Stuurlieden (Mates) Arent Martensz and Jan Jansz, dispatched under order and command of the Noble Lord General Jan Pietersen Coen, on behalf of their High Mightinesses the States-General, His Excellency the Prince of Orange and Messrs. the Directors of the United East India Company; and we have also on the 4th day of the same taken possession of the island for the above mentioned Highnesses. Likewise the Chiefs and People have placed themselves under the protection and rule of the aforesaid Lords and saluted the Princely flag.

In 1642 the carpenter, Pieter Jacobszn, swam from ship to shore at Blackman's Bay and raised the Prince flag. Looking remarkably dry in the nineteenth-century illustration, he took formal possession of the land which later bore Tasman's name — Tasmania. (From *Picturesque Atlas of Australasia*, Mitchell Library, State Library of New South Wales.)

The VOC instructed explorers to look out for harbours for settlements but none saw any considered worth reporting; one factor here was probably the fact that a staging point between the Cape of Good Hope and Batavia was not needed.

In 1717, Jean Pierre Purry, a Swiss adventurer who had worked for the VOC in Batavia, proposed to the directors a colonisation of Pieter Nuyts Land. The consequences of such a settlement would have been incalculable for Australia because the VOC, if it had foreseen commerce in it, would almost certainly have settled Malays there. Purry argued that the climate should prove most suitable to the production of fruits and wines. With the exception of South America, New Zealand and Kaffraria (a region of South Africa), there was in the whole 'Antarctic hemisphere only the Land of Nuyts, in which I include Leeuwin and Edelsland'. He continued:

> Who knows what there is in *New-Holland*, and whether that Country does not perhaps contain richer Mines of Gold or Silver than, perhaps, *Chile*, *Peru* or *Mexico*...Whence should it be, that all the other Countries of the Earth which are situate under this Climate, should be good, and this [Nuyts Land] alone with nothing? (Purry, 32)

Purry's plan was to disembark 500 or 600 men, all good soldiers, to spy out the land to see whether the Nuytsians had fortified towns and more terrible machines of war, or were giants in stature, in intelligence and knowledge so prodigious that their likes have never been seen or heard of in any other country. Purry was a most persistent planter of settlements. He could not get his ideas for Nuyts Land taken up in Europe, but with other Swiss he later founded a colony 'on the English coast of America' in Carolina, where a town he named after himself, Purrisburg, survives.

William Dampier's responses to the west coast of the continent were similar to those of the Dutch. As an inducement to his patrons to support his voyage, he said he 'considered...New Holland a country likely to contain gold', a statement wild but prophetic enough. However, though he added little to knowledge of the countryside, his wry comment on it is memorable: 'If it were not for that sort of pleasure which results from the discovery even of the barrenest spot on the globe, this coast of New Holland would not have charmed me much'.

Dampier was more interested in the Aborigines, botany, zoology and hydrography. Like the VOC mariners, he did not explore very far inland. Of his 1688 visit he wrote:

> *New-Holland* is a very large Tract of Land. It is not yet determined whether it is an Island or a main Continent; but I am certain that it joyns neither to *Asia, Africa,* nor *America.* This part of it that we saw is all low even Land, with Sandy Banks against the Sea, only the Points are rocky, and so are some of the Islands in this Bay.
>
> The Land is of a dry sandy Soil, destitute of Water, except you make Wells; yet producing divers sorts of Trees; but the Woods are not thick, nor the Trees very big. Most of the Trees that we saw are Dragon-Trees, as we supposed; and these too are the largest Trees of any there. They are about the bigness of our large Apple-trees, and about the same heighth; and the Rind is blackish, and somewhat rough. The Leaves are of a dark Colour; the Gum distils out of the Knots or Cracks that are in the Bodies of the Trees. We compared it with some Gum-Dragon or Dragon's Blood that was aboard, and it was of the same colour and taste. The other sorts of Trees were not known by any of us. There was pretty long Grass growing under the Trees; but it was very thin. We saw no Trees that bore Fruit or Berries. (Dampier, 1968, 312)

And of his 1699 visit of five weeks, mainly in August, he had even less to say about the countryside:

> The Land is of an indifferent Heighth, so that it may be seen 9 or 10 Leagues off. It appears at a Distance very even; but as you come nigher you find that there are many gentle Risings, tho' none steep nor high. 'Tis all a steep Shore against the open Sea.' In the archipelago named after him Dampier expressed a slight interest in minerals: 'among so many Islands, we might have found some Sort of rich Mineral, or Ambergreece, it being a good Latitude for both these. (Dampier, 1906, 424, 434).

Dampier also offered an apologia for his failure to attempt the discovery of the continent's eastern coast, in which he anticipated Purry's outlook:

> thus having ranged about, a considerable time, upon this Coast, without finding any good fresh water, any convenient Place to clean the Ship, as I had hop'd for: And it being moreover the heighth of the dry Season, and my Men growing scorbutick for want of Refreshments, so that I had little encouragement to search further; I resolved to leave this Coast, and accordingly in the beginning of September set sail towards Timor...
>
> I had spent about 5 Weeks in ranging off and on the Coast of New-Holland, a Length of about 300 Leagues: and had put in at 3 several Places [Shark Bay, Rosemary Island and Lagrange Bay], to see what there might be thereabouts worth discovering; and at the same Time to recruit my Stock of fresh Water and Provisions for the further Discoveries I purposed to attempt on the Terra Australis. This large and hitherto almost unknown Tract of Land is situated so very advantageously in the richest Climates of the World, the Torrid and Temperate zones; having in it especially all the Advantages of the Torrid Zone, as being known to reach from the Equator it self (within a Degree) to the Tropick of Capricorn, and beyond it; that in coasting round it, which I design'd by this Voyage, if possible: I could not but hope to meet with some fruitful Lands, Continent or Islands, or both, productive of any of the rich Fruits, Drugs or Spices (perhaps Minerals also, &c.) that are in the other Parts of the Torrid Zone, under equal Parallels of Latitude; at least a Soil and Air capable of such, upon transplanting them hither, and Cultivation. I meant, also to make as diligent a Survey as I could, of the several smaller Islands, Shores, Capes, Bays, Creeks and Harbours, fit as well for Shelter as Defence, upon fortifying them; and of the Rocks and Shoals, the Soundings, Tides, and Currents, Winds and Weather, Variation, &c. Whatever

might be beneficial for Navigation, Trade or Settlement; or be of use to any who should prosecute the same Designs hereafter; to whom it might be serviceable to have so much of their Work done to their Hands; which they might advance and perfect by their own repeated Experiences. As there is no Work of this Kind brought to Perfection at once, I intended especially to observe what Inhabitants I should meet with, and to try to win them over to somewhat of Traffick and useful Intercourse, as there might be Commodities among any of them that might be fit for Trade or Manufacture, or any found in which they might be employed. Though as to the New Hollanders thereabouts, by the Experience I had had of their Neighbours formerly, I expected no great Matters from them.

With such Views as these, I set out at first from England; and would, according to the Method I proposed formerly have gone Westward, through the Magellanick Streight, or round Terra del Fuego rather, that I might have begun my Discoveries upon the Eastern and least known Side of the Terra Australis. But that way 'twas not possible for me to go, by Reason of the Time of Year in which I came out; for I must have been compassing the South of America in a very high Latitude, in the Depth of Winter there. I was therefore necessitated to Eastward by the Cape of Good Hope; and when I should be past it, 'twas requisite I should keep in a pretty high Latitude, to avoid the general Trade-winds that would be against me, and to have the Benefit of the variable Winds: By all which I was in a Manner unavoidably determin'd to fall in first with those Parts of New Holland I have hitherto been describing. For should it be ask'd why at my first making that Shore, I did not coast it to the Southward, and that way try to get round to the East of New Holland and New Guinea; I confess I was not for spending my Time more than was necessary in the higher Latitudes; as knowing that the Land there could not be so well worth the discovering, as the Parts that lay nearer the Line, and more directly under the Sun. Besides, at the Time when I should come first on New Holland, which was early in the Spring, I must, had I stood Southward, have had for some Time a great deal of Winter-weather, increasing in Severity, though not in Time, and a Place altogether unknown; which my Men, who were heartless enough to the Voyage at best, would never have born, after so long a Run as from Brazil hither.

For these Reasons therefore I chose to coast along to the Northward, and so to the East, and so thought to come round by the South of Terra Australis in my Return back, which should be in the Summer-season there: And this Passage back also I now thought I might possibly be able to shorten, should it appear, at my getting to the East Coast of New Guinea, that there is a Channel there coming out into these Seas, as I now suspected near Rosemary Island: Unless the high Tides and great Indraught thereabout should be occasion'd by the Mouth of some large River; which hath often low Lands on each Side of its Outlet, and many Islands and Sholes lying at its Entrance. But I rather thought it a Channel or Streight, than a River: And I was afterwards confirmed in this opinion, when by coasting New Guinea, found that other Parts of this great tract of Terra Australis, which had hitherto been represented as the Shore of a Continent, where certainly Islands; and 'tis probably the same with New Holland: Though for Reasons I shall afterwards shew, I could not return by the way propos'd to my self, to fix the Discovery. All that had now seen from the Latitude of 27 d. South to 25, which is Shark's Bay; and again from thence to Rosemary Islands, and about the Latitude of 20; seems to be nothing but Ranges of pretty large Islands against the Sea, whatever might be behind them to the Eastward, whether Sea or Land, Continent or Islands. (Dampier, 1906, 444, 457–60)

The last of the Dutch explorers, Lieutenant Jean Etienne Gonzal of the *Ridjer* (Horseman), made the only favourable report on the country, in 1756. The first European to see the land about the Gulf of Carpentaria in more than 100 years, he wrote:

The land was overgrown with tall grass, and they saw a number of fine dells or valleys, through which flowed various small rills of fresh

> water; the trees were very tall and straight, of regular growth and of different kinds, some of which would…furnish excellent timber for ships' masts, yards etc. The soil was very rich and on the whole the country looked very promising. (Heeres, 92)

It is uncertain precisely which area Gonzal here described. The eastern coast of the gulf is mostly flat country, with lots of low branching shrubs, grasses and squat, irregularly shaped trees. It is possible that he was describing the Torres Strait islands off Cape York at the head of the gulf, on some of which occurs the hoop pine (*Araucaria cunninghamii*), which could have made masts.

But the VOC was unmoved, even by the promise of masts, and it finally closed its book on New Holland. The results of 150 years of discovery and exploration had been disappointing. Those who had sailed on deliberate exploration had been concerned almost exclusively with prospects of trade and profit. They were not naturalists with an intrinsic interest in plants and animals, nor were they ethnologists. As Nicolaas Witson commented to a friend at the beginning of the eighteenth century: 'You asked for information about Asia; but no, our people there are not interested in science, only in money'. More scientific observation and description of Australia were to come in the second phase of its discovery by Europeans.

3

The English and French, 1768–80

Though France and Spain remained rivals, Britain emerged from the Seven Years' War (1756–63) as the dominant maritime and colonial power. As soon as the war was over, Britain embarked on an ambitious program of exploration, to locate the supposed North-West Passage from the Atlantic to the Pacific Ocean, and the supposed Terra Australis. Between 1764 and 1768, Byron, Wallis and Carteret each sought for these prizes in vain, though Wallis did discover Tahiti, and thought he saw the mythical continent to the south of it. Wallis reached England again with this news when, with the help of King George III and the Admiralty, the Royal Society was mounting expeditions to observe the transit of Venus across the face of the sun, due on 3 June 1769.

This was a scientific task of considerable significance, for accurate measurements of the transit would enable mathematicians to know the precise distance of the earth from the sun, which in turn would lead to more accurate navigation. The authorities decided to join the two purposes, by observing the transit from Tahiti and then extending the search for the southern continent.

The Admiralty provided a commander — Lieutenant James Cook. His pay was five shillings a day. He was a Yorkshireman, aged 40 and the son of a Scottish farm labourer and a Yorkshire mother. His ship, a converted collier, became HM Bark *Endeavour*. Cook, who had been a seaman in colliers from Whitby, Yorkshire, joined the navy and rose from the lower deck, an uncommon achievement. He was an experienced navigator and hydrographer of the St Lawrence River, Newfoundland and Labrador, and capable of being co-observer of the transit of Venus with the Society's astronomer, Charles Green.

The Society had proposed one of its members, Alexander Dalrymple, as co-observer with its astronomer. A geographer, hydrographer and recorder of discoveries in the South Pacific, he found details of Torres Strait between Australia and New Guinea in Spanish documents captured in the Philippines in 1762. Dalrymple wished to take command, but the Admiralty insisted that an officer must command a Royal Navy ship.

As mentioned, the scientific expedition was an ostensible excuse for a fourth exploratory voyage to the Pacific. The Admiralty gave Cook secret supplementary instructions to follow the observation of the transit of Venus with a search in the South Seas for discoveries and commercial prospects. If this search failed, he was to fall in with the land Tasman had discovered in 1642 and called New Zealand, explore as much of its coast as possible, and return to England by way of Cape Horn or the Cape of Good Hope. The officers and petty officers were bound to hand over their journals and logs. Cook was expected to bring back all possible observations, charts, views and hydrographic details of countries he explored and more — the nature of soil and products, beasts, birds, fishes and minerals. The Admiralty wanted seeds of trees and fruits and grains; an account of the native inhabitants, if any, and friendly alliance and trade with them; and, with their consent, possession of convenient situations in the country in the name of the King of Great Britain

Sydney Parkinson, 'Venus Fort, Erected by the *Endeavour*'s crew to secure themselves during the observation of the Transit of Venus, at Otaheite [Tahiti]'. From *A Journal of a Voyage to the South Seas*..., 1773. (Facsimile edition, Libraries Board of South Australia, 1972.)

At the Royal Society's request, the Admiralty directed Cook to take supernumeraries in the complement—Joseph (later Sir Joseph) Banks, a Lincolnshire squire aged 25 years, a member of the Society and a dedicated botanist, and his suite of eight, consisting of two naturalists, two artists and four servants, along with two greyhounds. With the qualification that the French navigator, Louis Antoine de Bougainville, sailing simultaneously, also had scientists on board, Cook's was the first voyage of discovery to be equipped for the descriptive sciences of zoology, botany and ethnology. Fortunately, Cook, in his first commission, and Banks, a man of high spirits and tolerance, were compatible. The two men wrote more than 100 000 words in their journals about their experiences and observations in Australia. As authors, Banks was often the more graphic, Cook mostly matter-of-fact. Clearly, they discussed what they saw in detail, and similarities in their journals show that they sometimes copied each other. At first Cook was more dependent on Banks in this, but as the voyage progressed he came to rely less on his younger companion.

Banks had a library of natural history. The *Endeavour* had charts, including those printed in Dalrymple's *An Account of the Discoveries made in the South Pacifick Ocean previous to 1764* (London, 1767), which showed Torres Strait, and in Charles de Brosses' *Historie des Navigations aux Terres Australes* (Paris, 1756). De Brosses' charts showed southern and eastern Australia with hypothetical coastlines from Tasmania to Nuyts Land in the Great Australian Bight in the west, north-east to Espiritu

'Mr Banks'. Stipple engraving by John Smith (1752–1812). (Rex Nan Kivell Collection, National Library of Australia.)

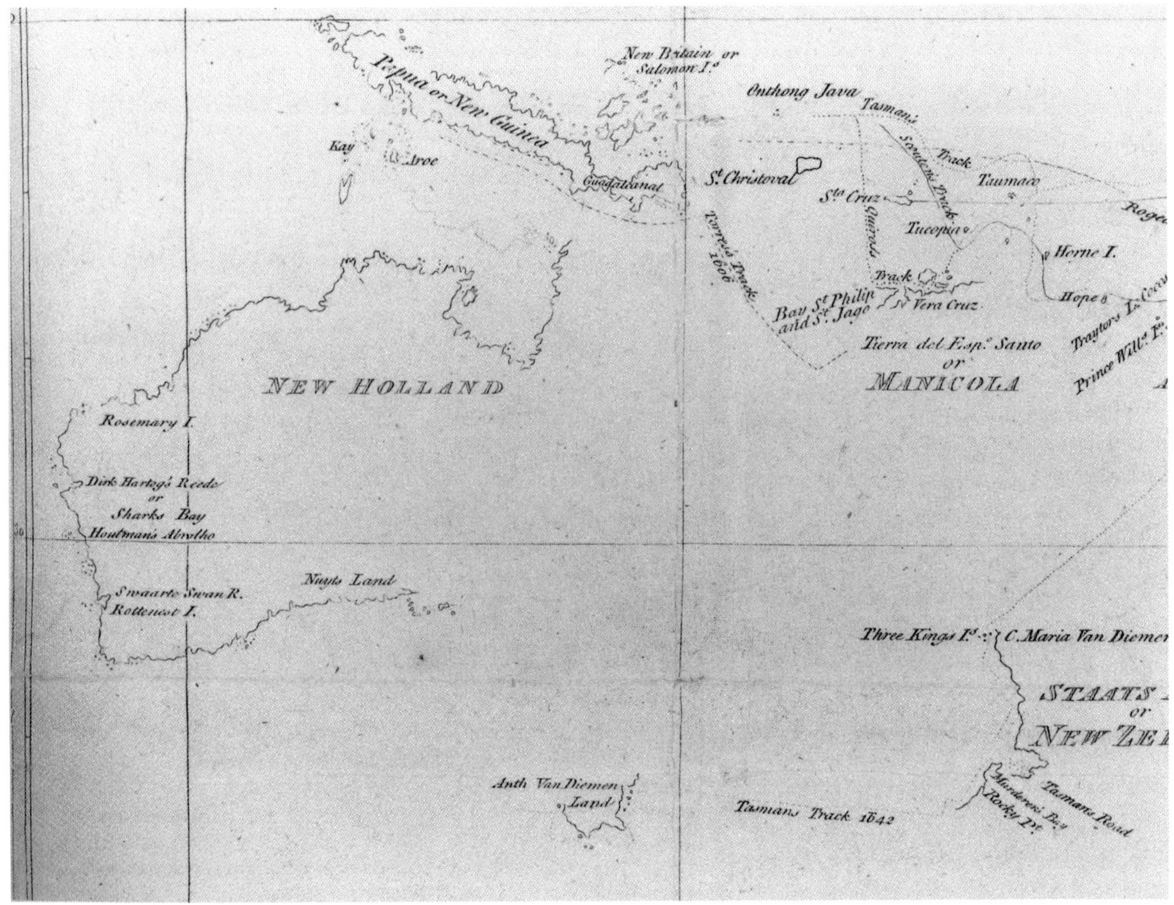

A section from Alexander Dalrymple's 'Chart of the South Pacifick Ocean', 1767. (British Library.)

Santo (the largest island in the group which Cook in 1774 named New Hebrides — nowVanuatu) and to a broad strait between Cape York and New Guinea. As well, the *Endeavour*'s library included works by Dampier and other navigators and geographers.

Whether Cook had any part in choosing the *Endeavour* is uncertain. However, experience of it showed him that it was just the type of ship needed for Pacific exploration:

> A ship of this kind must not be of a great draught of water, yet of sufficient burden and capacity to carry a proper quantity of provisions and necessaries for her complement of men and for the term requisite to perform the voyage. She must also be of a construction that will bear to take the ground and of a size, which, in case of necessity, may be safely and conveniently laid on shore to repair any accidental damage or defect. These properties are not to be found in ships of war of forty guns nor in frigates nor in East India Company's ships nor in a large three-decked West Indian ship, not, indeed, in other but north-country built ships, such as are built for the coal trade, which are peculiarly adapted for this purpose.

Cook's perspicacity as a mariner was proved by his choice of such ships for his second and third voyages. All three were Whitby-built, three of them converted colliers, and all performed very well.

The *Endeavour*, at four years old, cost £2800 and its conversion and stores raised its price to more than £8200. It was 32 metres long overall, with a burthen of 368 tons (1 ton=2.83 cubic metres). Having no figurehead and only a straight stem, it was designated a bark and was ship-rigged, with square sails on all three masts. Armament was ten carriage guns, twelve swivel guns (portable cannon mountable on a ship's bulwarks or boat's gunwales) and a quantity of muskets and ammunition.

The *Endeavour* had a 'long' boat (of 6.7 m) able to carry 20 people, water and stores; a pinnace 4.26 metres long, specifically for the commander's use and able to carry twelve people; and a yawl, the smallest boat. According to an anonymous letter from the *Endeavour*, she was 'the dullest sailing vessel...you will not find eight knots an hour upon our log-book in the whole voyage', but Cook said 'a better ship for such a Service I never would wish for' (Cook, I, 645, 506). Because of its qualities he was able to stay longer in the Pacific than any before him. On return to England the *Endeavour* served in the navy until sold to a foreign trader in 1774.

The *Endeavour*'s complement of 94 included fourteen marines and eleven civilians (Banks and his suite, the astronomer and his servant). The marines, who were guards ashore and afloat, got scant mention in Cook's and Banks' journals of their time on the Australian coast — occasional small arms exercise and the flogging of private Thomas Dunster with twelve lashes seven times for persistent thefts. The youngest midshipman was Isaac Manley, son of a lawyer who was a bencher of the Middle Temple. He later became a vice-admiral. A celebrated goat which provided milk to the officers was to complete its second voyage around the world, having previously been on board Wallis' *Dolphin*. The ship also had sheep, pigs and fowls aboard.

The expedition set out on 25 August 1768 and was away three years. They spent four and a half months at Tahiti. While it used to be said that the observation of the transit of Venus was a failure, modern analysis has shown that the results obtained from the *Endeavour* were surprisingly accurate. Afterwards, Cook searched the south-central Pacific for the Southland for two months, then spent nearly six months on the coast of New Zealand, being nine weeks in all ashore at eight landing places. He circumnavigated the 4500 kilometres of coastline of the north and south islands.

Having complied fully with the Admiralty's instructions, Cook had to decide which way to go home — 'either around the Cape of Good Hope, or Cape Horn, as from Circumstances you may judge the Most Eligible way'. In unforeseen emergencies, his instructions said, 'you are...toproceed, as upon advice with your Officers you shall judge most advantageous to the Service on which you are employed' (Cook, I, cclxxxiii). A man of infinite resource and curiosity, Cook gave his reasons in his journal for the decisions he made:

John Noble, portrait of Captain Cook. (Dixson Library, State Library of New South Wales.)

> To return by the way of *Cape Horn* was what I most wish'd, because by this rout we should have been able to prove the existence or non existence of a Southern Continent which yet remains Doubtfull; but in order to ascertain this we must have kept in a high latitude in the very depth of winter but the condition of the ship in every respect was not thought sufficient for such an undertaking. For the same reason the thoughts of proceeding directly to the Cape of Good Hope was laid aside especially as no discovery of any moment could be hoped for in that rout. It was therefore resolved to return by way of the East Indies by the following rout: upon leaving this coast

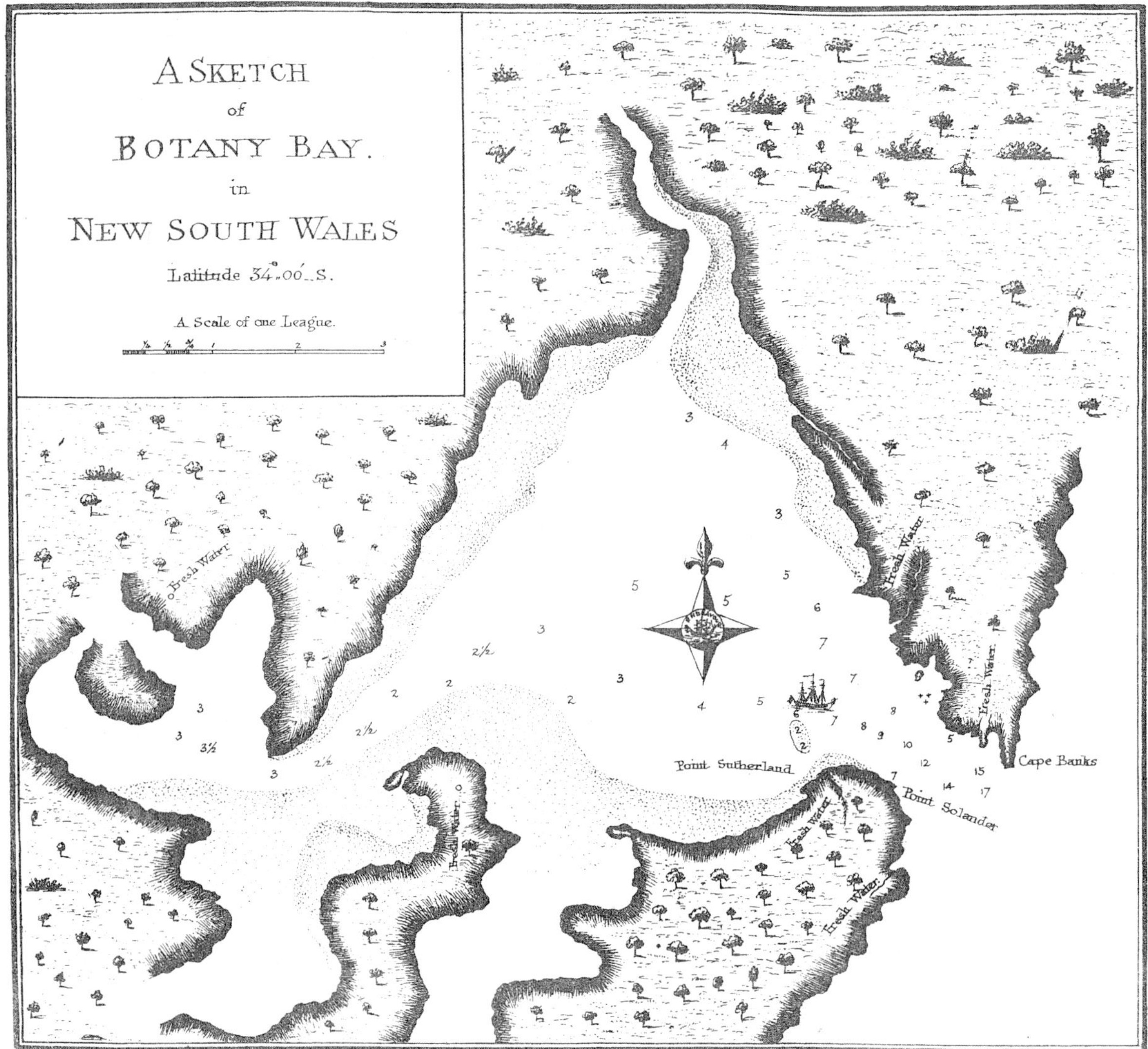

James Cook, 'A Sketch of Botany Bay in New South Wales', from *Historical Records of New South Wales, Facsimiles of Charts,* 1893. This facsimile of Cook's map has HM Bark *Endeavour* in the bay off Point Sutherland.

to steer to the westward untill we fall in with the East Coast of New Holland and then to follow the direction of that Coast to the northward or what other direction it may take untill we arrive at its northern extremity, and if this should be found impractical, then to endeavour to fall in with the land or islands discover'd by Quirós. With this View at day light in the morning we got under sail and put to sea. (Cook, I, 273)

(In Cook's journal, this entry appears under the date 31 March [1770]. Because ship's time ran from noon till noon, the morning referred to was that of 1 April — though it was actually 2 April, as Cook had crossed the international date line in the Pacific to the west and did not correct his journal until he reached Batavia.)

Cook was embarking on the second longest discovery of Australia's coastline to date, during which he was to survive two extraordinary misadventures. He tried to meet the coast of Van Diemen's Land where Tasman left it so as to continue the charting of the coast of New Holland. Gales drove the *Endeavour* northwards until at 6 a.m. on 20 April, Lieutenant Zachary Hicks sighted land which, according to Cook's log, was 'extending from NE to West at the distance of 5 or 6 Leagues'. This land was the east coast of New Holland and the locality was in what became East Gippsland, a region of Victoria 69 kilometres from that state's border with New South Wales.

Cook was on the east coast of New Holland for more than four months — 27 days on the Victorian and New South Wales coasts and 100 days on the Queensland coast, a total lineal distance of 4000 kilometres. As the Dutch had traversed 18 850 kilometres of the north, west and south coasts of New Holland from Cape York to Nuyts Archipelago in the Great Australian Bight, only 1740 kilometres from the Bight to Point Hicks were undiscovered — until 1800. Cook was to make eleven landings and bestow more than 100 place names. His 'Chart of the Sea Coast of New South Wales', although it had some errors, was remarkable for the accuracy of its positions, considering he did not have a chronometer. Not having imperative instructions to explore, as he had in New Zealand, Cook had turned for home and was not tarrying unduly. Sailing northward he looked for a harbour, as much for scraping the *Endeavour*'s fouled bottom as for exploration. He noted one bay (Jervis Bay, 352 kilometres north of Point Hicks) that was not favourable enough to 'induce me to loose time beating up to it'. On 30 April Cook discovered 'a Bay which appear'd to be tollerably well shelter'd from all winds in to which I resolved to go with the Ship'. This was Botany Bay, 500 kilometres from Point Hicks. In seven days there Cook explored the country, obtained wood and water, and had the ship scrubbed and cleaned and sails repaired. In his first encounter with the Aborigines he was unable to

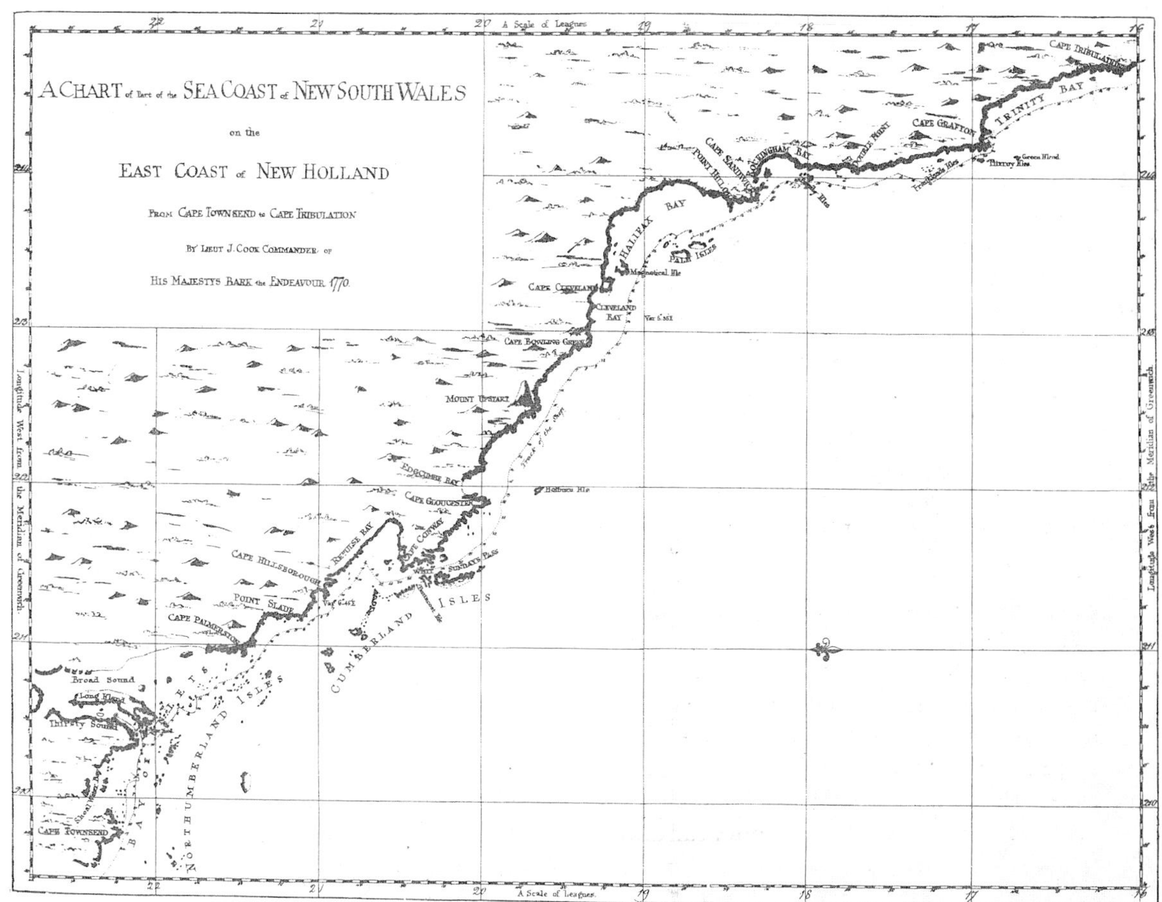

James Cook, 'A Chart of the Sea Coast of New South Wales on the East Coast of New Holland from Cape Townshend to Cape Tribulation', 1770, from *Historical Records of New South Wales, Facsimiles of Charts*, 1893

communicate with them. Banks collected plants.

Eighteen days later and 1290 kilometres farther north, Cook anchored at Bustard Bay, north of the present Bundaberg in Queensland, and went ashore exploring for two days. He was under way again on 26 May and nearing the end of plain sailing and the beginning of incomparable feats of navigation and seamanship. Involuntarily, he was to traverse the Great Barrier Reef, by far the largest coral reef of its kind, for almost its entire length of 1850 kilometres northwards along the coast to the Gulf of Papua. It is 207 000 square kilometres of reefs strewn with flat coral islets or atolls and mountainous islands. From about 180 kilometres off the coast in central Queensland reefs scattered over a wide area with deep channels between them got closer to the coast. From Cairns to Torres Strait the reef is one monolithic rampart, broken only by small openings. Its distance from the coast narrows progressively from 80 kilometres to 25 kilometres in the far north.

Cook did not know the reef existed. Nearly three months later he was to say:

> After having been intangled among them more or less ever sence the 26th of May, in which time we have saild 360 Leagues without ever having a Man out of the cheans heaving the Lead when the Ship was under way, a circumstance that I dare say never happen'd to any Ship before and yet here it was absolutely necessary. (Cook, I, 375)

In this predicament, Cook was unlikely to anchor for exploration, only to search for water as he did at Thirsty Sound, between Rockhampton and Mackay; at Quail Island, south of Whitsunday Passage, for coconuts; at Palm Island, north of Townsville, and again for water at Yarrabah, near Cairns.

Cook had charts which showed the Torres Strait between New Holland and New Guinea, but of course he did not know how far north the reefs extended. If the strait could not be confirmed he would need to sail around the north of New Guinea to Batavia, with time to spare so as to escape the north-west monsoon. There was also the question of Quirós' islands and, early in June, Cook decided to look for them:

> At this time we shortend sail and hauld off shore ENE and NEBE close upon a wind. My intention was to stretch off all night as well to avoid the dangers we saw ahead as to see if any Islands lay in the offing, especialy as we now begin to draw near the Latitude of those discover'd by Quirós which some Geographers, for what reason I know not have thought proper to tack to this land. (Cook, I, 343)

This decision led to Cook's first misadventure. Quirós' islands were actually 2160 kilometres to the east. Two months later Cook had occasion to correct their position: 'The Islands discover'd by *Quirós* called by him Australia del Espiritu Santo lays in this parallel but how far to the East is hard to say, most charts place them as far to the West as this Country, but we are morally certain that he never was upon any part of this coast' (Cook, I, 376). This was 12 June, the seventeenth day of sounding and 1167 kilometres north of Bustard Bay. Cook had turned the *Endeavour* offshore at nightfall because of the dangers he saw. At first the water deepened safely from 25 to 38 metres, but then, says Cook:

> we fell into 12, 10 and eight fathom. At this time I had every body at their stations to put about and come too an anchor but in this I was not so fortunate for meeting again with deep water I thought there could be no danger in standg on. Before 10 o Clock we had 20 and 21 fathom and continued in that depth untill a few Minutes before a 11 when we had 17 and before the Man at the lead could heave another cast the Ship Struck and stuck fast. Emmidiatly upon this we took in all our sails hoisted out the boats and sounded round the Ship, and found that we had got upon the SE edge of a reef of Coral rocks. (Cook, I, 344)

The *Endeavour* was on what became known as Endeavour Reef, sixteen nautical miles from shore, 4610 kilometres from the nearest help at Batavia in Indonesia. It had boats for only half of the complement to save themselves and leave the others 'on a barbarous coast', as Sydney Parkinson, one of Banks's artists, called the country. 'If the ship had been wrecked, and we had escaped the perils of the sea, we should have fallen into the rapacious hands of savages'.

Cook described first emergency measures:

> the Ship being quite fast, upon which we went to work to lighten her as fast as possible which seem'd to be the only means we had left to get her off as we went a shore about the top of high-water. We not only started water but throw'd over board our guns Iron and stone ballast Casks, Hoops staves oyle Jars, decay'd Stores &c., many of these last articles lay in the way at coming at heavyer. All this time the Ship made little or no water. At a 11 o Clock in the am being high-water as we thought we try'd to heave her off without success, she not being a float by a foot or more notwithstanding by this time we had thrown overboard 40 or 50 Tun weight; as this was not found sufficient we continued to Lighten her by every method we could think off. As the Tide fell the Ship began to make water as much as two Pumps could free. At Noon she lay with 3 or 4 Strakes heel to Starboard. (Cook, I, 344–5)

Six of the guns which were on deck were thrown overboard. According to Parkinson: 'we fixed buoys to them, intending, if we escaped, to have heaved them up again; but, on attempting it, we found it was impracticable' (Parkinson, 143). In 1969 members of the Academy of Natural Sciences of Philadelphia, Pennsylvania, U.S.A., located the guns. They retrieved three of them and Australian skindivers found the others. The guns are at Cooktown; Kurnell, Cook's landing place at Botany Bay; Sydney; New Zealand; Philadelphia; and the National Maritime Museum, Greenwich, London. Australian skindivers also recovered an anchor in 1972. It is at Cooktown and a replica is at Kurnell.

Cook was puzzled that the next tide did not allow him to take off the lightened ship. (On this coast only every alternate tide rises to a full height.) As he ran on the reef at the top of the higher of the two waters he had to wait 24 hours to take the ship off on 13 June.

By contrast with the unemotional account of the near disaster which Cook wrote, Banks's description of it was most dramatic:

> [10 June]...[we] went to bed in perfect security, but scarce were we warm in our beds when

'Coasted the shore to the Northward through the most dangerous Navigation that perhaps ever ship was in...' (Cook). This illustration by Geoffrey C. Ingleton appeared in *The Explorations of Captain James Cook in the Pacific*, edited by A. Grenfell Price, Limited Editions Club, 1957. (Mitchell Library, State Library of New South Wales.)

we were calld up with the alarming news of the ship being fast ashore upon a rock, which she in a few moments convincd us of by beating very violently against the rocks. Our situation became now greatly alarming: we had stood off shore 3 hours and a half with a pleasant breeze so knew we could not be very near it: we were little less than certain that we were upon sunken coral rocks, the most dreadfull of all others on account of their sharp points and grinding quality which cut through a ships bottom almost immediately. The officers however behavd with inimitable coolness void of all hurry and confusion; a boat was got out in which the master went and after sounding round the ship found that she had ran over a rock and consequently had Shole water all round her. All this time she continued to beat very much so that we could hardly keep our legs upon the Quarter deck; by the light of the moon we could see her sheathing boards &c. floating thick round her; about 12 her false keel came away...

[11 June] The most critical part of our distress now aproachd: the ship was almost afloat and every thing ready to get her into deep water but she leakd so fast that with all our pumps we could just keep her free: if (as was probable) she should make more water when hauld off she must sink and we well knew that our boats were not capable of carrying us all ashore, so that some, probably the most of us, must be drownd: a better fate maybe than those would have who should get ashore without arms to defend themselves from the Indians or provide themselves with food, on a countrey where we had not the least reason to hope for subsistance had they even every convenence to take it as netts &c, so barren had we always found it; and had they even met with good usage from the natives and food to support them, debarrd from a hope of ever again seing their native countrey or conversing with any but the most uncivilizd savages perhaps in the world.

The dreadfull time now approachd and the anxiety in every bodys countenance was visible enough: the Capstan and Windlace were mannd and they began to heave: fear of Death now stard us in the face; hopes we had none but of being able to keep the ship afloat till we could run her ashore on some part of the main where out of her materials we might build a vessel large enough to carry us to the East Indies. At 10 O'Clock she floated and was in a few minutes hawld into deep water where to our great satisfaction she made no more water than she had done, which was indeed full as much as we could manage tho no one there was in the ship but who willingly exerted his utmost strength.

[12 June] The people who had been 24 hours at exceeding hard work now began to flag; myself unused to labour was much fatigued and had laid down to take a little rest, was awakd about 12 with the alarming news of the ships having gaind so much upon the Pumps that she had four feet water in her hold: add to this that the wind blew off the land a regular land breeze so that all hopes of running her ashore were totaly cut off. This however acted upon every body like a charm: rest was no more thought of but the pumps went with unwearied vigour till the water was all out which was done in a much shorter time than was expected, and upon examination it was found that she never had half so much water in her as was thought, the Carpenter having made a mistake in sounding the pumps...

During the whole time of this distress I must say for the credit of our people that I beleive every man exerted his utmost for the preservation of the ship, contrary to what I have universaly heard to be the behavior of sea men who have commonly as soon as a ship is in a desperate situation began to plunder and refuse all command. This was no doubt owing intirely to the cool and steady conduct of the officers, who during the whole time never gave an order which did not shew them to be perfectly composd and unmovd by the circumstances howsoever dreadfull they might appear. (Banks, II, 77–81)

An operation known as fothering had saved the ship. Both Banks and Parkinson say a midshipman, Jonathan Monkhouse, suggested it. Cook gave him credit in his description of this operation:

> The Leak now decreaseth but for fear it should break out again we got the Sail ready fill'd for fothering. The manner this is done is thus, we Mix oacham & Wool together (but oacham alone would do) and chop it up small and then stick it loosly by handfulls all over the sail and throw over it sheeps dung or other filth. Horse dung for this purpose is the best. The sail thus prepared is hauld under the Ships bottom by ropes and if the place of the Leak is uncertain, it must be hauld from one part of her bottom to a nother untill the place is found where it takes effect; while the sail is under the ship the oacham &c is washed off and part of it carried along with the water into the leak and in part stops up the hole. Mr Munkhouse one of my Midshipmen was once in a Merchant ship which sprung a leak and made 48 inches water per hour but by this means was brought home from Virginia to London with only her proper crew, to him I gave the deriction of this who exicuted it very much to my satisfaction. (Cook, I, 347)

Cook sent the master with two boats to look for a harbour 'where we could repair our defects and put the Ship into a proper Trim' (Cook, I, 348). The first prospect, Weary Bay, proved to be too shallow, but a second seemed suitable. Banks wrote: 'We now began to consider our good fortune; had it blown as fresh the day before yesterday or before that we could never have got off but must inevitably have been dashd to peices on the rocks' (Banks, II, 81). Of this second harbour, Endeavour River, Banks wrote:

> The Captn and myself went ashore to view the Harbour and found it beyond our most sanguine wishes: it was the mouth of a river the entrance of which was to be sure narrow enough and shallow, but when once in the ship might be moord afloat so near the shore that by a stage from her to it all her Cargo might be got out and in again in a very short time; in this same place she might be hove down with all ease, but the beach gave signs of the tides rising in the springs 6 or 7 feet which was more than enough to do our business without that trouble. The meeting with so many natural advantages in a harbour so near us at the very time of our misfortune appeard almost providential; we had not in the voyage before seen a place so well suited for our purpose as this was, and certainly had no right to expect the tides to rise so high here that did not rise half so much at the place where we struck, only 8 Leagues from this place; we therefore returnd on board in high spirits and raisd the spirits of our friends on board as much as our own by bringing them the welcome news of aproaching security. (Banks, II, 81–2)

On 18 June the *Endeavour* entered a harbour but ran ashore twice — of no consequence, Cook said — and was moored alongside a steep beach the following day. Cook named the river running into the harbour after the ship. The harbour was later named Cooktown. An inspection showed that the reef had broken through four planks and damaged three more. Cook wrote:

> scarce a splinter was to be seen but the whole was cut away as if it had been done by the hands of Man with a blunt edge tool. Fortunatly for us the timbers in this place were very close, other ways it would have been impossible to have saved the ship...A large piece of Coral rock was sticking in one hole and several pieces of the fothering, small stones, sand &c had made its way in and lodged between the timbers which had stoped the water from forceing its way in in great quantities. Part of the sheathing was gone from under the larboard bow, part of the false keel was gone and the remainder in such a shatter'd condition that we should be much better of if it was gone also; her fore foot and some part of her Main keel was also damaged but not materialy. (Cook, I, 350–1)

The ship was delayed 50 days at Endeavour River and the voyage continued on 7 August. The reef ahead as far as Torres Strait Cook was to call The Labyrinth on his chart. He and his officers looked for channels through it from the masthead and from hills at Lookout Point, 70 kilometres north of Cooktown and 50 kilometres from the reef, and two offshore islands, Eagle and Lizard. Cook said: 'I saw that we were surrounded on every side with shoals and no such thing as a passage to Sea but through the winding channels between them, dangerous to the highest degree in so much that I was quite at a loss which way to steer' (Cook, I, 370). The prospect of beating southward against the wind was daunting, so he decided to press on to the north.

At Lizard Island Cook surveyed the scene from the highest hill. Of the outermost shoals he wrote: 'I did not doubt but what I should be able to get without them for there appear'd to be several breaks or Partitions in the reef and deep water between it and the Islands' (Cook, I, 373). Because of haze he camped on the island and hoped for a clearer view in the morning. The weather remained hazy but at 3 a.m. he sent one of the ship's mates in the pinnace to examine a channel. The mate reported that it seemed to him very narrow but Cook thought he had seen it at a disadvantage and said he was not discouraged.

The channel, 22 kilometres north of the island, is now known as Cook's Passage and is one of the safest and best for ships on routes between Australia and Papua New Guinea. Cook rejoiced because he was out of the reef, but he also left it rather wistfully:

> It was with great regret I was obliged to quit this coast unexplored to its Northern extremity which I think we were not far off, for I firmly believe that it doth not join to *New Guinea*, however this I hope yet to clear up being to get in with the land again as soon as I can do it with safety and the reasons I have before assigned will I presume be thought sufficient for my haveing left it at this time. (Cook, I, 375–6)

Unfortunately, Cook was once more too venturesome and his second misadventure was near. Banks described how Cook got into his predicament outside the reef which moved him more than running on to Endeavour Reef did:

> [15 August] The Captn was fearfull of going too far from the Land, least he should miss an opportunity of examining whether or not the passage which is layd down in some charts between New Holland and New Guinea realy existed or not, steerd the ship west right in for the land; about 12 O'Clock it was seen from the Mast head and about one the Reef laying without it in just the same manner as when we left it. He stood on however resolving to stand off at night after having taken a nearer view, but just at night fall found himself in a manner embayd in the reef so that it was a moot Point whether or not he could weather it on either tack; we stood however to the Northward and at dark it was concluded that she would go clear of every thing we could see. The night however was not the most agreable: all the dangers we had escapd were little in comparison of being thrown upon this reef if that should be our lot. A Reef such a one as I now speak of is a thing scarcely known in Europe or indeed any where but in these seas: it is a wall of Coral rock rising almost perpendicularly out of the unfathomable ocean, always overflown at high water commonly 7 or 8 feet, and generaly bare at low water; the large waves of the vast ocean meeting with so sudden a resistance make here a most terrible surf Breaking mountain high, especialy when as in our case the general trade wind blows directly upon it. (Banks, II, 104–5)

Cook was uncommonly graphic in his description of the predicament:

> [16 August] A little after 4 oClock the roaring of the Surf was plainly heard and at day break the vast foaming breakers were too plainly to be seen not a Mile from us towards which we found the Ship was carried by the waves surprisingly fast. We had at this time not an air of wind and the depth of water was unfathomable so that there was not a possibillity of Anchoring, in this distressed situation we had nothing but Providence and the small Assistance our boats could give us to trust to; the Pinnace was under a repair and could not immidiately be hoisted out, the Yawl was put in the water and the Long-boat hoisted out and both sent ahead to tow which together with the help of our sweeps abaft got the Ships head round to the northward which seem'd to be the only way to keep her off the reef or at least to delay time, before this was effected it was 6 oClock and we were not above 80 or 100 Yards from the breakers, the same Sea that

washed the side of the Ship rose in a breaker prodigiously high the very next time it did rise so that between us and distruction was only a dismal Vally the breadth of one wave and even now no ground could be felt with 120 fathoms. The Pinnace was by this time patched up and hoisted out and sent ahead to tow; still we had hardly any hopes of saving the Ship and full as little our lives as we were full 10 Leagues from the nearest Land and the boats not sufficient to carry the whole of us, yet in this truly terrible situation not one man ceased to do his utmost and that with as much calmness as if no danger had been near. All the dangers we had escaped were little in comparison of being thrown upon this Reef where the Ship must be dashed to peices in a Moment. A Reef such as is here spoke of is scarcely known in Europe, it is a Wall of Coral Rock rising all most perpendicular out of the unfathomable Ocean, always overflown at high-water generally 7 or 8 feet and dry in places at low-water; the large waves of the vast Ocean meeting with so sudden a resistance makes a most terrible surf breaking mountains high especially as in our case when the general trade wind blowes directly upon it. At this critical juncture when all our endeavours seem'd too little a small air of wind sprung up, but so small that at any other time in a Calm we should not have observed it, with this, and the assistance of our boats we could observe the Ship to move off from the Reef in a slanting direction, but in less than 10 Minutes we had as flat a Calm as ever when our fears were again renewed for as yet we were not above 200 Yards from the breakers. Soon after our friendly Breeze Viseted us again and lasted about as long as before. A small opening was now seen in the reef about a quarter of a Mile from us which I sent one of the Mates to examine, its breadth was not more than the length of the Ship but within was smooth water, into this place it was resolv'd to push her if possible haveing no other probable Views to save her, for we were still in the very jaws of distruction, and it was a doubt whether or no we could reach this opening, however we soon got off it when to our surprise we found the Tide of Ebb gushing out like a Mill stream so that it was impossible to get in; we however took all the advantage possible of it and it carried us out about a 1/4 of a Mile from the breakers, but it was too narrow for us to keep in long; how ever what with the help of Ebb and our boats we by noon had got an offing of one and a half or two Miles, yet we could hardly flater our selves with hopes of getting clear even if a breeze should spring up as we were by this time imbayed by the Reef, and the Ship in spite of our endeavours driving before the Sea into the bight, the Ebb had been in our favour and we had reason to suppose that the flood which was now making would be againest us, the only hopes we had was another opening we saw about a Mile to the Westward of us which I sent Lieutenant Hicks in the Small boat to examine.

[17 August] While Mr Hicks was examining the opening we strugled hard with the flood sometime gaining a little and at other times looseing. At 2 oClock Mr Hicks returned with a favourable account of the opening, it was immidiately resolved to try to secure the Ship in it, narrow and dangerous as it was, it seem'd to be the only means we had of saving her as well as our selves. A light breeze soon after sprung up at ENE which with the help of our boats and a flood tide we soon enter'd the opening and was hurried through in a short time by a rappid tide like a Mill race which kept us from driving againest either side, tho the channel was not more than a quarter of a Mile broad, we had however two boats a head to direct us through, our depth of water in the Channell was from 30 to 7 fathom very erregular soundings and foul ground untill we had got quite within the Reef where we anchor'd in 19 fathom a Corally & Shelly Bottom. (Cook, I, 377–80)

Cook named the site of his escape Providential Channel. It is opposite Cape Weymouth, 40 kilometres from the reef, a quarter of a mile wide and has a rock nearly in the middle. It is so short that transition from the heavy ocean sea to smooth water is almost instantaneous. Cook had been out of sight of the coast for 370 kilometres.

Admiral W.J.L. Wharton, who edited a version of Cook's journal in 1893, recorded a sidelight to this drama. It involved the Royal Society's astronomer, Charles Green, Charles Clerke, master's mate, who was with Cook in his three voyages of exploration, and Stephen Forwood, the gunner:

> As a proof of the calmness which prevailed on board, it may be mentioned that when in the height of the danger, Mr Green, Mr Clerke, and Mr Forwood the gunner, were engaged in taking a Lunar, to obtain the longitude. The note in Mr Green's log is: 'These observations were very good, the limbs of sun and moon very distinct, and a good horizon. We were about 100 yards from the reef, where we expected the ship to strike every minute, it being calm, no soundings, and the swell heaving us right on.' (Wharton, 305)

Cook reflected on his second narrow escape from disaster:

> [17 August] [I was] happy once more to incounter there shoals which but two days ago our utmost wishes were crowned by geting clear of, such are the Visissitudes attending this kind of service and must always attend an unknown Navigation: Was it not from the pleasure which naturly results to a Man from his being the first discoverer, even was it nothing more than land and Shoals, this service would be insuportable especialy in far distant parts, like this, short of Provisions and almost every other necessary. The world will hardly admit of an excuse for a man leaving a Coast unexplored he has once discover'd, if dangers are his excuse he is than charged with *Timorousness* and want of Perseverance and at once pronounced the unfitest man in the world to be employ'd as a discoverer; if on the other hand he boldly incounters all the dangers and obstacles he meets and is unfortunate enough not to succeed he is than charged with *Temerity* and want of conduct. The former of these aspersins cannot with Justice be laid to my charge and if I am fortunate enough to surmount all the dangers we may meet the latter will never be brought in question. I must own that I have ingaged more among the Islands and shoals upon this coast than may be thought with prudence I ought to have done with a single Ship and every other thing considered, but if I had not we should not have been able to give any better account of the one half of it than if I had never been able to give any better account of the one half of it than if we had never seen it, that is we should not have been able to say whether it consisted of main land or Islands and as to its produce we must have been totally ignorant of as being inseparable with the other. (Cook, I, 379–80)

As had Torres and Bougainville before him, Cook discovered the hazards of Coral Sea navigation. This area of the Pacific Ocean consists of scattered reefs and islands, often little more than sandbanks, spreading over a sea area of 1 035 995 square kilometres with only a few square kilometres of land. Some of the islands have a cover of grassy scrub-type type vegetation.

Cook's ordeal by reefs continued for fifteen days sailing of almost 740 kilometres from the Endeavour River to the northern extremity of the east coast of New Holland at Cape York which they reached on 22 August. The next day, at Possession Island, Cook took possession of what he eventually named New South Wales:

> [I] may land no more on the Eastern coast of *New Holland*, and on the Western side I can make no new discovery the honour of which belongs to the Dutch Navigators; but the Eastern Coast from the Latitude of 38°S [Point Hicks] down to this place [10 ½°S] I am confident was never seen or viseted by any European before us. (Cook, I, 387)

Possession Island is 30 kilometres west of Cape York and at the entrance to Endeavour Strait, one of nine channels in the Torres Strait. After two days of sounding his way through 93 kilometres of Endeavour Strait, Cook landed at the western entrance to Booby Island on 24 August. It was the eleventh and last landing on the coast. He was the first navigator for 164 years to pass through the strait since Torres traversed it through a channel farther north. Cook's observation from this island:

> left me no room to doubt but we were got to the Westward of *Carpentaria* or the Northern

> extremity of *New-Holland* and had now an open Sea to the westward, which gave me no small satisfaction not only because the danger and fatigues of the Voyage was drawing near to an end, but by being able to prove that New-Holland and New-Guinea are two Seperate Lands or Islands, which untill this day hath been a doubtfull point with Geographers. (Cook, I, 390)

He later wrote of his passage:

> It is also very probable that among these Islands are as good if not better passages than the one we have come thro', altho one need hardly wish for a better was the Access to it from the Eastward less dangerous, but this difficulty will remain untill some better way is found out than the one we came...
>
> With respect to the Shoals that lay upon this Coast I must observe for the benifit of those who may come after me, that I do not beleive the one half of them are laid down in my chart, for it would be obsurd to suppose that we could see or find them all. (Cook, I, 391–2)

As well as surviving the hazards of the Great Barrier Reef, Cook had not lost a man from scurvy for he insisted on the general regimen proposed by James Lind. The tragedy of the voyage was the incidence of malaria and a virulent type of dysentery (known as the bloody flux) during two months spent at Batavia for necessary repairs to damage the ship received on Endeavour Reef. In this pestilential place seven of the crew died and 23 more on the way to Cape Town, including astronomer Green, Midshipman Monkhouse, who fothered the hole in the ship at the reef, and the incorrigible marine Dunster. Alone in the complement a 70-year-old seaman, who was an inebriate, did not become ill there. Hicks, who was the first European to sight the east coast of Australia, died of consumption before reaching England.

Cook's report on the condition of the *Endeavour*'s hull as revealed at Batavia read:

> [9 October] In the PM Hove the Larboard side of the Ship Keel out and found her bottom to be in a far worse condition than we expected, the False Keel was gone to within 20 feet of the stern post, the Main Keel wounded in many places very considerably, a great quantity of Sheathing [off], several planks much damaged especially under the Main channell near the Keel, where two planks and a half near 6 feet in length were within 1/8 of a Inch of being cut through, and here the worms had made their way quite into the Timbers, so that it was a Matter of Surprise to every one who saw her bottom how we had kept her above water; and yet in this condition we had saild some hundreds of Leagues in as dangerous a Navigation as is in any part of the world, happy in being ignorant of the continual danger we were in. In the Evening righted the Ship, Having only time to patch up some of the worst places to prevent the water geting in in large quantitys for the present. In the Morning hove her down again and most of the

Sydney Parkinson, the artist-draughtsman (1745?–71) who specialised in botanical drawings, made at least 1300 sketches as he travelled with Cook and Banks in the *Endeavour*. Parkinson died when only 26 of fever contracted at Batavia. (From Sydney Parkinson, *A Journal of a Voyage to the South Seas*, 1773, facsimile edition, Libraries Board of South Australia, 1972.)

'The Lad Taiyota, Native of Otaheite [Tahiti] in the Dress of his country'. This flute-playing child boarded the *Endeavour* at Tahiti with the priest-navigator, Tupaia, to whom he was servant. Tupaia acted as an interpreter between Cook and the Maoris, and tried to communicate with the Aborigines without success. Both priest and boy died of fever at Batavia, as did seven of Cook's crew. (From Sydney Parkinson, *A Journal of a Voyage to the South Seas*, 1773, facsimile edition, Libraries Board of South Australia, 1972.)

> Carpenters and Caulkers in the yard (which are not a few) were set to work upon her bottom, and at the same time a number of slaves were employ'd bailing the water out of the hold. Our people altho they attend were seldom called upon, indeed by this time we were so weakend by sickness that we could not muster above 20 Men and officers that were able to do duty, so little should we have been able to have hove her down and repair'd her our selves as I at one time thought us capable of. (Cook, I, 438)

Cook struck a note of pride in his report from Batavia to the Admiralty: 'after all [we] put to Sea with a Leaky ship and afterwards Coasted the Shore to the Northward through the most dangerous navigation that perhaps ever Ship was in untill we found a Passage into the Indian Sea' (Cook, I, 500).

The *Endeavour* returned to England on 12 July 1771, after three years absence. Newspapers took more interest in Banks and Solander's botanical specimens than in Cook's discoveries in New Zealand and Australia. However, the kangaroo taken at the Endeavour River did arouse comment. 'Upon this barbarous shore,' said one report, 'we took an uncommon curious animal, which weighed upwards of 80 pounds; it was formed like a rat in the face, and run erect upon its hinder legs' (Cook, I, 654)

An enterprising publisher produced a surreptitous and anonymous book two months after Cook returned. It was entitled *A Journal of a Voyage round the World, In his Majesty's Ship ENDEAVOUR, In the years 1768, 1769, 1770 and 1771.* An official account of the voyage and its predecessors, compiled by John Hawkesworth, came out nearly two years later — *An Account of the Voyages undertaken...for making Discoveries in the Southern Hemisphere.* Books about Cook's voyages were bestsellers for decades thereafter.

The Board of Admiralty praised Cook for his work, its secretary writing:

> Having laid the same [your journals and charts] before my Lords Commissioners of the Admiralty I have the pleasure to acquaint you that their Lordships extremely well approve of the whole of your proceedings and that they have great satisfaction in the account you have given them of the good behaviour of your Officers and Men and of the chearfulness and alertness with which they went through the fatigues and dangers of their late voyage. (Cook, I, 635)

The Admiralty promoted him to the rank of commander. As a plain man, Cook perhaps did not expect any more. His distinction was to become known as the 'great circumnavigator'.

Cook made a modest assessment of the results to the Admiralty:

> Altho' the discoveries made in the Voyage are not great, yet I flatter my self that they are such as may merit the attention of their Lordships, and altho' I have faild in discovering the so much talk'd Southern Continent (which

John Webber, the artist on Cook's third voyage, painted this portrait of Captain James Cook (oil on canvas) in 1776. (Courtesy of the Museum of New Zealand Te Papa Tongarewa.)

The bark, *Earl of Pembroke*, later *Endeavour*, leaving Whitby Harbour in 1768. Oil on canvas by Thomas Luny (1759–1837), 1790. (National Library of Australia.)

HM Bark *Endeavour* careening. This 1973 oil painting by Oswald L. Brett recreates the scene at Cooktown in 1770. The ship is at right. At left are Banks and Solander in Banks' skiff. On the river a yawl returns from fishing on the reef, and an Aborigine is ready with a spear in an outrigger canoe. Banks' greyhound, Lady, is on the foreshore, and on land the launderers dry linen in the sun. All incidents are mentioned in the journals. (Courtesy of the artist, transparency lent by the owner, Mrs Douglass C. Fonda, Jnr.)

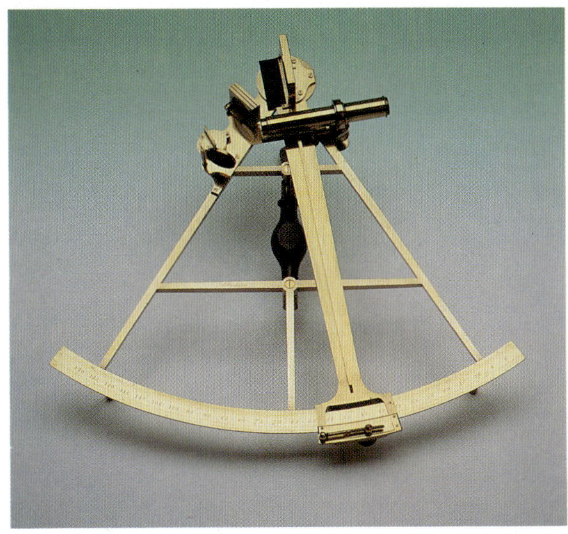

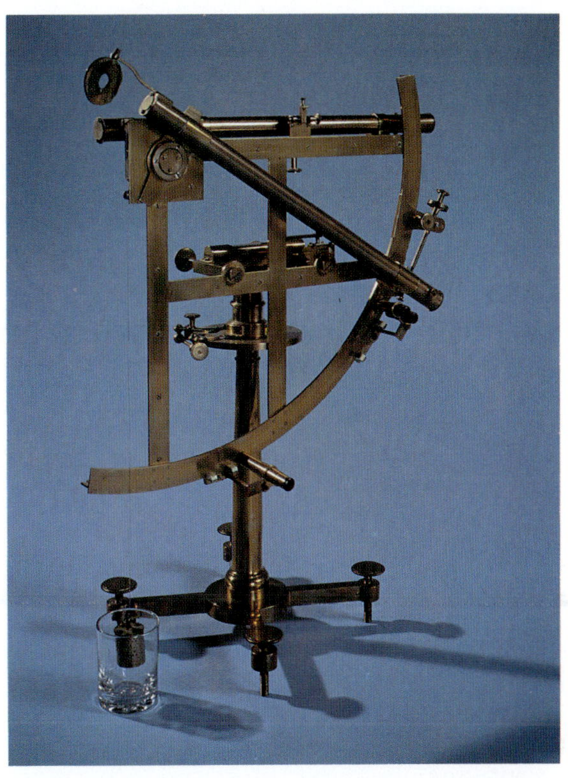

Above: Sextant, made about 1770. Cook took this on his third voyage.

Right: Astronomical quadrant used in observing the transit of Venus in Cook's first voyage.

Below: Model of HM Bark *Endeavour*.

Georg(e) Forster, 'Ice Islands with Ice Blink', 1773, gouache. The artist, only eighteen when he made this brilliant study of Antarctic light, sailed in the *Resolution* on Cook's second voyage. His father, Johann Reinhold Forster, was naturalist on the same ship. (Mitchell Library, State Library of New South Wales.)

Antoine Phelippeaux (1767–*c.*1830), 'Tableau des découvertes du Capne Cook & de la Perouse…', Paris, *c.*1798, hand-coloured engraving. (Rex Nan Kivell Collection, National Library of Australia.)

The Royal Society's Medal. (Mitchell Library, State Library of New South Wales.)

> perhaps do not exist)...I am confident that no part of the failure of such discovery Can be laid to my Charge ...
>
> In Justice to the officers and the whole crew I must say that they have gone through the fatigues and dangers of the whole voyage with that cheerfulness and allertness that will always do honour to British seamen. (Cook, I, 501)

Cook did not see New Holland, for all its size, as the Terra Australis Incognita that he and others had looked for. Indeed, by the time he had reached New Zealand, Cook came to think this continent did not exist. And he finished the voyage with a plan to settle the matter once and for all:

> Now I am upon the subject of discoveries I hope it will not be taken a Miss if I give it as

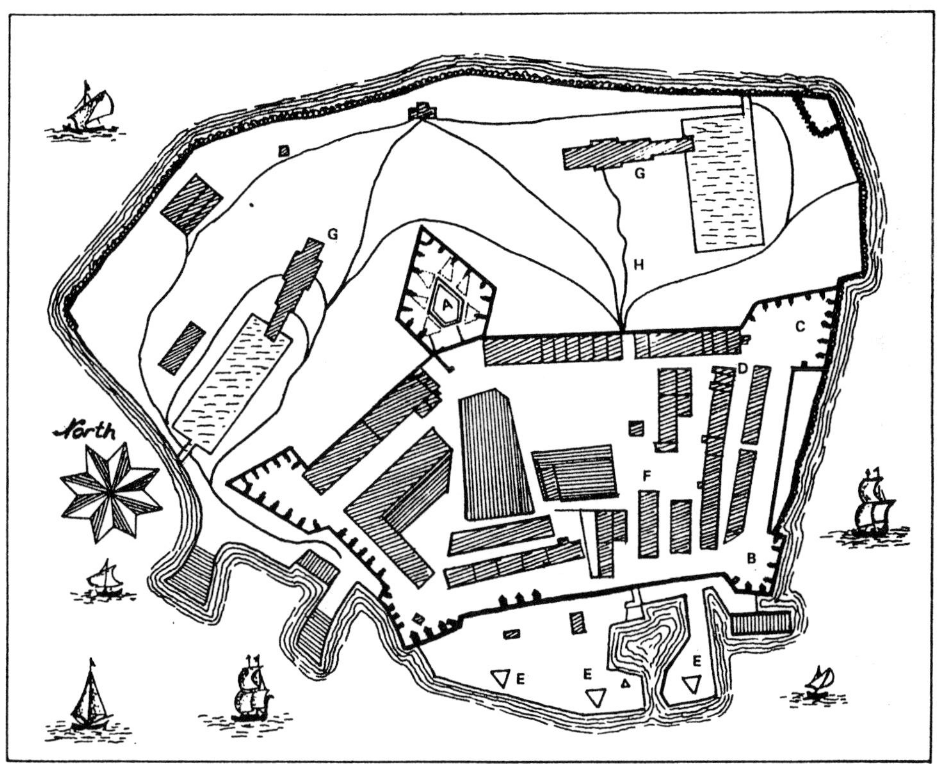

'I do not believe there is a Marine Yard in the world where work is done with more alertness,' Cook wrote of the marine yard on the island of Onrust where the *Endeavour* was careened and repaired. Map by J.W.Heydt around 1740, three decades before Cook's arrival. On the map are (A) ammunition depot and battery (B) Bastion Beekhuis, (C) Bastion Touwpunt, (D) rice and arak magazines (E) three cranes, (F) church, (G) two sawmills and (H) the flagpole. (From *Historical Sites of Jakarta*, by A. Heuken, SJ. Published by Cipta Loka Caraka, Jakarta, 1982.)

my opinion that the most feasable Method of making further discoveries in the South Sea is to enter it by the way of New Zeland, first touching and refreshing at the Cape of Good Hope, from thence proceed to the Southward of New Holland for Queen Charlottes Sound where again refresh Wood and Water, takeing care to be ready to leave that place by the latter end of September or beginning of October at farthest, when you would have the whole summer before you and after geting through the Straight might, with the prevailing Westerly winds, run to the Eastward in as high a Latitude as you please and, if you met with no lands, would have time enough to get round Cape Horne before the summer was too far spent, but if after meeting with no Continent & you had other Objects in View, than haul to the northward and after visiting some of the Islands already discover'd, after which proceed with the trade wind back to the Westward in search of those before Mintioned thus the discoveries in the South Sea would be compleat. (Cook, I, 479)

This scheme formed the basis for Cook's second circumnavigation. Banks made elaborate plans to join Cook on this voyage, with the *Resolution* being altered to accommodate him and his suite, but because the additions would have made it top-heavy and unseaworthy, they were removed. Banks tried unsuccessfully to persuade the navy to get another ship which could accommodate his suite but had to withdraw from the voyage.

On his second and third voyages Cook had a secondary interest in New Holland and Van Diemen's Land, especially whether a strait separated them. In 1773, after traversing the Antarctic for four months, he resolved to make his way in the *Resolution* to New Holland to 'injoy some short repose in a harbour where I can procure some refreshments for my people' (Cook, II, 106). The wind took him to New Zealand instead. His second in command, Captain Tobias Furneaux, in HMS *Adventure*, who

William Hodges, '*Resolution* and *Adventure* among bergs, 1773'. (Mitchell Library, State Library of New South Wales.)

had become separated from him, coasted Van Diemen's Land from South West Cape for 800 kilometres to East Sister Island until the east coast trended to the west. He believed it trended to a deep bay; actually it was into Bass Strait. Furneaux spent five days at Adventure Bay on the east coast of Bruny Island in the south-east of Tasmania. He did not see Aborigines, but from traces of them he concluded them to be 'a very Ignorant and wretched set of people, tho' natives of a country capable of producing every necessary of life, and a climate the finest in the world' (Cook, II, 735).

In 1777, during his third voyage, again in HMS *Resolution* with 21-year old William Bligh as master, Cook spent three days at Adventure Bay, Tasmania. It was an intermediate call on his way to New Zealand to refresh his people. He added little to the known geography of Van Diemen's Land. 'I need hardly say,' he said, 'it is the Southern point of New Holland which, if not a Continent is one of the largest islands in the World' (Cook, III, 56).

In this same period (1768–80), there were four French voyages towards New Holland and Van Diemen's Land. In 1768, continuing on his circumnavigation in *La Boudeuse* and *L'Etoile* westwards from Tahiti, Louis Antoine de Bougainville came upon the islands (now Vanuatu) discovered 160 years earlier by Quirós, then crossed the Coral Sea to the Great Barrier Reef. Bougainville viewed the violence of the sea breaking against the coral as 'the voice of God, and we were obedient to it'. He wrote:

> these numerous shoals, running out to sea, are signs of a low land; and when I see Dampier abandoning in our very latitude of 15°35', the western coast of this barren region, where he did not so much as find fresh water, I conclude that the eastern coast is not much better. (Bougainville, 304–5)

Short of stores, and believing that it would contain nothing of value, Bougainville forewent an opportunity to claim the east coast of New Holland for France. Instead, he sailed north-east through the Coral Sea, and then above New Guinea.

In 1769, seeking to establish trade with the newly discovered Tahiti, Jean-François-Marie de Surville skirted the Coral Sea on his way from Pondicherry and Canton south towards New Zealand. While de Surville did not actually see it, he passed to the west of Lord Howe Island, and when in the latitude of Broken Bay, just north of Sydney, was as close as 300 kilometres to the east coast of Australia.

Then, in 1771–72, there were two expeditions in search of the southern continent. Yves Joseph de Kerguelen-Trémarec led two ships out from Mauritius into the southern Indian Ocean. Kerguelen claimed falsely that he had found the fabled land, and cut short his quest. Separated from his commander, Comte Louis François Alesne de Saint Allouarn crossed to Western Australia in the *Gros Ventre.* He was the first explorer on the west coast for more than 70 years.

The ship's log records that he sighted land near Cape Leeuwin, on 17 March, 1772, was unable to land, and sailed north until anchoring in the locality of Shark Bay. A boat landed at a bay and an officer, M. de Mings, took possession of the land — the third claim after Tasman in Tasmania in 1642 and Cook on the east coast in 1770 — hoisting a flag and causing notification of the fact that he had taken possession of the land to be read. The document was put in a bottle and buried with two crowns of six francs each at the foot of a tree. The log refers to this bay as the Baie de Prise de Possession. It is the Bay of Turtles in the vicinity of Cape Inscription in the extreme north of Dirk Hartog Island. A gunner's mate named Massicot, who died of scurvy, was buried ashore, probably at Bernier or Doree Island.

An officer named M. de Rosily recorded these impressions of the country:

> From the top of this [hill] we perceived a landscape extending away for seven or eight leagues. The land rose imperceptibly, and we penetrated for about two and a half leagues inland. We saw there many burnt trees and others where it appeared that one had set fire to the foot of them. I do not believe that it is the heat of the sun that sets fire to these trees, for they are very green, and in the night there is a very heavy dew that refreshes them and gives them nourishment. We thought that we saw traces of men and of children, but we could hardly distinguish them, because of the very shifting nature of the sand. There was in particular one place as if it appeared that people

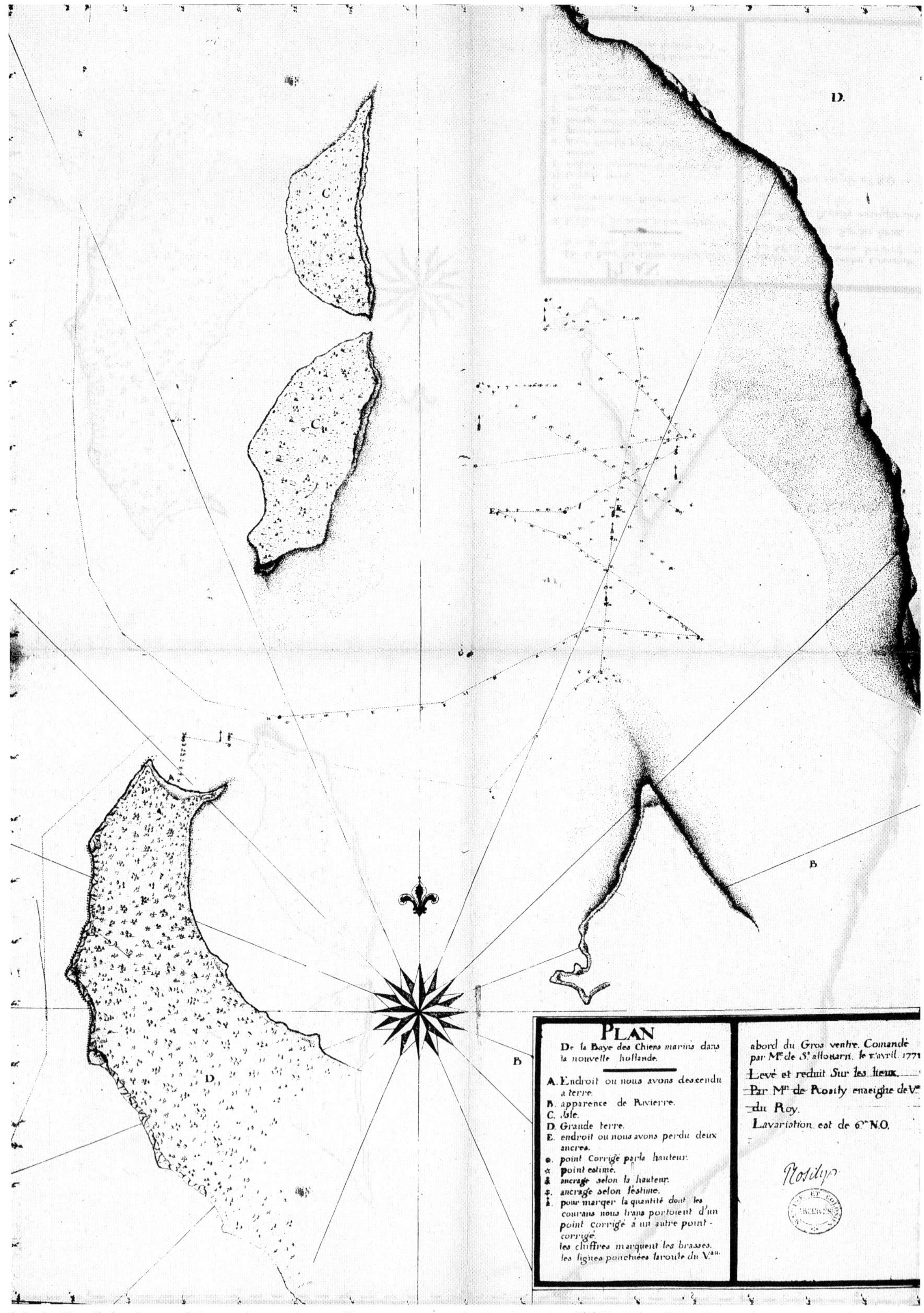

M. de Rosily's chart of the western Australian coast, made during the 1772 visit of the French commander, Saint Allouarn in the ship *Gros Ventre.* (Surveyor-General, Western Australia.)

> had danced in a ring. We saw there animals like makis [long-tailed monkeys] and others like mangoustes [the ichneumon or Pharaoh's rat], and several birds, including a kind of goose which had difficulty in flying, but never allowed us to approach within gun shot. Generally speaking, all the animals that we saw were very wild. We found no water at all. I believe that the animals drink only at night, taking advantage of the dew. We found on the beach thousands of little tortoises no bigger than your hand. The persons who passed the night in catching them saw a large animal in the shape of a dog which was scratching in this place in a search for the eggs of the tortoises. We caught many very good fish with the line, but could not succeed with the seine, the shore being very steep.

The log reported that they found only a kind of thyme and some sage.

Saint Allouarn followed the coast northwards until 3 May, when, in the vicinity of Melville Island, he turned north-west for the East Indies. As they proceeded, the French landed at intervals, but while they saw signs of humans (fire and a corroboree ground), they had no actual contact with the Aborigines.

Saint Allouarn died on the return journey at Mauritius. He was 35 and had made a valid claim to Western Australia for the King of France, Louis XV. (The fact of the French claim to territory was not published until early in this century after a copyist for the late Professor Ernest Scott, of Melbourne University, reported it from the Paris archives.)

Simultaneously, another expedition left Mauritius to look for the supposed Terra Australis. This was commanded by Marc-Joseph Marion du Fresne, who wrote at its commencement: 'I shall set my course...to reconnoitre the southern lands and find out if they exist, as I think they do... [I] shall neglect nothing in relation to the customs of the natives and various productions, for which I shall keep a most exact journal' (Duyker, 1992, 110).

This expedition also had the purpose of returning Aotourou, the Tahitian taken by Bougainville to France. Marion du Fresne sailed with two ships in October 1771 and proceeded first to the island of Bourbon (Réunion), where Aotourou sickened with smallpox and died. From here, Marion du Fresne went to the Cape of Good Hope, then, at the end of December, sailed on. Crossing the southern Indian Ocean in *c.* 45°S latitude, he found only the isolated Crozet Islands until he sighted the south-west coast of Van Diemen's Land on 3 March 1772. Following the coastline east and then north, he rounded Tasman Peninsula, to anchor in North Bay on 6 March. He and his companions had noted fires along the coast and now, the first Europeans to do so, they made contact with Tasmanian Aborigines. A group of 30 met the French landing parties and Marion du Fresne sent two sailors ahead, naked, through the surf, to reassure the Aborigines of their visitors' humanity. After initial friendly contact, however, violence erupted, with the Aborigines stoning the visitors, and the French shooting one Aborigine dead and wounding others. After inspecting some nearby islands and making a probe further north on 10 March, Marion du Fresne sailed for New Zealand, where he was killed.

Cook made one other discovery which may be seen as Australian. In October 1774, during his second voyage, he found Norfolk Island, about 1500 kilometres east of Sydney. He spent one day ashore there. In making a landing, he was luckier than some who followed, because all but 1.6 kilometres of the coastline of 32 kilometres is inaccessible cliffs. Coral reefs make the approach to the island hazardous, and there are no sheltered harbours. Cook wrote in his journal:

> After dinner hoisted out two boats in which my self, some of the officers and gentlemen went to take a view of the Island and its produce, we found no difficulty in landing behind some rocks which lined part of the coast and defended it from the Surf. We found the Island uninhabited and near a kin to New Zealand, the Flax plant, many other Plants and Trees common to that country was found here but the chief produce of the isle is Spruce Pines [Norfolk Island Pine, *Araucaria excelsa*]...Here then is a nother Isle where Masts for the largest Ships may be had...
>
> The Coast is not distitute of Fish, our people caught some which were excellent while in the

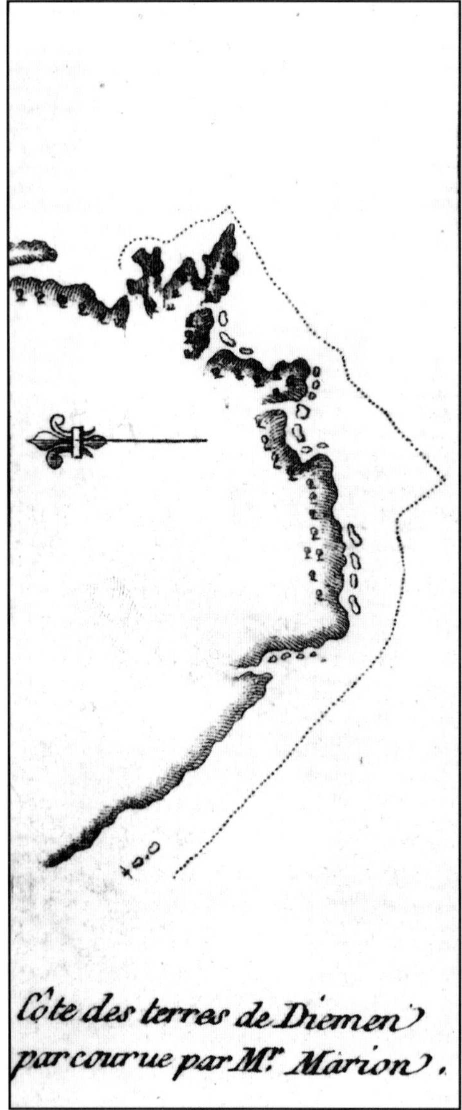

Two plates from J. Crozet's *Nouveau Voyage à la mer du sud* (1783). The first, 'Côte des terres de Diemen par courue par Mr Marion', shows the coast of Van Diemen's Land as charted by the French expedition under Marc-Joseph Marion du Fresne in 1772. The second, 'Habillemens des Insulaires de la Nouvelle Zelande', depicts 'dress of the islanders of New Zealand'. Marion du Fresne, who sailed to New Zealand from Van Diemen's Land, was killed there by the Maoris. (Mitchell Library, State Library of New South Wales.)

> boats a long-side the rocks. I took posission of this Isle as I had done of all the others we had discovered, and named it *Norfolk Isle*, in honour of that noble family [the Howard family, Dukes of Norfolk].
>
> ...the isle is supplied with fresh Water and produceth a bundance of small Cabbage Palms, we cut down and brought off as many as the little time we had would admit. Upon the whole here are many good refreshments to be got but we had no time to benefit by them. (Cook, II, 565–8)

William Wales, an astronomer in the complement, said Cook named the island after the Duchess of Norfolk. Of this place he wrote:

> Near the shores the Ground is covered so thick with the New-Zeeland flax-Plant that it is scarce

possible to get through it. This Plant was now nearly in its greatest perfection, the flowers being just opening, and as might naturally be expected from the Climate vastly more exuberant than at New Zealand; but a little way in-land the woods were perfectly clear and easy to walk in. The Soil seemed to be exceeding Rich and deep resembling that of New Zealand, and like it probably formed chiefly bye decay of its Vegetable Production...I took on shore with me a Bag which I soon filled with Wood sorrel [a species of the *Oxalis cornclulata* group] Sow-Thistle [probably *Actites megalocarpa*, 'Dune Thistle'], and Samphire [probably *Sarcocornia quinqueflora*] with which the shores in some places abound; but the greatest rarity we met with here was the Cabbage Tree, of which there are many, and we brought the Cabbages on board...This vegetable is not only wholesome but extremely palatable also, and proved the most agreeable repast we had had for some Time. (Cook, II, 865–9)

Cook's reports of trees suitable for ships' masts and yards and New Zealand flax (*Phormium tenax*) for textiles fibre at Norfolk Island were important in the British government's later decision to colonise Australia. Governor Phillip was instructed to begin cultivation of the flax plant immediately on arrival, and he sent Lieutenant Philip Gidley King with a ship to Norfolk Island within a month of arriving at Botany Bay in January 1788. For various reasons this scheme to obtain naval materials did not succeed. This small island (34 sq. kilometres) was a penal settlement from 1788 to 1813 and again from 1825 to 1856. Then 194 descendants of the mutineers of the *Bounty* were transferred there from Pitcairn Island. Now, the main business is tourism.

Polynesians killed Cook on 14 February 1779, in the Hawaiian Islands which he had discovered the previous year. News of his death did not reach England for 20 months. His widow, Elizabeth, survived him for 56 years. Three of their six children died in infancy; three sons died before marrying, two of them at sea while serving in the navy, so Cook had no direct descendants.

W. Henderson, 'Portrait of Mrs Elizabeth Cook', 1830. Mrs Cook and her husband had six children, all of whom died before her, as did Cook. (Mitchell Library, State Library of New South Wales.)

4

More Inviting Coasts

While they qualified their opinions, and were distinctly less enthusiastic about some parts, the explorers of the later eighteenth century certainly did find the eastern coasts of the continent and eastern Tasmania more inviting than had the Dutch and Dampier the western ones.

Cook wrote of the coast of New South Wales seen on the first day: '[it] appears rather low and not very hilly, the face of the Country green and woody but the sea shore is all a white sand'. A few days later, he added:

> The weather being clear gave us an oppertunity to View the Country which had a very agreeable and promising Aspect, the land is of a moderate height diversified with hills, ridges, planes and Vallies with some few small lawns, but for the most part the whole was cover'd with wood, the hills and ridges rise with a gentle slope, they are not high neither are there many of them. (Cook, I, 299, 300)

Banks whimsically compared the country to 'the back of a lean Cow, coverd in general with long hair, but nevertheless where her scrawny hip bones have stuck out farther than they ought accidental rubbs and knocks have intirely bard them of their share of covering'. (He was not to know he was describing a future dairying region!) A day later, he wrote: 'Land today more barren in appearance than we hade before seen it: it consisted cheifly of Chalky cliffs something resembling those of old England; within these it was flat and might be no doubt as fertile' (Banks, II, 51–2).

The pair's descriptions of the environs of Botany Bay were similarly mixed. Banks wrote:

> The Soil wherever we saw it consisted of either swamps or light sandy soil on which grew very few species of trees, one which was large yeilding a gum much like *sanguis draconis*, but every place was coverd with vast quantities of grass...
>
> Myself in the afternoon ashore on the NW side of the bay, where we went a good way into the countrey which in this place is very sandy and resembles something our Moors in England, as no trees grow upon it but every thing is coverd with a thin brush of plants about as high as the knees. The hills are low and rise one above another a long way into the countrey by a very gradual ascent, appearing in every respect like those we were upon. (Banks, II, 57, 60)

Cook wrote:

> we made an excursion into the country which we found deversified with woods, Lawns and Marshes; the woods are free from under wood of every kind and the trees are at such distance from one a nother that the whole Country or at least great part of it might be cultivated without being oblig'd to cut down a single tree; we found the soil every where except in the Marshes to be a light white sand and produceth a quantity of good grass which grows in little tufts about as big as one can hold in ones hand and pretty close to one another, in this manner the surface of the ground is coated in the woods between the trees...

> We found the face of the Country much the same as I have before described but the land much richer, for in stead of sand I found in many places a deep black Soil which we thought was capable of produceing any kind of grain, at present it produceth besides timber as fine meadow as ever was seen. (Cook, I, 307, 309)

Particularly because the officers of the First Fleet found the Botany Bay region to be very different — 'the fine meadows talked of in Captain Cook's *Voyage* I could never see, though I took some pains to find them out', John White wrote bitterly (White, 110) — these descriptions have caused historians much heartburn, and raised questions about precisely which areas the explorers described. After much investigation, C.H. Bertie concluded:

> We cannot trace the movements of Cook accurately during this week, as his record is indefinite occasionally, but from his journal we know that he explored the country about and to the south of Kurnell, in the vicinity of La Perouse and Cook's River, and that he spent a day exploring the upper reaches of the bay in the locality of Sans Souci and Tom Ugly's Point...
>
> On the evidence available and stretching 'almost' almost to breaking point, we might say that Sans Souci was the site of Cook's meadows...we can say definitely...that Lieutenant James Cook did not mistake a bog for a meadowland.

Sans Souci is at the south-western extremity of Botany Bay, whose northern and western suburbs were once Sydney's market gardens. This last fact suggests that Cook's and Banks' descriptions were not nearly so inaccurate as has often been supposed, and that we should look for the explanation of the discrepancies between what they saw and what the First Fleet people saw in the different times of the year when these visits were made.

As the *Endeavour* proceeded north, Cook and Banks saw areas that were distinctly less fertile. 'Bustard Bay,' Cook wrote, 'was vissibly worse than at the last place we were at.' And his comments about the Endeavour River were lukewarm:

> The Country as far as I could see is deversified with Hills and Plains and these with Woods and Lawns. The soil of the Hills is hard dry and very stoney yet it produceth a thin Coarse grass and some wood; the soil of the Plains and Vallies is sandy and in some Clay and in many Parts very Rocky and stoney as well as the hills, but in general the land is pretty well clothed with long grass, wood, shrubs etc. The Country in general is not badly water'd. (Cook, I, 325, 368)

Having had time for only fleeting observations of the country in four months on the coast, Cook and Banks wrote considered opinions of it after passing through Endeavour Strait into plain sailing in the Arafura Sea. Here, certainly, were no gold, silver, maize, potatoes or tobacco, such as America had to excite explorers.

Cook wrote temperately:

> In the Course of this Journal I have at different times made mention of the appearance or Aspect of the face of the Country, the nature of the Soil, its produce, &c. By the first it will appear that to the Southward of 33° or 34° [the latitude of Sydney] the Land in general is low and level with very few Hills or Mountains, further to the northward it may in some places be called a Hilly, but hardly anywhere can be call'd a Mountainous Country, for the Hills and Mountains put together take up but a small part of the Surface in comparison to what the Planes and Vallies do which intersect or divide these Hills and Mountains: It is indefferently well watered, even in the dry Seasons, with small Brooks and springs, but no great Rivers, unless it be in the wet Season when the low lands and Vallies near the Sea I do suppose are mostly laid under water; the small brooks may then become large Rivers but this can only happen with the Tropick. It was only in *Thirsty Sound* where we could find no fresh Water, excepting one small pool or two which Gore saw in the woods, which no doubt was owing to the Country being there very much intersected with Salt creeks and Mangrove land.
>
> The low land by the Sea and even as far in land as we were, is for the most part friable, loose, sandy Soil; yet indefferently fertile and cloathed with woods, long grass, shrubs, Plants, &c. The Mountains or Hills are Checquered with woods and Lawns. Some of the Hills are

wholy covered with flourishing Trees; others but thinly, and the few that are upon them are small, and the spot of Lawns or Savannahs are Rocky and barren, especially to the northward where the Country did not afford or produce near the Vegetation that it does to the southward, nor were the Trees in the woods half so tall and stout.

The Woods do not produce any great variety of Trees, there are only 2 or 3 sorts that can be call'd Timber; the largest is the Gum Tree which growes all over the Country, the Wood of this Tree is too hard and ponderous for most common uses. The Tree which resembles our Pines, I saw no where in perfection but in Botany Bay, this wood as I have before observed is something of the same nature as American Live Oak; in short most of the large Trees in this Country are of a hard and ponderous nature and could not be applied to many purposes. Here are several sorts of the Palm kind, Mangroves and several other sorts of small Trees and shrubs quite unknown to me besides a very great Variety of Plants hetherto unknown, but these things are wholy out of my way to describe, nor will this be of any loss sence not only Plants but everything that can be of use to the Learn'd World will be very accurately described by Mr Banks and Dr Solander. The Land naturaly produces hardly anything fit for man to eat and the Natives know nothing of Cultivation. There are indeed growing wild in the wood a few sorts of fruit (the most of them unknown to us) which when ripe do not eat a miss, one sort especially which we call'd Apples, being about the size of a Crab-Apple; it is black and pulpy when ripe and tastes like a Damson, it hath a large hard stone or kernel and grows on Trees or Shrubs.

In the Northern parts of the Country as about *Endeavour River*, and probably in many other places, the Boggy or watery Lands produce Taara or Cocos which when properly cultivated are very good roots, without which they are hardly eatable, the tops however make very good greens. (Cook, I, 392–4)

Cook attributed variations of his compass on three occasions to iron ore. On a hilltop at Thirsty Sound he wrote of 'Iron ore in the hill, visible signs of which appear'd not only here but in several other places'. At Cape Upstart, between Bowen and Ayr, he 'judged that it was owing to Iron ore or other Magnetical Matter Lodged in the earth'. Magnetic Island, nine kilometres north east of Townsville, got its name from Cook's naming '*Magnetical head* or *Isles* as it had much the appearance of an Island and the Compass would not travis well when near it'. (Cook, I, 331, 338)

Having mainly a naturalist's interest in the Aborigines and other animals and plants, Banks had even less to say specifically about the country:

> For the whole lengh of coast which we saild along there was a sameness to be observd in the face of the countrey very uncommon; Barren it may justly be calld and in a very high degree, that at least that we saw. The Soil in general is sandy and very light: on it grows grass tall enough but thin sett, and trees of a tolerable size, never however near together, in general 40, 50, or 60 feet assunder. This and spots sometimes very large of loose sand constitutes the general face of the countrey as you sail along it, and indeed of the greatest part even after you have penetrated inland as far as our situation would allow us to do. The Banks of the Bays indeed are generaly clothd with thick mangroves sometimes for a mile or more in breadth; the soil under these is rank mud always overflowd every spring tide. Inland you sometimes meet with a bog upon which the grass grows rank and thick so that no doubt the soil is sufficiently fertile. The Valleys also between the hills where runs of water come down are thick clothd with underwood, but they are generaly very steep and narrow, so that upon the Whole the fertile soil Bears no kind of Proportion to that which seems by nature doomd to everlasting Barrenness.
>
> Water is here a scarce article or at least was so while we were there, which I beleive to have been in the very hight of the Dry season; some places we were in where we saw not a drop, and at the two places where we filld for the ships use it was done from pools not brooks. This drought is probably owing to the dryness of a soil almost intirely composd of sand in which

high hills are scarce. That there is plenty however in the rainy season is sufficiently evincd by the channels we saw cut even in rocks down the sides of inconsiderable hills; these were in general dry, or if any of them containd water it was such as ran in the woody valleys, and these seldom carried water above half way down the hill. Some indeed we saw that formd brooks and ran quite down to the sea but these were scarce and in general brackish a good way up from the beach.

> A Soil so barren and at the same time intirely void of the helps derivd from cultivation could not be supposd to yeild much towards the support of man. We had been so long at sea with but a scanty supply of fresh provisions that we had long usd to eat every thing we could lay our hands upon, fish, flesh, or vegetable which only was not poisonous; yet we could but now and then procure a dish of bad greens for our own table and never but in the place where the ship was careend met with a sufficient quantity to supply the ship. (Banks, II, 112–13)

Nonetheless, this was not Banks's final view. In a short paragraph, he conceded that the country was not without resources:

> Upon the whole New Holland, tho in every respect the most barren countrey I have seen, is not so bad but that between the productions of sea and Land a company of People who should have the misfortune of being shipwrecked upon it might support themselves, even by the resources that we have seen. Undoubtedly a longer stay and visiting different parts would discover many more. (Banks, II, 122)

Despite its limitations, Cook did not hesitate to take possession of the region he termed New South Wales. He described how, at Possession Island:

> Notwithstanding I had in the Name of his Majesty taken posession of several places upon this coast, I now once more hoisted English Coulers, and in the Name of His Majesty King George the Third took posession of the whole Eastern coast from the above Latitude [38ºS] down to this place by the name of *New South Wales*, together with all the Bays, Harbours Rivers and Islands, situate upon the said coast, after which we fired three Volleys of small Arms which were Answered by the like number from the Ship. (Cook, I, 387–8)

Other journals reported that the occasion was 'cheared three times'.

Cook took possession from the highest hill 'of no great height, yet not less than twice or thrice the height of the Ships Mast heads [about 76 m]'. Practically on the spot where he planted his flagstaff a vein of auriferous quartz was discovered in 1895 and was mined for some years. Had Cook known he was standing on a gold mine, the development of Australia might have proceeded from north to south instead of south to north!

The general European response to the southeast coast of Tasmania in the 1770s was similar to that of Cook and Banks to the southern coast of New South Wales. Here is Crozet's description of the land adjacent to Frederick Hendrik (now Marion) Bay:

> We remained six days at Frederick Henry Bay, during which time we did not cease to make searches for fresh water — in vain. The land here is sandy like that at the Cape of Good Hope; it is covered with heath and small trees, most of which we found stripped of bark by the savages, who make use of it for cooking their shellfish. We found traces of fire everywhere; the ground seemed covered with ashes. In the midst of these trees stripped of their bark and mostly burnt at the foot, we noticed a species of pine a little less tall than ours, which appeared well preserved — probably because the savages gained something useful from it, and did not maltreat it as they did other trees. It seemed to us that in going further away from the sea and penetrating the interior, we should find in the valleys these same pines of a height and thickness sufficient to be used in masting ships.
>
> In the areas which had not been burnt, the soil was covered with grass and fern, similar to that of Europe, and also with sorrel and wood sorrel. There was little game, and we presumed that the fires made by the savages in this area had driven them inland. (Duyker, 1992, 26)

And here is Le Dez's:

> We spent the following two days visiting the bay. In the west we discovered a port which we had not perceived before; its opening was hidden by a big promontory jutting out a little. At its entrance there are 3½ to 4½ fathoms of water. On shore we saw a little mountain or rock, which seemed to be a very beautiful marble. We also visited an island to the NNE. We found a few miserable inhabitants there, more like animals than men. They ran away from us. It is astonishing that in such a large expanse of countryside we have not found the least little stream of fresh water, but as it is swampy in several places, water could easily be procured by making wells. I say swampy because we found reeds and other aquatic plants there. The soil seemed good, but almost all the trees are softwood and very light. I think they are little able to be worked and we did not see one which bore fruit. Although we found the tracks of several animals, we encountered only one which was a sort of tiger cat. There are numerous birds and a lot of pelicans which go in flocks in the woods; their cry is like the sound of a trumpet. It would appear to be this which Tasman thought he had heard. (Duyker, 1992, 33)

The next year, Furneaux described the same region even more favourably:

> We found the country very pleasent, the soil of a black rich, tho' thin one; the sides of the hills covered with large trees and very thick, growing to a great height before they branch off: they are all of them of the Ever-green kind of a different sort to any I ever saw; the wood is very brittle and easily split, there is very little variety of sort, having seen but two, the leaves of one is long and Narrow, the seed (of which I got a few) was in the shape of a Button, and has a very agreeable smell: the Leaves of the other are like the bay and has a seed like the white thorn, with an agreeable spicy taste and smell. Out of the trees we cut down for Fire wood there issued some Gum, which the Surgeon called Gum lac. The trees are mostly burnt or scorched near the ground, occasioned by the natives seting fire to the under wood in the most frequented places, and by these means have rendered it easily walking. (Cook, II, 734)

In 1777, Cook remarked that the land about Adventure Bay was 'for the most part of a good height, diversified with hill and Vally and every where of a greenish hue, it is well wooded...not badly water [i.e. watered]' (Cook, III, 56). He looked for grass for the cattle he was taking to Tahiti. What he first saw was scarce and coarse but he later found an excellent crop. He left it to the *Resolution*'s surgeon, William Anderson, who was also a naturalist, to compose a fuller description:

> At the bottom of [Adventure] Bay is a beautifull sandy beach above two mile long, excellently adapted for hauling a Seine which both ships did repeatedly with success. Behind this is a plain or flat with a salt or rather brackish pool running with the beach almost its whole length, in which are a great number of whitish Bream many of which we caught with angling rods and some small trout. The other parts are quite hilly and both those and the flat is an entire forest of very tall trees, render'd almost impassible by shrubs, brakes of fern and fallen trees except on the sides of some of the hills where the trees are but thin and only a coarse grass to interrupt you. To the northward of the bay there is low land stretching farther than the eye can reach, which is only cover'd with wood in certain spots, but we had no oppurtunity to examine in what respects it differ'd from the hilly country. The soil on the flat land is either sandy or of a yellowish mould and in some places a reddish clay. The same is found on the lower part of the hills, but farther up especially where there are few trees it is of a grey tough cast to appearance very poor. In the valleys between the hills the water drains down from their sides and at last in some places forms small brooks such as that we water'd at, but they are by no means of that size we might expect in so extensive a country, especially as it is both hilly and well wooded. Upon the whole it has many marks of being naturally a very dry country and might (independent of its wood) perhaps be compard with more justice to Africa about the Cape of good hope than any other, though

> that lyes ten degrees farther northward. For if we take new Zealand on the other side in the same Latitude we shall find every valley however small furnish'd with a considerable run of water. The heat too appears to be great as the Thermometer stood at 64, 70, and once at 74 and it was remark'd, that birds were seldom kill'd an hour or two before they were almost cover'd with small Maggots, which I would rather attribute this merely to the heat than any peculiar disposition of the climate to render substances soon putrid, which we have not any reason to suppose. (Cook, III, 790–1)

While not wildly enthusiastic, these descriptions were certainly favourable enough to justify the belief that eastern Australia might support a European colony. Because they have not attended closely enough to what Banks subsequently said in support of this idea, nor noted his careful qualifications, historians have supposed that time spread a romantic glow over the landscape he had seen in 1770.

In 1779, Banks told the House of Commons Committee investigating transportation that he was at Botany Bay:

> in the End of *April* and Beginning of *May* 1770, when the Weather was mild and moderate;... the Climate... was similar to that about *Toulouse*, in the South of *France*...The Proportion of rich Soil was small in Comparison to the barren, but sufficient to support a very large Number of People; there were no tame Animals, and he saw no wild Ones during his Stay of Ten Days...there were no Beasts of Prey; and he did not doubt but our Oxen and Sheep, if carried there, would thrive and increase; there was great Plenty of Fish, he took a large Quantity by hauling the Seine, and struck several Stingrays, a kind of Skate, all very large...The Grass was long and luxuriant, and there were some eatable Vegetables...the Country was well supplied with Water; there was Abundance of Timber and Fuel, sufficient for any Number of Buildings, which might be found necessary. (*Journal of the House of Commons*, 37 [1778–80], 311)

Banks added that, to support themselves, colonists should take with them food, tools, animals, grains and vegetables.

In 1785, he told another committee that he had 'no doubt that the Soil of many Part of the Eastern Coast of New South Wales between the Latitudes of 30 & 40 is sufficiently fertile to support a Considerable Number of Europeans who could cultivate it in the Ordinary Modes used in England' (Beauchamp Committee Minutes, Public Record Office, London, HO 7/1). When we notice that Banks confined his recommendation to the south-eastern coast of Australia, approximately from Broken Bay down to Wilson's Promontory, we may see that in fact there had been very little, if any, change in his view.

PART II: RESULTS OF DISCOVERY

Introduction

Between the Dutch voyages in the first half of the seventeenth century and those of Captain James Cook there occurred very significant changes in European consciousness. The modern scientific outlook emerged, and Europeans began to assess non-European cultures more in their own terms, and less in terms of how they compared with the European matrix.

One of the signs of the new age was a navigation much more precise in its methods and more reliable in its results. Another was the methodical collection of botanical and zoological specimens, and their subsequent scientific classification. A third was a growing interest in non-European peoples, and a changed attitude towards them. All these developments were reflected in the remarkable advice offered to Cook and Banks by Lord Morton, the President of the Royal Society, before the *Endeavour* sailed:

> *Hints offered to the consideration of Captain Cooke, Mr Bankes, Doctor Solander, and the other Gentlemen who go upon the Expedition on Board the 'Endeavour'*
>
> To exercise the utmost patience and forbearance with respect to the Natives of the several Lands where the Ship may touch.
>
> To check the petulance of the Sailors, and restrain the wanton use of Fire Arms.
>
> To have it still in view that sheding the blood of those people is a crime of the highest nature: – They are human creatures, the work of the same omnipotent Author, equally under his care with the most polished European; perhaps being less offensive, more entitled to his favor.
>
> They are the natural, and in the strictest sense of the word, the legal possessors of the several Regions they inhabit.
>
> No European Nation has a right to occupy any part of their country, or settle among them without their voluntary consent.
>
> Conquest over such people can give no just title; because they could never be the Agressors.
>
> They may naturally and justly attempt to repell intruders, whom they may apprehend are come to disturb them in the quiet possession of their country, whether that apprehension be well or ill founded.
>
> Therefore should they in a hostile manner oppose a landing, and kill some men in the attempt, even this would hardly justify firing among them, 'till every other gentle method had been tried.
>
> There are many ways to convince them of the Superiority of Europeans, without slaying any of those poor people. — for Example. —
>
> By shooting some of the Birds or other Animals that are near them; – Shewing them that a Bird upon wing may be brought down by a Shot. — Such an appearance would strike them with amazement and awe. — Lastly to drive a bullet thro' one of their hutts, or knock down some conspicuous object with great Shot, if any such are near the Shore.
>
> Amicable signs may be made which they could not possibly mistake. — Such as holding up a jug, turning it bottom upwards to shew them it was empty, then applying it to the lips in the attitude of drinking. — The most stupid from such a token, must immediately

Hints offered to the Consideration of Captain Cooke, Mr Banks, Doctor Solander, and the other Gentle=men who go upon the Expedition on Board the Endeavour.

To exercise the utmost patience and forbearance with respect to the Natives of the several Lands where the Ship may touch.

To check the petulance of the Sailors, and restrain the wanton use of Fire Arms.

To have it still in view that sheding the blood of those people is a crime of the highest nature: — They are human creatures, the work of the same Omnipotent Author, equally under his care with the most polished European; perhaps being less offensive, more entitled to his favor.

They are the natural, and in the strictest sense of the word, the legal possessors of the several Regions they inhabit.

No European Nation has a right to occupy any part of their country, or settle among them without their voluntary consent.

Conquest over such people can give no just title; because they could never be the Agressors.

They

Hints offered to Capt Cook, Mr Banks and Dr Solander by James Douglas, Earl of Morton, 1768. (National Library of Australia.)

comprehend that drink was wanted.

Opening the mouth wide, putting the fingers towards it, and then making the motion of chewing, would sufficiently demonstrate a want of food.

They should not at first be alarmed with the report of Guns, Drums, or even a trumpet. — But if there are other Instruments of Music on board they should be first entertained near the Shore with a soft Air.

If a Landing can be effected, whether with or without resistance, it might not be amiss to lay some few trinkets, particularly looking Glasses upon the Shore: Then retire in the Boats to a small distance, from whence the behaviour of the natives might be distinctly observed, before a second landing were attempted.

Other and more important considerations of this kind will occurr to the Gentlemen themselves, during the course of the Expedition.

Upon the whole, there can be no doubt that the most savage and brutal Nations are more easily gained by mild, than by rough treatment.

As resistance may in some emergencies become absolutely necessary for self defence. — Training the men to fire at a mark, as was practised during one part of Lord Ansons voyage, and giving premiums or conferring some mark of distinction upon those who are most adroit, might have good effect, if it raised only emulation without animosity. The last by all means should be carefully avoided.

If during an inevitable skirmish some of the Natives should be slain; those who survive should be made sensible that it was done only from a motive of self defence: for which reason no rancour should appear to continue on account of their having attacked or perhaps killed some of the Crew when on Shore, or having opposed their Landing: But the Natives when brought under should be treated with distinguished humanity, and made sensible that the Crew still considers them as Lords of the Country. — Such behaviour would soon conciliate them to a familiarity with the Crew, and raise friendly sentiments towards supplying their wants.

But caution should be observed, as to the partaking of any food or liquors they may tender; unless the natives themselves do first taste of the same.

From the reports handed about concerning some of the late Expeditions, it should seem that upon one or two occasions, some of the Natives had been wantonly killed without any just provocation: – *Particularly*, a single man, who was killed in attempting to Swim towards one of the Boats. – If this account be true there was not the colour of a pretence for such a brutal Massacre: – A naked man in the water could never be dangerous to a Boats Crew.

Ships of so small a rate, not being furnished with Chaplains, it were to be wished that the Captain himself, would sometimes perform that Office, and read prayers, especially on sundays, to the Crew; that they may be suitably impressed with a sense of their continual dependance upon their *Maker*, and all who are able on board, Passangers and others should be obliged to attend upon those occasions.

The primary object of the Expedition is to take a correct observation of the Transit of Venus on the 3d of June. — No time therefore should be lost in getting to the station fixed upon for that purpose, there being many preparatory operations absolutely requisite, which may take up six weeks, or two months, previous to the day of the transit.

Least the state of the Sky should happen to prove unfavorable, for some days preceeding the 3d of June; – It might perhaps be advisable to pitch upon two places at some miles distance from each other, verifying before hand by repeated observations their different Longitudes and Latitudes. — When these are well ascertained, should the morning of the Transit, or even the day before, appear unfavorable, An observer might be stationed at each of those places; because one of those Observers might possibly see the Phaenomenon while the other could not.

As there is but one Clock, that certainly should be fixed in the portable Observatory; – But that deficiency in the other place might in part be remedied, by adjusting a good second Watch, marking its rate of going and its variation from the Clock for eight or ten days before the day of the Transit.

When that business is finished, other matters may be attended to, *Particularly*, the discovery of a Continent in the Lower temperate Latitudes;- A Continent in the higher Latitudes, or in a rigorous climate, could be of little or no advantage to this nation.

There are different indications described by Navigators, for judging whether Land descried be an Island or part of a large Continent.

Very high Mountains within Land, at a great

distance from the Shore, give strong symptoms of a large Continent.

The mouths of large Rivers, with Bars of Sand, unequally disposed; and at a considerable distance from the Shore, give likewise the presumption of a Continent.

The most populous Nations are generally found on large Continents.

Populous nations are commonly the most civilized.

The Hottentots at the Cape of Good Hope, are described to be in no great number.

The same observation holds with respect to the Savage Nations in North America.

If the Ship should fortunately discover any part of a well inhabited Continent, many new subjects in Natural History might be imported, and usefull branches of Commerce set on foot, which in process of time might prove highly beneficial to Brittain.

The natural Dispositions of the people; Their progress in Arts or Science, Especially their *Mechanics*, Tools, and manner of using them:- Their notions of Astronomy &c are principal objects of attention.

Or if they have any method of communicating their thoughts at a distance, As the *Mexicans* are said to have done by painting, and the Peruvians by the Quipos.

Next, the Character of their Persons
Features
Complection
Dress
Habitations
Food
Weapons
Then may be considered, their
Religion
Morals
Order
Government
Dinstinctions of Power
Police

Their token for Commerce and if they have any currency that passes among them in lieu of money, to bring home several Specimens from the highest to the lowest denomination

Lastly, the Natural productions of the Country, in the
Animal
Vegetable and
Mineral Systems.

These open so vast a field, that there is no room in this place for descending to particulars.

In general where an animal is to be described or figured, the name by which it goes in the Country, with all circumstances that can be collected relating to its nature, disposition, and character, should be minutely noticed.

VEGETABLES

Their powers in Medicine, whether Salutary or noxious, — The other uses to which they are put by the Natives. —

Particularly, such as give vivid or lasting colours for dyeing.

If any attempt should be made in the latter part of the Voyage, to bring home live plants in Pots, it might be usefull to mark upon the Stem of the plant the Exposition of it, taken correctly by applying a small Mariners compass to the side of the Stem, and observing which part of the Plant fronts the South.

In noting down such observation, the variation of the Compass at that particular place should be specified: Also the Latitude under which the plant grew, and whether to the South or North of the Equator.

Virgil gives a very judicious caution with respect to the transplanting Vines, and which would equally hold in the transplanting other trees, tho' hardly ever observed by English Gardiners.

Quin etiam ca[e]li regionem in cortice signant:

Ut, quo quaeque modo steterit, quâ parte calores

Austrinos tulerit, quae terga obverterit axi,

Restituant. adeò in teneris consuescere multum est.

[What's more, he may even carve on the bark four points of the compass

So that, when a plant is transferred, it shall turn the same face

To north or South as it turned

From birth: so important are habits developed in early days.]

Upon glancing over this article, the same

appears to be superfluous; because it is scarce to be imagined that Mr Bankes or Dr Solander will attempt the bringing home plants in pots.

The Latitudes in which seeds are collected, might also be noted with the nature of the Soils in which they grew:- And if earths could be brought in Boxes, it might tend to promote natural knowledge.

MINERALS & FOSSILLS

To examine if not at too great a distance within the Country the places where such are found.

It has been alledged by some Naturalists that Gold is not found in Veins, as other Metals.

If that, or any other Metal should be met with, it would be curious and Instructive, to examine minutely how they lye in the Earth in their Brute State, and how the Veines *Hade*, as well with respect to the angle of their declivity, as their bearing to the Mariners Compass.

Precious stones make a curious and valuable part of Natural History, and are therefore a considerable object of enquiry.

Mr Hamilton his Majestys Envoy Extraordinary at Naples, after repeated and accurate Observations upon Mount Vesuvius during a Course of three years; and Doctor Morris very lately, after analyzing many of the substances found in that Volcano, did concurr in opinion (tho without having had any mutual correspondence with each other by letter or otherwise) that all precious stones, not excepting even Diamonds, were the production of Volcanos.

If any precious stones therefore should be met with during the Course of the Voyage, it might be expedient to enquire particularly into the nature of the places where they are found, and if possible to view the places themselves.

Islands, or other Lands thrown up by Volcanos, if they lye in the Warmer or temperate Climates, do in process of time, change their nature and appearance very considerably.

In the year 1707 (I think it was) a new Island was formed by a Volcano in the Archipelago a few miles distant from the Port of Santerin.

For some years after, it was only a large mass of Cinders: I have been lately told, that it is now well cultivated with different plants growing upon it.

There is an account of the formation of that Island, in the Abrigment of the Philosophical Transactions by Jones Vol. 5 part 2d page 196, and if the report of its present condition be true, it may be very possible, that those places in the Kingdom of Golconda, or in the Brazils where diamonds are found, Or in Pegu, where the finest Rubies are found, may in very remote ages have been Volcanos, tho' the present face of those countries should give no such appearance.

Gravel and Sand found at the mouths of Rivers, help to give a notion of the Minerals and Fossils of the Countrys thro' which those Rivers take their course, such therefore should be carefully collected and separately kept, noting the names and situation of the Rivers where they are found.

Lastly, to form a Vocabulary of the names given by the Natives, to the several things and places which come under the Inspection of the Gentlemen.

The foregoing hints, hastily put together; and probably very incorrect, are however humbly submitted to the consideration of the Captain Cooke and the other Gentlemen, by their hearty wellwisher and

Most obedt Servant
MORTON
10th August 1768
(Cook I, 514 – 19)

The scientific enlightment of the second half of the seventeenth and first half of the eighteenth centuries, then, constitutes a great divide in the first European reconnaissance of Australia. Before it, there was little systematic collection and (with the partial exception of Dampier) scientific description. After it, there was both, which led to Australian specimens being incorporated into European systems of classification, and the beginnings of reliable ethnography.

The materials presented in the following chapters are arranged accordingly.

5

Botany

Seventeenth Century

The plants seen by the VOC explorers and Dutch merchants seemed to have no commercial value; neither did they arouse much curiosity, so they received scant attention. And now, precise identification of what they did observe is sometimes difficult. Sandalwood (*Santalum lanceolatum*) was the only obvious product they could have used in trade if explorers had realised it was growing on the northern and western coasts. It makes fragrant incense for Buddhist rites; oil; and is used for making ornaments. Carstensz was told to enquire where he landed whether sandalwood was growing, but he could not communicate with the Aborigines. Although sandalwood grows on hillsides and in scrubs behind the beaches he traversed, he did not report it. Sandalwood was cut and exported from a number of Pacific Islands and North Queensland in the nineteenth century and early in the twentieth century.

Carstensz wrote that at one place on the west coast of Cape York in 1623 they 'gathered excellent vegetables or pot-herbs' (Heeres, 40). Most likely this was wild jachu bean (*Canavalia rosea*). He also gathered what he described as herbs. If he was meaning aromatic herbs as in the sense of 'herbs and spices' they could have been some of the native mint relatives. *Anisomeles malabarica*, a strongly aromatic native, would then be most likely.

In the same region 133 years later, Gonzal wrote that the natives mainly subsisted on the roots of trees and wild fruits, such as yams, tubers or berries. (Yams of *Vigna* spp. and *Dioscorea* spp. and fruits of the cocky apple [*Planchonia careya*]; nonda [*Parinari nonda*] and white apple [*Syzygium suborbiculare*] are known dietary items of Aborigines in the area in more recent times.) Gonzal also said that he saw excellent timber for ships' yards, etc. This was the only favourable reference made by a Dutch explorer to the timber on the continent. It was almost certainly to hoop pine on the Torres Strait islands.

Of Blackman Bay, his landing place on the east coast of Tasmania, Tasman wrote of his crew

> bringing [aboard ship] various types of greens (which they had seen growing in plenty), some [probably *Tetragonia tetragoniaidess*, New Zealand spinach] not unlike a certain green which grows at the [Cape of Good Hope] and is suitable to use as vegetables another being long and salty, which has not a bad likeness to sea parsley [probably *Apium prostratum*]...also a little (to the eye) good gum which is dripping from trees and had a *Zwijim of Goomalacca* [literally 'swoom of gummy substance']. (Sharp, 75–6)

Shellac has the product of the lac insect; the gum was almost certainly from a Eucalyptus species, probably stringy-bark (*Eucalytpus obliqua*), or the grasstree, species Xanthorrhoea, possibly *Xanthorrhoea australis*.

In 1658 Jacob Pieterszoon Peerboom made the first known reference to a plant in Western Australia. This was on the south-west coast. He described a 'gum or glue used by the Aborigines in making stone axes' which 'after it has been rubbed a bit [is] of a pleasant smell and red in colour' (Sharp, 95). This was either the kino or *Eucalyptus calophylla*, marri or red gum, or resin from *Xanthorrhoea preissii*, black boy. Forty years later, at Rottnest Island in 1696–97, de Vlamingh found trees for firewood 'in abundance and very fine in fragrance just like rosewood' (Schilder, 123). This was probably *Callitris preissii*, Rottnest Island cypress pine.

De Vlamingh's expedition also gathered natural history specimens which went to Europe. The VOC officials reported:

> We are also sending some large and small pieces of wood which the skipper Willem de Vlamingh also brought here to us from the South-land...that it was a species of fragrant wood, which quality could not be judged here, although we did have some of it distilled first, and have handed over to Commodore Bichon a bottle of that oil for Your Honours' speculation. (Schilder, 211)

Two pressed plants were described and depicted by N.L. Brenman in his *Flora Indica* in 1768. They were *Synaphea spinulosa*, which is preserved in Genoa, and *Acacia truncata*, now lost.

The author of a journal of the *Nijptangh*, one of de Vlamingh's ships, reported an experience with a poisonous plant, *Macrozamia riedlei*, at the Swan River:

> I was offered the Kernel of a certain fruit not unlike the Driaens in appearance, and tasting like our Dutch broad beans and those which were less ripe, like a hazel nut. I ate five or six and drank some of the water from one of the aforesaid holes, but after an interval of about three hours I and five more of the of the others who had also eaten of the said fruit began to vomit so violently that there was hardly any distinction between death and us. (Schilder, 155)

The pith of *Macrozamia riedlei* in Western Australia has been used for starch, its poisonous properties (contained in the pith as well as the roots, leaves and seeds) being readily removed by washing and cooking. All species of *Macrozamia* are poisonous to stock, causing the 'staggers' or 'wobbles'.

Subsequently, the VOC officials at Batavia sent back 'a small chest containing shells collected on the beaches, fruits, plants, etc.' However, they added: '[These] are of little importance and may be found elsewhere in the Indies of a much better quality' (Schilder, 211).

Dampier collected a number of plant specimens during his stays, some of which are preserved in collections in England and Italy. The botanist A.S. George has observed generally of these specimens:

> Dampier's collection is largely of historical interest, as he was the first Englishman to make a collection of plants in Australia. Whether he was the first person ever is conjectural; there are no earlier recorded collections, but there are in the herbarium of the Geneva Botanic Garden two specimens which were described as ferns by the Dutch botanist Burmann in 1768. The locality was given as Java, but the plants are in fact sterile specimens of *Acacia truncata* (Burm. f.) Hort. ex Hoffmag. and *Synaphea spinulosa* (Burm. f.) Merrill, which are endemic in south-western Australia. They were probably collected when a Dutch ship stopped here on its way to Java. Although it is impossible to determine when this occurred, a strong possibility is the expedition of Willem Vlamingh who explored the Swan River in 1697, two years before Dampier's visit to the North-west. Both the plants concerned occur in coastal areas near Perth.
>
> Dampier's descriptions from his first visit, to King Sound in 1688 are brief — e.g. 'the Woods are not thick, nor Trees very big. Most of the Trees that we saw are Dragon-Trees [Kino of *Eucalyptus* sp., a Bloodwood] as we supposed'. (Dampier, 1968, 312)

However, those from his second visit, in 1699, to Shark Bay, the Dampier Archipelago, and Lagrange Bay, are much more extensive. Some of these are reproduced following, with A.S. George's remarks in square brackets. Of Shark Island, where he spent five days, Dampier wrote:

> The Mould is Sand by the Sea-side, producing a Sort of Sampier, which bears a white Flower. [This was probably *Nitraria billardieri* DO the Nitre Bush, a succulent-leaved shrub which occurs there and has some resemblance to the European Samphire, *Crithmum maritimum* L.]...The Grass grows in great Tufts, as big as a Bushel, here and there a Tuft: Being intermix'd

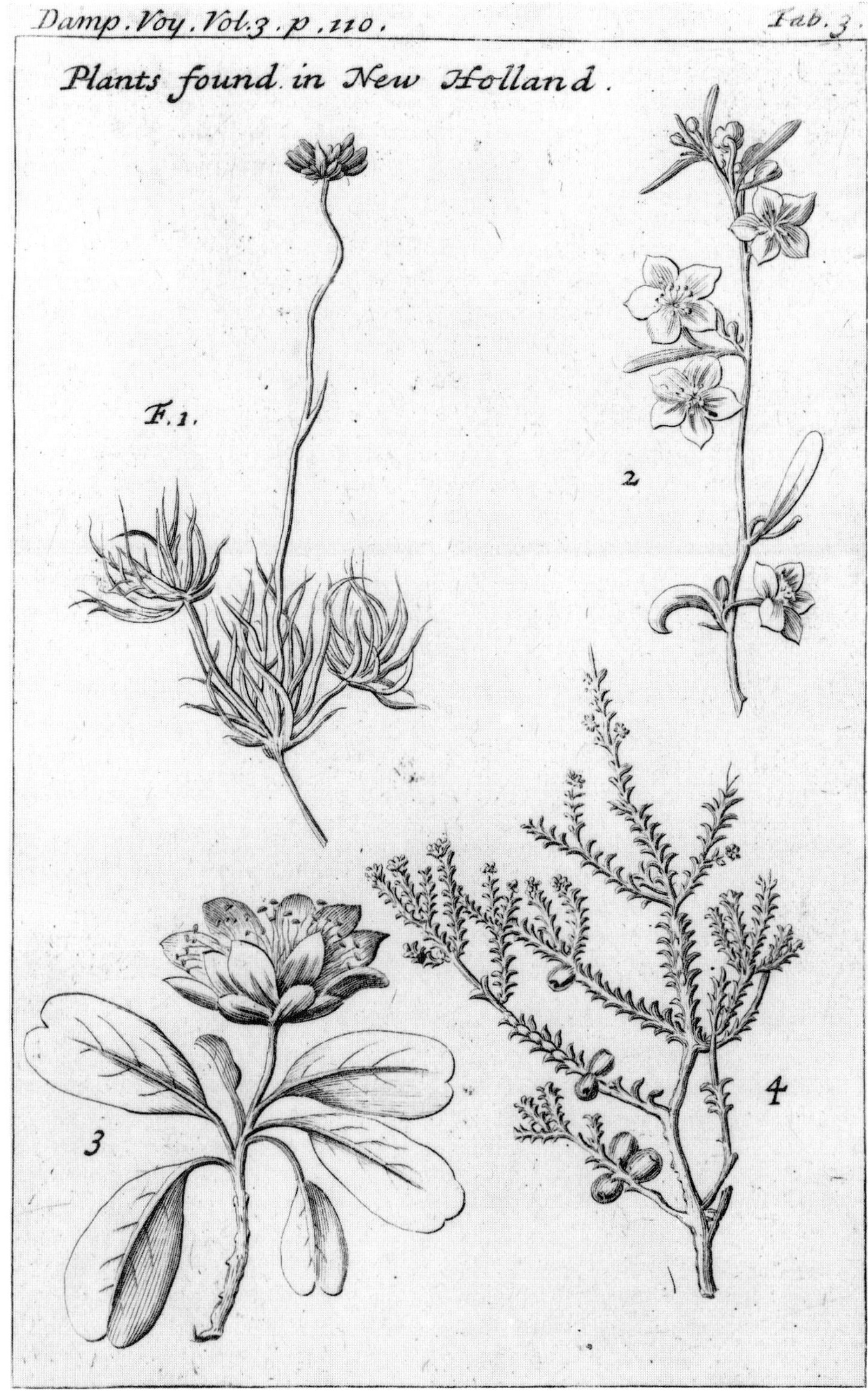

Anonymous, 'Plants found in New Holland'. From William Dampier, *A Voyage to New Holland*, London, 1729. (British Library, London.)

with much Heath, much of the kind we have growing on our Commons in England. [This could refer to *Spinifex longifolius* R.Br., *Triodia plurinervata* N.T. Burbridge or *Plectrachne danthonioides*, the first of which is common on the coastal dunes and the other two behind the foredunes. Dampier collected the Plectrachne].

Of Trees or Shrubs here are divers Sorts; but none above 10 Foot high: Their Bodies about 3 Foot about, and 5 or 6 Foot high before you come to the Branches, which are bushy and compos'd of small Twigs there spreading abroad, tho' thick set, and full of Leaves; which were mostly long and narrow. The Colour of the Leaves was on one Side whitish. and on the other green; and the Bark of the Trees was generally of the same Colour with the Leaves, of a pale green. [This would be *Pittosporum phylliraeoides*, referred to as Weeping Pittosporum, Native Willow, Bottlebrush or Melmaei.]

Some of these Trees were sweet-scented, and reddish within the Bark, like the Sassafras, but redder. Most of the Trees and Shrubs had at this Time either Blossoms or Berries on them. The Blossoms of the different Sort of Trees were of several Colours, as red, white, yellow, &c. but mostly blue: And these generally smelt very sweet and fragrant, as did some also of the rest. There were also beside some Plants, Herbs, and tall Flowers, some very small Flowers, growing on the Ground, that were sweet and beautiful, and for the most part unlike any I had seen elsewhere. (Dampier, 1906, 424–5)

Of the Archipelago Islands Dampier wrote:

There grow here 2 or 3 Sorts of Shrubs, one just like Rosemary; and therefore I called this Rosemary Island, Coastal Daisybush [which is also referred to as Native Rosemary]. It grew in great Plenty here, but had no Smell. Some of the other Shrubs had blue and yellow Flowers; and we found 2 Sorts of Grain like Beans [would have been in the species of *Acacia*]. The one grew on Bushes; the other on a Sort of a creeping Vine that runs along on the Ground, having very thick broad Leaves, and the Blossoms like a Bean Blossom, but much larger, and of a deep red Colour, looking very beautiful. (Dampier, 1906, 434–5)

Mueller identified *Canavalia obtustralia* DC (also known as *C. maritima* but now known as *Crosea* (swartz) DC and commonly called wild jack bean) — a 'creeping vine that runs along the Ground, having very thick broad leaves, and the Blossom like a Bean Blossom, but much larger, and of a deep red Colour, looking very beautiful'. The flowers are obviously those of *Clianthus*, this being the only creeping legume in the area with large red flowers, but it has relatively small, soft leaflets. Dampier must have confused the foliage with that of another creeper growing with it. *Canavalia*, having thick leaflets, is a possibility, but so also is *Ipomoea pes-caprae* (L.) R.Br., (now known as *I. brasiliensia* (L.) sweet, is commonly called goat's foot or beach morning glory), a common morning glory of the north-west coast. Dampier's other plant with 'Grain like Beans which grew on Bushes' was possibly a species of *Crotalaria cunninghamii* (which has the common name green birdflower). Mr George's list of Dampier's 23 Plants in the Sherardian Herbarium follows, with common names provided by Mr T.E.H. Aplin, Senior Botanist, Western Australian Herbarium:

Acacia coriacea DC. Grevillea sp. (Osborn-Gardner) Uncertain locality. Desert oak, dogwood and winewood

Acacia rostellifera Benth. A. salicina Lindl. (Mueller). Shark Bay. A coastal wattle

Adriana tomentosa Gaud. Uncertain locality

Beaufortia dampieri. A. Cunn. ex Hook. Shark Bay

Brachycome ciliocarpa. W.V. Fitzg. Shark Bay

Calandrinia liniflora. Fenzl. Shark Bay. A 'Parakeelya'

Clianthus formosus (G. Don) Ford et Vickery. C. dampieri A. Cunn. Sturt pea. (Mueller). C. speciosus (G. Don) Aschers et Graebn. (Osborn-Garner). Dampier Archipelego

Conostylis candicans. Endl. var. leptophylla Benth. Shark Bay

Dampiera incana. R. Br. Shark Bay

Diplolaena grandiflora Desf. D. dampieri Desf. (Mueller, Osborn-Gardner). Shark Bay

Frankenia pauciflora D.C. Shark Bay

Hannafordia quadrivalvis F. Muell. Shark Bay

Lotus cruentus Court. Tephrosia sp. (Osborn-Gardner). Shark Bay. Redflower lotus. The

James Gillray (1757–1815), 'The great south sea caterpillar transform'd into a Bath butterfly'. (Hand-coloured etching, 34.5 x 2.48 cm, London, R. Humphrey, 1795.) (Rex Nan Kivell Collection, National Library of Australia.)

specimen is sterile and cannot be definitely determined

Melaleuca cardiophylla F. Muell. Shark Bay

Myoporum acuminatum R. Br. M. montanum R. Br. (Mueller). A boobialla

Olearia axillaris D.C. Aster axillaris F. Muell. (Mueller). Dampier Archipelago. Coast daisy-bush

Paractaenum novae-hollandiae Beauv. Shark Bay. Common name reverse grass, reflexed panic grass

Pittosporum phylliraeoides D.C. Probably Marianthus pictus Lindl. (Mueller). Shark Bay

Plectrachne danthonioides (F. Muell.) D.E. Hubb. Plectrachne sp. (Osborn-Gardner) Shark Bay

Sida calyxhymenia J. Gay. Sida virgata Hook. (Mueller). Uncertain locality

Solanum orbiculatum Dun. Shark Bay

Thryptomene baeckeacea F. Muell. Shark Bay

Thrachymene elachocarpa (F. Muell.) B.L. Burtt. Didiscus pusillus (dC). F. Muell. (Osborn-Gardner). Shark Bay

Eighteenth Century

Between the seventeenth-century piecemeal natural history gatherings and those on the *Endeavour* in 1770 stands the towering figure of the Swedish naturalist, Carolus Linnaeus. From early in the 1730s Linnaeus developed and then refined his system of classifying plants according to their reproductive parts into class, order, genus and species, using a binomial system. Developing a passion for botany while a student at Oxford, Joseph Banks learnt the basics of the Linnaean system; and he took with him on the *Endeavour* one of Linnaeus's disciples, Dr Daniel Solander. Banks also engaged two draughtsmen/artists, Sydney Parkinson and Alexander Buchan, to depict the specimens collected.

Having inherited a large fortune, Banks was able to spare no expense, and the pair made elaborate preparations for their work. The contemporary natural historian John Ellis has left this description of Banks' and Solander's preparations:

> No people ever went to sea better fitted out for the purpose of Natural History, nor more elegantly. They have got a fine library of Natural History; they have all sorts of machines for catching and preserving insects; all kinds of nets, trawls, drags and hooks for coral fishing; they have even a curious contrivance of a telescope, by which, put into the water, you can see the bottom to a great depth, where it is clear. They have many cases of bottles with ground stoppers, of several sizes, to preserve animals in spirits. They have the several sorts of salt to surround the seeds; and wax, both beeswax and that of the *Myrica*; besides there are many people whose sole business it is to attend them for this very purpose. They have two painters and draughtsmen, several volunteers who have a tolerable notion of Natural History; in short Solander assured me this expedition would cost Mr Banks ten thousand pounds. (Banks, I, 30)

This is how Banks himself described their procedure during the voyage:

> We had a suitable stock of books relating to the natural history of the Indies with us; and seldom was there a storm strong enough to break up our normal study time, which lasted daily from nearly eight o'clock in the morning till 2 in the afternoon. From 4 or 5, when the cabin had lost the odour of food we sat till dark by the great table with our draughtsman opposite and showed him in what way to make his drawings and ourselves made rapid descriptions of all the details of natural history while our specimens were still fresh.

Usually Banks and Solander gathered specimens jointly, Solander described and classified them, and a clerk, probably Sporing, recorded them. Parkinson sketched the plants' shape, size, coloration and principal parts of foliage and flora, and made notes on the back of the outlines for guidance in finishing the job. Banks supervised their pressing and drying between a publisher's discarded unbound sheets of Addison's *Commentary* on Milton's *Paradise Lost*. On returning to England Solander wrote a full description of the plants.

It was with the *Endeavour*'s voyage that Australia really came to the attention of European science.

Captain Tobias Furneaux. This twentieth-century oil on canvas portrait by Dorofield Hardy (?–1937) was acquired in 1928, and is now in the Parliament House Art Collection, Canberra.

This cannon from the *Endeavour* is now at the Australian National Maritime Museum. (Photograph by Jenni Carter, Australian National Maritime Museum.)

'*Banksia serrata*', gathered Botany Bay, Australia, 12 April–6 May 1770'. Line engraving by G. Smith after Sydney Parkinson (1770) and J.F. Miller (1773). Plate 285 from *Banks' Florilegium.* (Alecto Historical Editions in association with the British Museum [Natural History].)

Banks and Solander collected plants at ten of their eleven landing places in 1770, with time spent at each varying from about an hour to six and half weeks in the Endeavour River area. They were at Botany Bay for seven and a half days.

Judging by Banks's journal, he was most interested in the Aborigines in his first two days ashore at Botany Bay, as he merely said he had found many plants in the woods. However, on the third day he wrote:

> The Captn, Dr Solander, myself and some of the people, making in all 10 musquets, resolvd to make an excursion into the countrey. We...walkd till we compleatly tird ourselves...The Soil wherever we saw it consisted of either swamps or light sandy soil on which grew very few species of trees, one of which was large yeilding a gum much like *sanguis draconis* but every place was coverd with vast quantities of grass. (Banks, II, 57)

This first tree Banks specified was probably a variety of eucalyptus, kaikur (*Eucalyptus alba*), its gum likening it to the dragon tree (*Dracaena draco*) of the Maderias and the Canary Islands. Two days later:

> Our collection of Plants was now grown so immensly large that it was necessary that some extrordinary care should be taken of them least they should spoil in the books. I therefore devoted this day to that business and carried all the drying paper, near 200 Quires of which the larger part was full, ashore and spread them upon a sail in the sun, kept them in this manner exposd the whole day, often turning them and sometimes turning the Quires in which were plants inside out. By this means they came on board at night in very good condition. (Banks, II, 58)

This collection included the genus *Banksia*; and the stamp used by the Botany Department, Natural History Museum is based on *Banksia serrata.*

Banks then resumed 'botanizing as usual, now quite void of fear as our neighbours have turned out to be such rank cowards'. He recorded Cook and Solander's finding trees 'which bore fruit of the Jambosa kind [probably *Eugenia banksii*], much in colour and shape resembling cherries; of these they eat plentifully and brought home also abundance, which we eat with much pleasure tho they had little to recommend them but a light acid'. With excellent tripe of stingray they had 'a dish of the leaves of *tetragonia coirnuta* [*Tetragonia expansa*] boild, which we eat as well as spinage or near it'. Banks introduced this plant to England on his return (Banks, II, 59, 61).

Although the proliferation of plants inspired Cook to change the harbour's name to Botany Bay, Banks himself specified only three of them in his journal—the dragon tree, the 'cherries' and the spinach, leaving descriptions to his staff. He did not write any general impressions of the botany of the place, as Cook did briefly:

> Altho wood is here in great plenty yet there is very little variety; the largest trees are as large or larger than our Oaks in England and grows a good deal like them and yields a redish Gum; the wood itself is heavy hard and black like Lignum Vitae [possible *Casuarina glauca*, swamp oak]. Another sort that grows tall and Strait some thing like Pines, the wood of this is hard and Ponderous and something of the Nature of America live oaks, these two are all the Timber trees I met with. There are a few sorts of Shrubs and several Palm trees, and Mangroves about the head of the harbour. (Cook, I, 311)

Banks wrote little more than a sentence in his journal for seven days after leaving Botany Bay, undoubtedly because he was preoccupied with plants: 'This evening we finishd Drawing the plants got in the last harbour, which had been kept fresh till this time by means of tin chests and wet cloths' (Banks, II, 62).

At Bustard Bay, Banks' second landing:

> We found a great variety of Plants, several however the same as those we ourselves had before seen in the Islands between the tropicks and others known to be natives of the east Indies, a sure mark that we were upon the point of leaving the Southern temperate Zone and for the future we must expect to meet with plants &c. a part of which at least have been before seen by Europeans. The Soil in general was very sandy and dry: tho it producd a large variety of Plants yet it never was coverd with a thick verdure...

'The simpling Macaroni' (London, Darly, 1772). This caricature is of the Swedish naturalist Dr Daniel Solander, former pupil of Linnaeus and assistant to Joseph Banks on the *Endeavour*. In eighteenth-century Britain, the word 'macaroni' meant a dandy who affected foreign manners. (Rex Nan Kivell Collection, National Library of Australia.)

'The fly catching Macaroni', a caricature of Banks. Etching. (Rex Nan Kivell Collection, National Library of Australia.)

> Upon the sides of the hills were many of the trees yeilding a gum like *Sanguis draconis*: they differd however from those seen in the last harbour in having their leaves longer and hanging down like those of the weeping willow, tho notwithstanding that I beleive that they were of the same species. There was however much less gum upon them; only one tree that I saw had any upon it, contrary to all theory, which teaches that the hotter a climate is the more gums exsude. The same observation however held good in the plant yeilding the Yellow gum of which tho we saw vast numbers we did not see any that shewd signs of gum. (Banks, II, 65–6)

The next seventeen days were uneventful from a botanical point of view. They found the figs from Bustard Bay, either the cluster or Moreton Bay fig, to be impregnated by insects. Sand burrs made walking almost intolerable at Thirsty Sound. They saw much seaweed with very fine leaves (probably agardh) all through one day. And what were thought to be cocoa nut trees at Palm Island turned out to be nothing more than bad Cabbage Trees.

At Endeavour River Banks and Solander went ashore to gather plants before the ship was moored preparatory to being careened. This collecting continued intermittently for 41 days until Banks wrote: 'Botanizing with no kind of success. The Plants were now intirely compleated and nothing new to be found' (Banks, II, 100). Nevertheless, he specified in his journal only nine of the numerous plants collected:

> 27 [June]. Some of the Gentlemen who had been out in the woods Yesterday brought home the leaves of a plant which I took to be *Arum Esculentum*, the same I beleive as is calld Coccos in the West Indies [i.e. Taro]. In consequence of this I went to the place and found plenty; on

tryal however the roots were found to be too acrid to be eat, the leaves however when boild were little inferior to spinage. In the same place grew plenty of Cabbage trees [*Livistona australis*] a kind of Wild Plantain [*Musa banksii*] whose fruit was so full of stones that it was scarce eatable, another fruit about as large as a small golden pippin but flatter, of a deep purple colour; these when gatherd off from the tree were very hard and disagreable but after being kept a few days became soft and tasted much like indiferent Damsons [*Pleiogynium cerasiferum*, Burdekin plum].

28 [June]. Tupia by Roasting his Coccos very much in his oven made them lose intirely their acridity; the Roots were so small that we did not think them at all an object for the ship so resolvd to content ourselves with the greens which are calld in the West Indies Indian Kale [*Colocasia esculenta*]. I went with the seamen to shew them the Place and they Gatherd a large quantity...

The Wild Plantain trees, tho their fruit does not serve for food, are to us a most material benefit; we made Baskets of their stalks (a thing we learnd of the Islanders) in which our plants which would not otherwise keep home remain fresh for 2 or 3 days; indeed in a hot climate it is hardly Practicable to go on without such baskets which we call by the Island name of Papa Mya [*paepae meia*, woven of banana leaves]. Our Plants dry better in Paper Books than in Sand, with this precaution, that one person is intirely employd in attending them who shifts them all once a day, exposes the Quires in which they are to the greatest heat of the sun and at night covers them most carefully up from any damps, always carefull not to bring them out too soon in a morning or leave them out too late in the evening...

...the Banks were steep and coverd with trees of a Beautifull verdue particularly what is calld in the West Indies Mohoe or Bark tree (*Hibiscus tiliaceus*)...

...these [turtles] when killd were always found to be full of Turtle Grass (a kind of Conferva I beleive) [*Thalassia hemprichii*?] ...

The Dr and me were obligd to go very far for any thing new; to day we went several miles to a high hill where after sweating and broiling among the woods till night we were obligd to return almost empty. But the most vexatious accident imaginable befel us likewise: traveling in a deep vally, the sides of which were steep almost as a wall but coverd with trees and plenty of Brush wood, we found marking nuts (*anacardium orientale*) [*Semecarpus australiensis*] laying on the ground, and desirous as we were to find the tree on which they had grown, a thing that I beleive no European Botanist has seen, we were not with all our pains able to find it; so after cutting down 4 or 5 trees and spending much time were obligd to give over our hopes. (Banks, II, 85, 88, 94, 99)

After leaving Endeavour River Banks spent a night with Cook on Lizard Island: 'On it I found some few plants which I had not before seen'. However, he specified only one — *Blepharocarya involucrigera* (Banks, II, 103).

Banks wrote his conclusions about the botany of the country on the way from Torres Strait to Batavia:

> indeed Palm cabbage and what is calld in the West Indies Indian Kale were in tolerable plenty, as was also a sort of Purslane. The other plants we eat were a kind of Beans, very bad, a kind of Parsley and a plant something resembling spinage, which two last grew only to the Southward. I shall give their botanical names as I beleive some of them were never eat by Europeans before: first Indian Kale [*Arum Esculentum*], Red flowerd purslane [*Sesuvium Portulacastrum*], Beans [*Glycine speciosa*] [*Canavalia maritima*], Parsley [*Apium*], Spinage [*Tetragonia cornuta*] [*Tetragonia expansa*]. Fruits we had still fewer; to the South was one something resembling a heart cherry only the stone was soft [*Eugenia*] [*Eugenia banksii*] which had nothing but a light acid to recommend it; to the Northward again a kind of Figs growing from the stalk of a tree, very indifferent [*Ficus caudiciflora*] [*Ficus glomerata*], a fruit we calld Plumbs like them in Colour but flat like a little cheese [ ] [Burdekin plum, *Pleiogynium cerasiferum*], and another much like a damson both in appearance and taste [probably *Plachonella obovata*], both these last however were so full of a large stone that eating them was but

an unprofitable business. Wild Plantanes we had also but so full of seeds that they had little or no pulp [*Musa banksii*].

For the article of timber, there is certainly no want of trees of more than the midling size and some in the valleys very large, but all of a very hard nature; our carpenters who cut them down for firewood complaind much that their tools were damaged by them. Some trees there were also to the Northward whose soft bark, which easily peels off, is in the East Indies applyd to the use of calking ships in Lieu of Oakum [probably *Melaleuca leucadendron*].

Palms here were of three different sorts. The first which grew plentifully to the Southward had leaves pleated like a fan; the Cabbage of these was small but exquisitely sweet and the nuts which it bore in great abundance a very good food for hogs [*Livistona australis*]. The second was very much like the real cabbage tree of the West Indies, bearing large pinnated leaves like those of a Cocoa nut; these too yeilded cabbage if not so sweet as the other sort yet the quantity made ample amends [*Areca monostachya*]. The third which as well as the second was found only in the Northern parts was low, seldom ten feet in hight, with small pennated leaves resembling those of some kinds of fern; Cabbage it had none but generaly bore a plentifull Crop of nutts about the size of a large chestnut and rounder [*Cycas media* or *Macrozamia spiralis*]. By the hulls of these which we found plentifully near the Indian fires we were assurd that these people eat them, and some of our gentlemen tried to do the same, but were deterrd from a second experiment by a hearty fit of vomiting and purging which was the consequence of the first. The hogs however who were still shorter of provision than we were eat them heartily and we concluded their constitutions stronger than ours, till after about a week they were all taken extreemly ill of indigestions; two died and the rest were savd with dificulty.

Other usefull plants we saw none, except perhaps two might be found so which yeild resin in abundance: the one a tree tolerably large with narrow leaves not unlike a willow which was very plentyfull in every place into which we went [probably *Eucalyptus creba*]; this yeilded a blood red resin or rather gum-resin very nearly resembling *Sanguis draconis*, indeed as *Sanguis draconis* is the produce of several different plants this may perhaps be one of the sorts. This I should suppose to be the gum mentiond by Dampier in his voyage round the world p. [463] and by him compard with *sanguis draconis*, as possibly also that which Tasman saw upon Diemens Land, where he says he saw gum of the trees and gum Lac of the ground...The other was a small Plant with long narrow grassy leaves and a spike of flowers resembling much that kind of Bulrush which is cald in England Cats tail [*Xanthorrhoea*, black boy or grass tree]; this yeilded a resin of a bright yellow colour perfectly resembling Gambouge only that it did not stain; it had a sweet smell but what its properties are the chymists may be able to determine.

Of Plants in general the countrey afforded a far larger variety than its barren appearance seemd to promise. Many of these have no doubt properties which might be usefull, but for Physical and oeconomical purposes which we were not able to investigate, could we have understood the Indians or made them by means our freinds we might perchance have learnt some of these; for tho their manner of life, but one degree removd from Brutes, does not seem to promise much yet they had a knowledge of plants as we plainly could percieve by their having names for them.

Thus much for plants: I have been rather particular in mentioning those which we eat hoping that such a remembrance might be of use to some or other into whose hands these papers may fall. (Banks, II, 114–16)

In general, Parkinson had little to say about the new plants. However, he did show some interest in those that were edible. At Botany Bay he wrote:

> The country is very level and fertile; the soil, a kind of grey sand; and the climate mild: and though it was the beginning of winter when we arrived, everything seemed in perfection. There is a variety of flowering shrubs; a tree that yields gum [any or all of several species of *Eucalyptus*, *Angophora*, *Acacia* and *Xanthorroea*]; and a species

of palm, the berries of which are of two sorts; one small, eaten by the hogs, and the other, as large as a cherry, has a stone in it; it is of a pale crimson colour, and has the taste of a sweet acid [a fan-leaved, *Livistona australia* (cabbage tree).] We also found a species of *Salvia fortea* [one of several plants of the mint family, Labiatae]. (Parkinson, 135)

Parkinson did not go ashore at Bustard Bay but wrote: 'We observed nothing worthy of note on land, excepting a great variety of plants; one of which bore a fruit like a small crab-apple, having a large stone in it [probably *Pleiogynium* (Burdekin plum)], the Eawharra of Otaheite [a Pandanus species]' (Parkinson, 138). At Thirsty Sound he saw 'many of the Yam-trees, the greater part of them having been stripped of the bark' (Parkinson, 140). These are not identifiable.

Parkinson made his longest statement about plants at Endeavour River:

> Of vegetables we found Glycine rosea, which yields a sort of bean purslain, that eats very well, boiled [*Canavalea rosea* (wild jack bean)]; Cicas circinalis, the kernels of which, roasted, tasted like parched pease; but it made some of our people sick, who ate it: of this fruit, they made a kind of sago in the East Indies: we cut down many of them for the cabbage, which is very good food [probably a Zamia, *Cycas media* or *Macrozamia spiralis*]. We found also a black purple fruit, with a kernel in it which had a sweet flat taste [probably Burdekin plums]; two sorts of fruit like pears, having stony sides, somewhat like the Guava, and of very indifferent taste [of the species of *Capparis* or _____ Passiflora (passionfruit)]; a small-leaved plant, that smelt like lemon and orange peel, and made an agreeable substitute for tea [of the Myrtaceae family: the small-leaved *Backea inbricata* _____ *Leptospermum fabricia* ________ or small-leaved paper-barked *Melaleuca quinquenervia* ________]; the Epeea, Taro, Eowhee and Epeepee of Otaheiti, [*Tacca leontopelaloides* ______ *Alocasia macrorrhiza* ________ *Castanospermum australe* _______ *Mucana gigas* _______ _____]; also wild Plaintain like the Meyia of Otaheiti which is very full of seed and has hardly any pulp [*Musa banksii* _______]; a sort of fig-tree, that bears fruit on the main stem, which tastes very insipid [*Ficus glomerata* _________]; the Etee and Eroa, of which the natives of Otaheiti make the best lines [*Cordyline* ________ *Dendrocnidee moroides* _______ ________]; many gum-trees [*Eucalyptus* and *Xanthorrhoea*], and a great number of other plants, among which was a beautiful Nymphea, with blue and white petals [*Nymphaea violacea*]. (Parkinson, 144)

The collections from the *Endeavour* voyage made a striking addition to European science. Banks himself wrote after his return:

> The number of Natural productions discover'd in this Voyage is incredible: about 1000 Species of Plants that had not been at all describ'd by any Botanical authority; 500 fish, as many Birds, and insects Sea and Land innumerable: out of these some considerable oeconomical purposes may be answer'd particularly with the fine Dyes of the Otaheitians and the Plants of which the new Zealanders make their Cloth of which we have brought over ye seeds. The fine red Colour us'd by the inhabitants of the Islands situated between the tropicks in the South Sea the tinge of which seems to be between that of Scarlet and a pink is made by mixing the juice of the Fruit of a Fig Tree suppos'd to be peculiar to those Islands with the juice of the Leaves of the *Cordia Sebestena orientalis Lenius.* (Banks, II, 328)

John Ellis went further, telling Linnaeus that Banks and Solander had returned 'laden with the greatest treasure of Natural History that ever was brought into any country at one time by two persons'. This news raised the old man's excitement to fever pitch. He wrote to Solander, pleading that the results be published, for they would 'delight and benefit' the world, and 'the foundations of true science will be strengthened, so as to endure through all generations' (Banks, I, 53; Linnaeus, I, 267).

Even now, no one knows precisely how many botanical specimens the pair brought back. Researchers at London's Natural History Museum, where most are deposited, are still, after more than 200 years, engaged in the seemingly endless task of tracking down and describing and classifying them. It is known that in his own herbarium Banks came to have more than 3600 species of plants, more than 1400 of them new to science, with a total of more than 30 000 specimens. In this collection the Australian specimens constituted a core.

The few significant botanical observations of Tasmania were restricted to the visits of Cook's second and third voyages to Adventure Bay, South Bruny Island, on the south-east corner of Tasmania, and to that of Marion du Fresne to North Bay in 1772. From Cook's second voyage Tobias Furneaux took seeds of two plants to England, *Eucalyptus obliqua* and *Leptospermum lanigerum*, with a specimen. A number of the keepers of journals wrote about these plants. James Burney said that:

> The Trees are mostly Evergreens, standing very thick and close together — many of the Small ones bore berries of a spicy flavour — the larger ones are quite Strait & Shoot up very high before they branch out. They are large enough for Masts large enough for any Ship in the Navy, but are rather brittle and heavy — they have a Soft thick bark which many of them have been strippd of by the Natives — the Wood is of a reddish cast & has a great deal of gum in it. (Cook, II, 748)

And Furneaux wrote that the 'large trees' grow

> to a great height before they branch off: they are all of them of the Ever-green kind of a different sort to any I ever saw; the wood is very brittle and easily split; there is a very little variety of sort, having seen but two, the leaves of one is long and Narrow, the seed (of which I have got a few) was in the shape of a Button, and had a very agreeable smell: the Leaves of the other are like the bay and has a seed like a white thorn, with an agreeable spicy taste and smell. Out of the tree we cut down for Fire wood there issued some Gum, which the Surgeon called Gum lac. (Cook, II, 734)

On Cook's third voyage, William Anderson, a surgeon-botanist, sailed in the *Resolution*, and David Nelson, a young gardener from the Royal Gardens at Kew, in the *Discovery*. Nelson was a collector of plants for Banks who, under royal patronage, was enlarging the Kew gardens.

The plants which Anderson saw in Tasmania did not impress him greatly:

> Amongst the Vegetable productions there is not one which we could find that afforded the smallest subsistence for mankind. The forest trees are all of one sort growing to a great height and in general quite straight, branching but little till towards the top. The bark is white which makes them appear at a distance as if they had been peel'd. It is thick and within it are sometimes collected pieces of a reddish transparent Gum or resin which has an Astringent taste. The leaves are long, narrow and pointed and it bears clusters of small white flowers whose cups were plentifully scatter'd about the ground at this time, with another sort resembling them somewhat in shape but much larger which makes it probable that there are two species of this tree. The bark, fruit and leaves, have an agreeable aromatic taste and smell and the wood seems fit for most purposes to which navigators can apply it. The most common next to this is a small tree about ten feet high, branching pretty much with narrow leaves &c a large yellow cylindrical flower, consisting only of a vast number of filaments which being shed leave a fruit like a pine top. [Probably *Banksia marginata*.] These are both unknown in Europe but the underwood consists chiefly of a species of Syringa, and a new species of the Melaleuca or the Cayaputs of Rumphuis which being burnt by the natives, perhaps to clear the country, smutt the traveller abundantly as he walks in the wood. Of other plants which are not very numerous there are of known sorts viz Gladiolus, Rushes, Bellflower, Glasswort, Anise tree which is very common, a small sort of sorrel and milkwort, both scarce, Cudweed, and Jobs tears. Of ferns and mosses there are several kinds as female fern, Spleenwort, Poly pody &c but the species are either common or at least found in some other country especially New Zeeland. (Cook, III, 791–2)

(Gladiolus would be of the *Iridaceae*; rush could be *Juncus* spp.; bell-flower, possibly *Wahlenbergia* sp.; samphire, *Salicornia quinqueflora*; wood sorrel, *Oxalis* sp.; milkwort, possibly *Comesperma* spp.; cudweed, possibly of the Compositae family; Job's tears, possibly *Gahnia psittacorum*.)

Staying six days, Marion and his companions had

time to observe the environs of North Bay. They recorded that the land was covered with 'heath and small trees', and saw 'a species of pine a little less tall than ours' (probably Oyster Bay pine, *Callitris rhomboidea*). They wrote also of 'grass and fern', 'sorrell and sorrel wood', 'daisies and dandelions' (Duyker, 1992, 26). However, they were not trained botanists, so their records did not leave sufficient detail to allow for confident modern identifications.

On Norfolk Island in October 1774, Cook found

> the Flax plant [*Phormium tenax*], many other Plants and Trees common to [New Zealand] was found here but the chief produce of the isle is Spruce Pines [*Araucaria excelsa*] which grow here in vast abundance and to a vast size, from two to three feet diameter and upwards, it is of a different sort to those in New Caledonia and also to those in New Zealand and for Masts, Yards &c superior to both. We cut down one of the Smallest trees we could find and Cut a length of the uper end to make a Topgt Mast or Yard. (Cook, II, 565–6)

As had Banks and Solander previously, the collectors on Cook's second and third voyages took seeds back to England.

At least nine species of Australian plants were cultivated in England before 1788. See table below.

Two Australian herbariums have collections of plants collected here by Banks and Solander. They are duplicates which the British Museum (Natural History) presented to them. The National Herbarium of New South Wales at the Royal Botanic Gardens, Sydney, received 585 plants in 1905. The National Herbarium of Victoria at the Royal Botanic Gardens, Melbourne, has fewer, unknown numbers of plants.

Species	*Locality*	*Year*	*Introducer*
Casuarina torulosa	New South Wales	1771	Banks
Pouteria sericea	New South Wales	1771	Banks
Eucalyptus obliqua	Van Dieman's Land	1774	Furneaux
Leptospermum lanigerum	Van Dieman's Land	1774	Furneaux
Casuarina stricta	New South Wales	1771	Banks
Acacia verticillata	Van Dieman's Land	1780	Anderson and Nelson
Atylosia reticulata	New South Wales	1771	Banks
Dianella aspera	New South Wales	1771	Banks

6

Zoology

Seventeenth Century

Although seventeenth-century Europeans had their first experiences of Australian animals at Torres Strait and Cape York, they gained most of their knowledge of them on the west coast. Most of the VOC explorers' and sailors' observations of nature were meagre. The Englishman Dampier had much more to say than any of them.

Gilbert P. Whitley, who was curator of fishes at the Australian Museum, Sydney, made an invaluable record of the early history of Australian zoology, which the Royal Zoological Society of New South Wales published in 1970 for the bicentenary of Cook's discovery of Australia's east coast. He says two dozen or so Australian animal species, including man, were known before Tasman; before Cook nearly 100 different species were reported. Some, such as small land birds or food-fishes, were mentioned in general terms but others were described in detail. Between 1606 and 1769 the following classes of animals had been mentioned from Australia: 8 species of mammals, 40 of birds, 8 of reptiles, 23 of fishes, 3 of insects, 3 of crustaceans and 12 of molluscs — 'to say nothing of possible lower animals, such as coral and sea-eggs and some indeterminables'. Whitley adds: 'One would have expected the old explorers to have populated Australia with fabulous beasts, instead of which their reports were sober and factual; therefore, we can in many cases identify their species precisely'.

The author thanks Mr Whitley and the Royal Zoological Society of New South Wales and also Mr W.B. Alexander, who was keeper of biology in the Western Australian Museum, for their efforts in identifying animals which explorers and merchantmen saw and reported. Their *dramatis animalia* follows in chronological order:

1606

Birds

Torres Strait pigeon (*Ducula bicolor spilorrhoa*). Whitley records them as the first truly Australian animals reported by Europeans. They fly in flocks between the islands and the mainland.

Fishes

A reasonable assumption is that the first Australian animals Europeans saw were fish. T.D. Mutch thinks that in the chart of his 1606 voyage Jansz showed a river flowing into the Gulf of Carpentaria, which he named R Vis, and that a cartographer extended this in 1622 to R Visch (Fish River). Mutch therefore assumes that Jansz's crew caught fish there.

Insects

Flies, cantharides (?*Musca vetustissima*). Diego de Prado, Torres's companion, wrote: 'So great was the number of flies [probably bush flies] that they seemed as if they wanted to eat the men up'.

Coelenterata

Coral shoals. Jansz would have seen them when crossing Torres Strait and Torres when discovering it.

1618

Birds

Black dove, perhaps the noddy (*Anous stolidus*); 'Tropick Bird' (*Phaeton* sp.); 'Scissor tails'. Skipper Claeszoon of the *Zeewolf* (Seawolf), the second ship to sight Western Australia, wrote for 17 April: 'We saw a black dove flying close by and around the ship which we thought must surely have come from an island'. His entry for 29 April ran: 'We saw numbers of birds many of which seemed to be land-birds, such as a white tropic-bird and a few scissor-tail ducks, so that I surmiz'd that we were near land' (Heeres, 12).

1623

Mammals

Dingo (*Canis familiaris*). Carstensz made two references to seeing footprints of large dogs on the west coast of Cape York Peninsula. He also wrote of seeing many dogs.

Birds

Heron (fam. Ardeidae); Curlew (*Numenius madagascariensis*). Carstensz saw great numbers of them on the west coast of Cape York Peninsula.

Fishes

Shark (perhaps *Galeocerda cuvier*, etc.); Swordfish (*Istiompas indicus*). Carstensz saw them and 'the like unnatural monsters' in the Gulf of Carpentaria. He added that they also caught plenty of 'delicious' fish. (Heeres, 39)

Mollusca

Tiny shells (unknown species). Hermanszoon, skipper of the *Leyden*, saw them sticking to tallow on the sounding line. He also noted the plankton of the north-west seas.

1627

Birds

Storm petrel, (fam. Hydrobatidae); Sanderling (*Calidris alba*). J. Van Roosenbergh, supercargo of the *Wapen van Hoorn*, in the vicinity of Shark Bay, Western Australia, 'saw a black bird with a white tail, having white streaks here and there under its wings...Three or four days before we also saw a number of Sanderlings' (Heeres, 53).

Mollusca

Cuttle (fam. Sepiidae, various species). Van Roosenbergh wrote: 'Close inshore we also saw a quantity of cuttlebone, but the pieces were very small and scattered' (Heeres, 53).

1629

Mammals

Dama wallaby (*Thylogale eugenii*), or pademelon. François Pelsaert, commander of the *Batavia*, wrote what is evidently the first description of an Australian marsupial:

> we found in these islands large numbers of a species of cats, which are very strange creatures; they are about the size of a hare, their head resembling the head of a civet-cat; the forepaws are very short, about the length of a finger, on which the animal has five small nails or fingers, resembling those of a monkey's forepaw. Its two hindlegs, on the contrary, are upwards of half an ell in length [Dutch ell: 68 centimetres], and it walks on these only, on the flat of the heavy part of the leg, so that it does not run fast. Its tail is very long, like that of a long-tailed monkey; if it eats, it sits on its hindlegs, and clutches its food with its forepaws, just like a squirrel or monkey. Their manner of generation or procreation is exceedingly strange and highly worth observing. Below the belly the female carries a pouch, into which you may put your hand; inside the pouch are her nipples, and we have found that the young ones grow up in this pouch with the nipples in their mouths. We have seen some young ones lying there which were only the size of a bean, though at the same time perfectly proportioned, so that it seems certain that they grow there out of the nipples of the mammae, from which they draw their food, until they are grown up and are able to walk. Still, they keep creeping into the pouch even when they have become very large, and the dam runs off with them, when they are hunted. (Heeres, 61)

Whitley comments:

> If the translation is trustworthy, Pelsaert inaugurated the fallacy that the young wallaby was born on the nipples of its mother. After

more than three centuries, some people still maintain that this is so in kangaroos, wallabies and other marsupials. Nowadays, we should know better, perhaps having seen films showing young kangaroos born at an early age, still an embryo in form, and 'swimming' through its mother's fur until its mouth reaches and fixes itself to a teat, which then enlarges in its mouth so that the baby does not fall off.

Seals (various Otariidae). Pelsaert named Robben-eyeland or Seals Island in Houtman Abrolhos.

Birds

Grey turtle dove, the brush bronzewing (*Phaps elegans*). Pelsaert saw them in the islands of Houtman Abrolhos.

Insects

Flesh flies (?*Musca australis*). These were probably of a different species from those which tormented Torres's men in 1606. Pelsaert wrote of his experience on the mainland: 'We also found such multitudes of flies here, which perched on our mouths and crept into our eyes, that we could not keep them off our persons' (Heeres, 57).

Termite (mounds). Palsaert wrote of seeing on the mainland: 'ant-hills [which] consisted of earth thrown up, and from afar somewhat resembled huts for the abode of men' (Heeres, 57).

Crustacea

Crab shells, probably crayfish. Being unable to land on a precipitous part of the coast of the mainland, six of Pelsaert's men swam ashore to search for water. Pelsaert wrote: 'It also seemed that a short time before there had been natives there, for we found some crab-shells lying about and here and there fire-ashes' (Heeres, 57).

1635

Birds

Saturn gull; gull (*Larus novaehollandiae*): W.G. de Jongh, skipper of the *Amsterdam*, off Dirk Hartog's Roads, Western Australia, saw 'a small Saturn-gull, and not above 6 or 7 other gulls' (Heeres, 63).

1636

Birds

Black swan (*Cygnus atratus*). Off the south-west coast of Western Australia, apparently near Bernier Island, Antonie Caen, skipper of the *Banda*, saw on the sea two stately black birds as large as swans, which had orange-yellow bills and were almost half a metre long. Major H.W. Whittell, author of *The Literature of Australian Birds*, thinks this is almost certainly the first report of the black swan.

1642

Mammals

Whales, probably Humpback whales (*Megaptera novaeangliae*). Tasman wrote, when west or south-west of Tasmania: '[We] saw also some whales at night in the dog watch' (Tasman, 86).

'Tiger' (perhaps *Thylacinus cynocephalus*). A landing party at Tasman's anchorage at Blackman Bay, south-east Tasmania, saw 'furrows of some animals in the earth not unlike the claws of a tiger ...also...some excrements of...four-footed animals' (Tasman, 110).

Birds

Wild duck (fam. Anatidae); goose, perhaps Cape Barren goose. Tasman reported seeing both at Blackman Bay.

Fishes

Tunny (*Thinnus maccoyii*). South of South Australia, Tasman reported 'great abundance of tunnies by and around the ship' (Tasman, 81). These were probably Southern Bluefin Tuna, the first record of this important commercial fish.

Mollusca

Mussel (*Mytilus planalatus*). Tasman's pilot, Francoijs Jacobszn, reported 'various mussels (in various places lying stuck together in clusters)' at Blackman Bay (Tasman, 111).

Coelenterata

Tasmanian coral. Tasman wrote of it at south-west Tasmania: 'three miles off the coast had 60 fathom coral bottom' (Tasman, 90).

1644

Reptiles

Crocodile (*Crocodylus porosus*). Tasman made the first reference to an Australian reptile when he named Crocodile Islands, off the Northern Territory coast.

Mollusca

Shells used for drinking, indeterminable. Tasman spoke of these on the north and north-west coasts of the continent, 'for drinking from, one uses here large shells'.

1656

Mammals

'*Cat resembling civet-cat*', wallaby (*Setonix brachyurus*). Samuel Volckertszoon, skipper of the *De Wakende Boei*, wrote of an island which he did not name (Rottnest Island, off Perth): 'here certain animals are found, since we saw many excrements, and besides two seals and a wild cat, resembling a civet-cat, but with browner hair' (Heeres, 79). This was the wallaby known as the quokka or short-tailed pademelon.

1658

Birds

Black gulls, Shearwaters (*Puffinus* sp.); wagtails. Pietersz Jonck, skipper of the *Emeloort*, reported these birds at Western Australia.

1688

Mammals

Dingo: Dampier wrote of his 1688 visit: 'We saw no sort of Animal, nor any Track of Beast, but once; and that seemed to be the Tread of a Beast as big as a great Mastiff-Dog' (Dampier, [1697], 312).

Dugong (*Dugong dugon*). Dampier wrote of King Sound, Western Australia: 'Here are a few small Land-birds, but none bigger than a Blackbird; and but few Sea-fowls. Neither is the Sea very plentifully stored with Fish, unless you reckon the Manates [i.e. dugong] and Turtle as such' (Dampier [1697], 312).

Reptiles

Turtle (*Chelonia mydas*). Dampier saw green turtles.

Mollusca

Cockle [fam. Cardiiae]; periwinkle [fam. Littorinidae]. Dampier wrote of the Aborigines: 'at Low-water they seek for Cockles, Muscles and Periwincles (Dampier [1697], 313)'.

1696–97

Mammals

Dingo. Willem de Vlamingh's men in 1697 saw 'a yellow dog jump out of the scrub and throw itself into the sea as if to enjoy a swim' (Schilder, 157). Nicolaas Witsen wrote of a report he received from de Vlamingh's voyage: 'No four-footed beasts [have been found], except one as great as a dog with long ears, living in the water as well as on the land' (Schilder, 221).

Quokka. On the basis of de Vlamingh's report on Rottnest Island 1696–97, Nicolaas Witsen wrote of the quokkas: 'Upon the island near the coast have been seen rats as great as cats, in an innumerable quantity; all of which had a kind of bag or purse hanging from the throat upon the breast downwards, into which one could put one's hand, without being able to understand to what end nature had created the animal like this: as soon as it was shot dead, this animal smelled terribly, so that the skins were not taken along' (Schilder, 222).

Birds

Black swan (*Cygnus atratus*). De Vlamingh saw black swans in the Swan River. An officer wrote: '[We] saw many swans (of which our boat shot some nine or ten)' (Schilder, 155). They caught several and took three to Batavia, the first Australian wildlife to be exported, but all died there.

Nightingale, possibly reedwarbler (*Acrocephalus stentoreus*). De Vlamingh heard it in the Swan River area in Western Australia.

Emu (*Dromaius novaehollandiae*) tracks. De Vlamingh's officer wrote of Jurien Bay, between Perth and Geraldton: '[We saw] no people, nor fresh water, but several human footprints and such as of a dog and cassowary [i.e. emu]' (Schilder, 157).

Osprey (*Pandion haliaetus*). Of Jurien Bay one of de Vlamingh's officers wrote: '[Our captain] brought along a large bird's head and related that they had seen two nests made of branches, some three fathoms big in circumference' (Schilder, 159). Witsen wrote later from Amsterdam: 'There were also found some bird's nests of a prodigious greatness, so that six men could not, by stretching out their arms, encompass one of them' (Schilder, 222).

Parrots (fam. Psittacidae); cormorant (*Phalacrocorax* sp.) (Four species in Western Australia); pelican

(*Pelecanus conspillatus*); cockatoo (fam. Psittacidae); parakeet (fam. Psittacidae); diver, probably musk duck (*Biziura lobata*), but grebes are also known as divers.

Reptiles
Red serpent (indeterminable). De Vlamingh reported this reptile.

Fishes
Angler or frogfish. De Vlamingh's officer wrote of 'a miraculous fish about two feet long with a round head and arms and legs of a kind, nay even something like hands' (Schilder, 153). This was most likely the anglerfish (fam. Antennariidae).

Sardines (probably *Sardinops neopilchardus*); grey rock bream (indeterminable). De Vlamingh reported them.

Crustacea
Lobsters (crayfish, *Panulirus cygnus*); crabs (*Decapoda* indeterminable). De Vlamingh reported them.

Mollusca
Baler shell (*Melo*); nautilus (*Nautilus*). De Vlamingh sent specimens of these shells to Amsterdam but they cannot be positively identified in references.

1699

Mammals
Whales (undetermined). '...in the Night Abundance of whales about the Ship, some a-head, others a-stern, and some on each side blowing and making a very dismal Noise' (Dampier, 1906, 430).

Dingo. Dampier recorded a sighting of a dingo in his second visit in 1699: 'my Men saw two or three Beasts like hungry Wolves, lean like so many Skeletons, being nothing but Skin and Bones' (Dampier, 1906, p. 433).

Dolphins (fam. Delphinidae). Dampier saw them off the coast of Western Australia: 'saw many small Dolphins and Whales' (Dampier, 1906, 430).

'Racoon', banded hare wallaby (*Lagostrophus fasciatus*). Dampier wrote: 'The Land-Animals that we saw here were only a Sort of Raccoons, different from those of the West Indies, chiefly as to their Legs; for these have very short Fore-Leg; but go jumping upon them as the others do, (and like them are very good Meat)' (Dampier, 1906, 425). The bands on the fur would recall the raccoon.

Birds
Dampier wrote of many birds, including:
Lapwings, Caspian tern (*Hydroprogne caspia*): 'Being still nearer the Land, we saw...a Sort of Fowls, the like of which we had not seen in the whole Voyage...These were as big as Lapwings; of a grey Colour, black about their Eyes, with red sharp Bills, long Wings, their Tails long and forked like Swallows; and they flew lapping their Wings like Lapwings' (Dampier, 1906, 420).

Booby or brown gannet (*Sula leucogaster*), crested terns (*Sterna bergii*): 'As we were standing in we saw several large Sea-fowls, like our Gannets on the Coast of England, flying 3 or 4 together; and a Sort of white Sea-Mews, but black about the Eyes, and with forked Tails' (1906, 422).

Eagle, wedgetail (*Aquila audax*). At Shark Bay: 'There were but few Land-Fowls; we saw none but Eagles, of the larger Sorts of Birds; but 5 or 6 Sorts of small Birds. The biggest Sort of these were no bigger than Larks; some no bigger than Wrens, all singing with great Variety of fine shrill Notes; and we saw some of their Nests with young Ones in them.'

He added: 'The Water-Fowls are Ducks, (which had young Ones now, this being the Beginning of the Spring in these Parts); Curlews, Galdens, Crab-Catchers [sea pie: *Haematopus ostralegus*], Cormorants, Gulls, Pelicans; and some Water-Fowl, such as I have not seen anywhere besides. I have given the Pictures of 4 several Birds on this Coast' (Dampier, 1906, 425).

The pictures were of the straw necked ibis (*Threskiornis spinicollis*), the red-necked avocet (*Recurvirostra novaehollandiae*), the pied oyster catcher/crab catcher, and a noddy, bridled tern (*Sterna anaethetus*).

At Rosemary Island they saw white parrots, little corellas (*Cacatua sanguinea*) which 'flew a great many together'. In the vicinity of Roebuck Bay:

> We saw also some Boobies [or Brown Gannets], and Noddy Birds; and in the Night caught one of these last. It was of another Shape and Colour than any I had seen before. It had a small long Bill, as all of them have, flat Feet like Duck's Feet; its tail forked like a Swallow, but longer and broader, and the Fork deeper than that of the Swallow, with very long Wings; the Top or Crown of the Head of this Noddy was Coal-

black, also having small black Streaks round about and close to the Eyes; and round these streaks on each Side, a pretty broad, white Circle. The Breast, Belly and upper part of its Wings of this Noddy were white, and the Back and upper part of its Wings of a faint black or smoak Colour...

> We saw here Crows [*Corvus coronoides*] (just such as ours in England) small Hawks and Kites; a few of each sort: But here are plenty of small Turtle-Doves, that are plump, fat and very good Meat. (Dampier, 1906, 437, 443)

Dampier reported pigeons (fam. Columbidae) and, leaving the coast, 'Abundance of Boobies and Man of War Birds, *Frigate Bird* [*Fregata ariel* or *F. minor*] flying about us all the Day'.

Reptiles

Guano, stumptail lizard (*Trachydosaurus rugosus*). At Shark Bay Dampier reported:

> a Sort of Guano's, of the same Shape and Size with other Guano's...but differing from them in 3 remarkable Particulars: For these had a larger and uglier Head, and had no Tail: And at the Rump, instead of the Tail there, they had a Stump of a Tail, which appear'd like another Head; but not really such, being without Mouth or Eyes: Yet this Creature seem'd by this Means to have a Head at each End; and, which may be reckon'd a fourth Difference, the Legs also seem'd all 4 of them to be Fore-legs, being all alike in Shape and Length, and seeming by the Joints and Bending to be made as if they were to go indifferently either Head or Tail foremost. They were speckled black and yellow like Toads, and had Scales or Knobs on their Backs like those of Crocodiles, plated on to the Skin, or stuck into it, as part of the Skin. They are very slow in Motion; and when a Man comes nigh them they will stand still and hiss, not endeavouring to get away. Their Livers are also spotted black and yellow: And the Body when opened hath a very unsavoury Smell. I did never see such ugly Creatures any where but here. The Guano's I have observ'd to be very good Meat: And I have often eaten of them with Pleasure; but tho' I have eaten of Snakes, Crocodiles and Allegators, and many Creatures that look frightfully enough, and there are but few I should have been afraid to eat of, if prest by Hunger, yet I think my Stomach would scarce have serv'd to venture upon these N. Holland Guano's, both the Looks and Smell of them being so offensive. (Dampier, 1906, 425–6)

Sea snake (*Pelamis platurus*): 'In passing out [of Shark Bay],' Dampier wrote, 'we saw three Water-Serpents swimming about in the Sea, of a yellow Colour, spotted with dark, brown Spots. They were each about four Foot long, and about the bigness of a Man's Wrist, and were the first I saw on this Coast, which abounds with several sorts of them.' Some days later: 'we saw a great many, of two different Sorts or Shapes. One Sort was yellow, and about the Bigness of a Man's Wrist, about 4 Foot long, having a flat Tail about 4 Fingers broad. The other Sort was much smaller and shorter, round and spotted black and yellow' (Dampier, 1906, 429, 432). Lizard and speckled snake (indeterminable).

Fishes

Dampier's fishes included:

Garfish long tom (fam. Belonidae): 'We saw a large Gar-fish leap 4 times by us, which seemed to be as big as a porpoise...I saw some Bonetas, [fam. Thinnadie], and some Skipjacks [*Katsuwonas pelamys*], a Fish about 8 Inches long, broad and sizeable, not much unlike a Roach; which our Seamen call so from their leaping about...Here [Shark Bay] are also Skates, [fam. Rajidae], Thornbacks, and other Fish of the Ray-kind [*Daemomanta alfredi*]; (one Sort especially like the Sea-Devil) and Gar-fish, Boneta's &c' (Dampier, 1906, 420, 426).

At Rosemary Island:

> we fish'd with Hook and Line, and caught good Store of Fish, viz. Snappers [*Chrysophrys unicolor*], Breams, Old Wives [fam. Aluteridae], and Dog-fish [fam. Squalidae]: When these came we seldom caught any others; for if they did not drive away the other Fish, yet they would be sure to stop them from taking our Hooks, for they would first have them themselves, biting very greedily, We caught also a Monk fish [*Squatina australis*]. (Dampier, 1906, 436)

Off the coast he saw paracoot, barracouta (*Sphyraena* sp.) and flying fish with two wings (*Exocoetus volitans*).

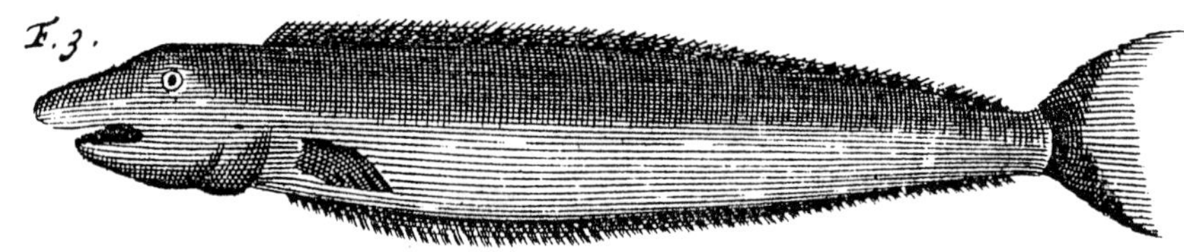

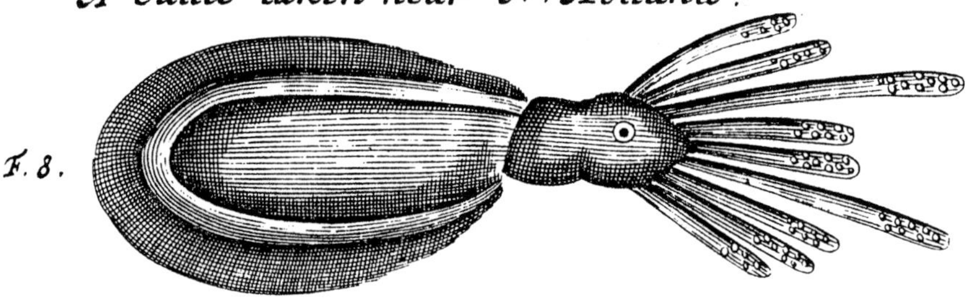

Anonymous, Fish, 1729. Fish recorded by Dampier. (From William Dampier, *A Voyage to New Holland,* London, 1729.)

Anonymous, Birds, 1729. Birds described by Dampier. (From William Dampier, *A Voyage to New Holland*, London, 1729.)

Mollusca

Limpet, pearl oyster (*Pinctada margarintifera*), edible oyster and Long Oyster (?*Ostrea scyphophylla*). 'Of Shell-fish we got here,' Dampier wrote, 'Muscles, Periwinkles, Limpets, Oysters, both of the Pearl-Kind and also Eating-Oysters, as well as the common Sort as long Oysters; besides Cockles, &c.' (Dampier, 1906, 426)

'Cuttle', calamary (*Sepioteuthis australis*). His artist drew one.

Echinodermata

Shell with rays or spikes, sea urchin, [?echinoderm]: 'I gather'd a few strange Shells; chiefly a sort not large, and thick-set all about with Rays or Spikes growing in Rows' (Dampier, 1906, 444).

Eighteenth century

Despite the growth of the modern scientific outlook, the zoological sightings and collections made on the eighteenth-century voyages are not as extensive as the botanical ones.

In 1768, when Bougainville's ships were in the Coral Sea, the naturalist Philibert Commerson reported sighting a wrasse, or parrot fish (perhaps *Lepidaplois diana*); and a large flying fish, 'black' with four 'red wings' (*Cypsibrus* sp.).

Then, in 1770, Cook, Banks and Solander made many sightings and collected extensively as they proceeded up the eastern coast. However, partly because Banks was more interested in plants than animals, what they collected was gradually dispersed to public and private ownership, and no central records kept. Emblematic is the case of the kangaroo. At Botany Bay, Solander 'had a bad sight of a small Animal something like a rabbit and we [i.e. Cook and others] found the dung of an Animal which must feed on grass and which we judged could not be less than a deer' (Cook, I, 307). However, it was not until the sojourn at Endeavour River that the explorers finally saw, and then shot, the elusive animal they learnt to call the 'kangooroo' or 'kanguru'.

Cook noted in his journal for Sunday 24 June:

> Early in the morning I sent a party of men into the Country under the direction of Mr Gore to seek for refreshments, they returnd about noon with a few Palm Cabbages and a bunch or two of wild Plantains, these last were much smaller then any I had ever seen and the Pulp full of small stones otherwise they were well taisted. I saw my self this morning a little way from the ship one of the Animals before spoke off, it was of a light Mouse colour and the full size of a grey hound and shaped in every respect like one, with a long tail which it carried like a grey hound, in short I should have taken it for a wild dog, but for its walking or runing in which it jumped like a Hare or a dear. (Cook, I, 351–2)

Three weeks later, one of the party succeeded in shooting one of these strange animals:

> Mr Gore being out in the Country shott one of the Animals before spoke of, it was a small one of the sort weighing only 28 pound clear of the entrails. The head neck and shoulders of this Animal was very small in proportion to the other parts; the tail was nearly as long as the body, thick next the rump and tapering towards the end; the fore legs were 8 Inch long and the hind 22, its progression is by hoping or jumping 7 or 8 feet at each hop upon its hind legs only, for in this it makes no use of the fore, which seem to be only design'd for scratching in the ground &c. The Skin is cover'd with a short hairy fur of a dark Mouse or Grey Colour. Excepting the head and ears which I thought was something like a Hare's, it bears no sort of resemblance to any European Animal I ever saw; it is said to bear much resemblance to the Gerbua excepting in size, the Gerbua being no larger than a common rat. (Cook, I, 359)

This was the great grey kangaroo (*Macropus giganteus*). The explorers found it 'excellent food'. Subsequently, Banks gave the skull to the eminent anatomist John Hunter. Later, this came to the Museum of the Royal College of Surgeons in London, where it was destroyed in one of the air raids of 1941.

Various entries in Cook's and Banks' journals, and in Sydney Parkinson's published account,

'*Barringtonia calyptrata*'. Plate 127 from *Banks' Florilegium*. (Alecto Historical Editions in association with the British Museum [Natural History]; lent by Mitchell Library, State Library of New South Wales.)

Above: Shells... *Turbo marmoratus* (Green snail from New Caledonia) and spiny *Murex ramosus* from Cooktown. (Photo by Kerry Dundas.)

Right: '*Epacris longiflora*'. Plate 197 from *Banks' Florilegium*. (Alecto Historical Editions in association with the British Museum [Natural History].)

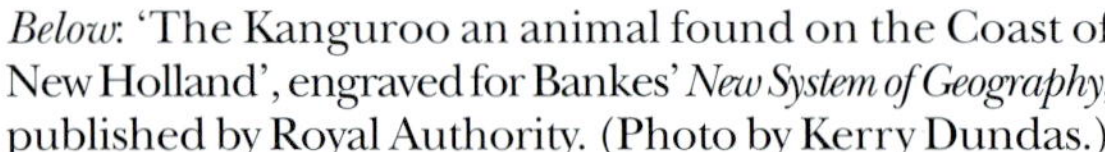

Below: 'The Kanguroo an animal found on the Coast of New Holland', engraved for Bankes' *New System of Geography*, published by Royal Authority. (Photo by Kerry Dundas.)

indicate that the explorers saw a great zoological variety during the *Endeavour*'s four months on the eastern Australian coast. At Botany Bay, for example, there were fish, stingrays, oysters and mussels. Cook added:

> in the wood are a variety of very boutifull birds such as Cocatoo's, Lorryquets, Parrots &c and Crows exactly like those we have in England. Water fowl are no less plenty about the head of the harbour where there are large flats of sand and Mud on which they seek their food, the most of these were unknown to us, one sort especialy which was black and white and as large as a goose but most like a pelican [i.e. *Pelecanus conspicillatus*]. (Cook, I, 311–12)

Then, along the coast, among many other species, the explorers saw brown boobies (*Sula leucogaster plotus*), and water snakes. At Bustard Bay, they saw 'Black & white Ducks' (*Tadora radjah rufitergum*) and 'Bustards such as we have in England one of which we killd that weigh'd 17½ pounds' (*Choriotis australis*). At Endeavour River, in addition to the kangaroo, they saw top-knot Pigeons (*Lofhalaimus antarcticus*), fruit bats (*Pteropus gouldi*), Greenback and Loggerhead turtles (probably *Chelonia*sp. and *Caretta caretta gigus*). There were also numerous fish. Cook wrote of 30 June: 'In the PM the People returnd from hauling the Sain having caught as many fish as came to 2½ pound a man' (Cook, I, 354). There were giant clams (*Tridacna gigus*), and the famous reptiles of Lizard Island (perhaps the monitor *Varanus semirex kinghorn*). And there were birds. Cook wrote as they were preparing to leave Endeavour River:

> The Land fowls we met with here which are far from being numerous were Crow, Kites, Hawks, Cockadores of two sorts the one white and the other brown, very beautifull Lorryquets of two or three sorts, Pidgions, Doves and a few other sorts of small bids. The Sea or water fowl are Herns, Whisling Ducks, which pearch

Anonymous, 'The Opossum found in the southern extremity of New Holland'. From Thomas Bankes et al., *A New Royal Authentic and Complete System of Universal Geography* (London, 1786–87).

> and I beleive roost on trees, Curlews &c and not many of these neither. Some of our gentlemen who were in the Country heard and saw wild Geese in the night. (Cook, I, 367)

Many of these references are too general to permit precise identifications. (For some attempts, interested readers are referred to J.C. Beaglehole's annotations in his editions of Cook's and Banks' journals.) However, it is known that Tupaia kept a rainbow lorikeet, and Banks gave a kookaburra to a French naturalist at the Cape of Good Hope.

At North Bay, Tasmania, in 1772, Marion du Fresne's crew saw:

> some crows similar to those in France; some blackbirds; thrushes; turtle doves; a parakeet, resembling a South American parrot with its plumage, and with a white beak. They killed all sorts of seabirds, above all pelicans, and a black bird with red beak and feet which Abel Tasman mentions in his journal. (Duyker, 1992, 26)

They also saw:

> catfish, red fish like gurnets, cod, wrasse, large numbers of very big rays, and many small fishes which were unknown to us... [also] many crayfish, lobsters, and very big crabs; the oysters were very good and abundant. The curious collected starfish, sea-urchins, scallops with long, spiny shells, wheels, olives and trumpets and several rare and very beautiful shells. (Duyker, 1992, 27)

About this time, on the opposite side of the continent, St Allouarn's people caught a glimpse of a small animal with a tail, which was probably a wallaby, a dingo, and many sharks, fish and turtles.

And at Norfolk Island, in October 1774, Cook found:

> the same sort of Pigions, Parrots and Parrokeets as in New Zeeland, Rails and some small birds. The Sea fowl are White Boobies, guls, Tern &c which breed undisturbed on the Rocks and in the Clifts. The Coast is not distitute of Fish, our people caught some which were excellent while in the boats a long-side the rocks. (Cook, II, 566–7)

The birds Cook and the astronomer William Wales mentioned in their journals were: Norfolk Island pigeon (*Hemiphega novaseelandiae spadicea*), now extinct; long-billed parrot (*Nestor productus*), now extinct; Norfolk Island parrot (*Cyanoramphus novaezelandiae cookii*); scarlet-breasted robin (*Petroeca multicolor*); masked or blue-faced booby (*Sula dactylatra personata*) and banded rail (*Rallus philippinensis*).

It is to be regretted that the records of these early gatherings of zoological specimens are not more complete, and their whereabouts better known.

By the time the First Fleet came to Australia the known number of animal species had increased from at least 98 on the north and west coasts to at least 616, an additional 518 having been recorded on the east coast. The species are:

22 mammals	4 other arthropods
93 birds	147 mollusca
14 reptiles	5 echinoderms
65 fishes	1 worm
3 ascidians	9 coelenterates
244 insects	1 sponge
8 crustaceans	

The Royal Zoological Society of New South Wales has most helpfully allowed extensive reproduction in this section of the zoology of Cook's 1770 voyage in the *Endeavour* from its publication, *Early History of Australian Zoology*, by Gilbert P. Whitley. The author has included extracts from Cook's and Bank's journals. Mr Whitley researched this material for more than 30 years.

Mr Whitley's *dramatis animalia* of the Cook period, roughly in order of their appearance:

Mammals

1710 'Animal like a rabbit'. ?Bandicoot, *Perameles.*

1770 'Polecat or weesel' = Native Cat, *Dasyurus quoll.*

1770 Porpoises, Delphinidae.

1770 Grampus, perhaps the whale *Megaptera australis.*

1770 Captain Cook's Kangaroo, *Wallabia canguru.*

1770 Flying Fox, *Pteropus* sp.

1770 Phalanger, *Pseudocheirus peregrinus.*

1770 Large animal, 80 lb. [Wallaroo, *Osphranter reginae*].

1770 Smaller animal, 8½ lb [Wallaby, *Macropus* sp.]

1770 Fer-de-cheval [Horseshoe Bat, genus indet.]

1772 Tiger Cat of Dufresne.

1772 Monkey-like and Mongoose-like animals.

1773 Tasmanian Possum *Pseudocheirus convolutor.*

Birds

1770 Port Egmont Hen [= Skua, *Catharacta skua lonnbergi*], well out to sea.

1770 Albatrosses, *Dionedea* sp., well out in Tasman Sea.

1770 Pintado Bird [= Cape Pigeon, *Daption capensis*], well out in Tasman Sea.

1770 Lorryquet, *Trichoglossus moluccanus.*

1770 Quail, [*Coturnix pectoralis*].

1770 *Nectris munda* [= Allied Shearwater, *Puffinus assimilis*].

1770 Bustard, *Eupodotis australis.*

1770 Black and White Duck [could be Pied Goose, *Anseranas semipalmata*, rather than Burdekin Duck, *Tadorna radjah rufitergum*].

1770 Egg Bird [= Sooty Tern, *Sterna fuscata*].

1770 *Nectris nugax* [= Audubon's Petrel, *Puffinus l'herminieri*].

1770 Pigeon, *Lopholaimus antarcticus.*

1770 Pigeon, = Bar-shouldered Dove, *Geopelis humeralis.*

1770 Crow = Raven, *Corvus orris.*

1770 Goatsucker or Churn Owl, *Caprimulgus* sp.

1770 Bee-eater, *Merops ornatus.*

1770 A small bird with wattles.

1770 A bird like a Tetrao [grouse-like bird]. [Probably *Alectura lathami*].

1770 Owl [*Ninox*].

1770 White-breasted Eagle of Lizard Island [*Haliaeetus leucogaster*].

1770 Oyster-cracker, *Haematopus unicolor.*

1770 Loxia of Parkinson [= Tooth-billed Cat Bird, *Scenopoeetes dentirostris*, fide H.J. de S. Disney, pers. comm.].

1770 Black and White Hawk [probably *Elanus scriptus*].

1770 Kite [*Milvus migrans*].

1770 Hawks (several species).

1770 White Cockadore [*Kakatoe galerita*].

1770 Brown Cockadore [*Calyptorhynchus banksii*].

1770 Scaly-breasted Loryquet, *Trichoglossus chlorolepidotus.*

1770 Doves (several species).

1770 Herns (several species).

1770 Whistling Ducks [*Dendrocygna arcuata* & *D. eytoni*].

1770 Shagg [any of 4 species of *Phalacrocorax*].

1770 Crane [probably Brolga, *Grus rubicunda*].

1770 Ducks, including *Anas superciliosa.*

[1770] 'Great Kingfisher of New Guinea' [= Kookaburra, *Dacelo gigas*].

1773 Crested Penguin, *Eudyptes cristatus.*

1773 Crow kind [= Black Currawong or Bell Magpie, *Strepera arguta*].

1773 Teal, *Anas* sp.

1773 Sheldrake [Mountain Duck, *Casarca tadornoides*].

1773 White form of the Grey Goshawk, *Accipiter novaehollandiae.*

1777 Small Tasmanian bird, Lae'renne. Indeterminable.

1777 Brown hawks or eagles [Probably *Falco berigora*].

1777 Yellowish Paroquet [= Green Rosella, *Platycercus caledonicus*].

1777 Pigeon, *Phaps chalcoptera.*

1777 Thrush [*Colluricincla harmonica*].

1777 Blue Wren, *Motacilla cyanea* = *Malurus cyaneus.*

1777 [Pacific] Gull, *Larus pacificus.*

1777 'Plover' = Hooded Dotterel, *Charadrius cucullatus.*

1777 [Yellow-winged Honeyeater, *Meliornis novaehollandiae canescens*].

1777 [Yellow-tipped Pardalote, *Pardalotus striatus*].

1777 [Black-faced Cuckoo Shrike, *Coracina novaehollandiae*].

Reptiles

1770 Loggerhead Turtle, *Caretta caretta gigas.*

1770 Lizard of Lizard Island. ? *Varanus simerix.*

1770 Water Snake, *Boa pelagica* [= *Aipysurus* sp.]

1773 Snakes, probably *Denisonia superba* & others.

1777 Large Lizard [= Bluetongue Lizard, *Tiliqua nigrolutea*].

1777 Small Lizard [*Lyosoma metallicum* rather than *Egernia whitii*].

Fishes

1770 Sharks of Botany Bay, including the whaler, *Squalus vulpecula* [= *Galeolamna macrurus*].

1770 Leatherjackets [*Scobinichthys granulatus* or *Monacanthus macrolepis*].

1770 Stingray [= Captain Cook's Stingray, *Bathytoshia brevicaudata*].

1770 Stingray [*Urolophus testaceus*].

1770 [Fiddler Ray, *Trygonorrhina fasciata*].

1770 [Shovelnose Ray, *Aptychotrema banksii*].

1770 Whip Ray [Eagle Ray, *Myliobatis australis*].

1770 [Mudskipper, *Euchoristopus kalolo*].

1770 Flying Fish [of N. Queensland, probably *Parexocoetus brachypterus*].

1770 'Flounders', indeterminable, also 'flatfish'.

1770 Fish from Endeavour River [*Drepanichthys punctatus*].

1770 Fish from Endeavour River [Mango Fish, *Eleutheronema tetradactylum*].

1770 Toadfish, etc. from Endeavour River.

1770 [Epaulette Shark, *Hemiscyllium ocellatum*].

1770 Large Skeat, or Skate [perhaps *Urogymnus*].

1770 *Raja radula* [= Rough Ray, *Urogymnus asperrimus solanderi*].
1770 Skate or ray fish marked with polygons [perhaps *Himantura toshi*].
1770 Skate of an orbicular figure [probably *Taeniura lymma halgani*].
1770 Sharks, dogfish, rockfish, etc. [Indeterminable. Some of the identifications quoted by Beaglehole are not satisfactory].
1770 Mullet [*Mugil dobula*].
1770 Scomber of Parkinson or Cavalhi [= Trevally, fam. Carangidae].
1770 Mack'rel or Mackarel [*Pneumatophorus australasicus*].
1770 Old Wives [*Enoplosus armatus*, not in Dampier's sense of the term].
1770 Five Fingers [Morwong or Jackass Fish, *Nemadactylus macropterus*].
1772 Cod of Dufresne.
1772 Catfish.
1772 Gurnet.
1772 Toadfish of St. Allouarn [*Pleuranacanthus sceleratus*].
1773 Tasmanian shark or dogfish [*Flakeus megalops*].
1773 Nurse [i.e. Spotted Dogfish, *Koinga lebruni*].
1773 Spratt [*Maugeclupea bassensis*].
1773 Trout [*Galaxias truttaceus*].
1777 Elephant Fish [*Calloryncbus milii*].
1777 Bream [?*Roughleyia australis*].
1777 Soles [probably *Rhombosolea* sp.].
1777 Tasmanian Flounder [*Ammotretis rostratus*].
1777 Gurnards of 2 sorts [*Currupiscis kumu* & *Paratrigla vanessa*]
1777 Spotted mullet [?*Upeneichthys lineatus*].
1777 *Atherina hepsettus* [Hardyhead, *Atherinason dannevigi*].
1777 Round and flat fish [= Flathead, *Trudis bassensis*].
1777 Boxfish [*Acarana aurita*].

Mollusca

1770 Violet Snail; between Australia and New Zealand, *Janthina janthina* [= *violacea*].
1770 Enormous cuttle [*Amplisepia verrauxi*].
1770 *Mimus volutator* [= Sea Lizard, *Glaucus lineatus*].
1770 Mud Oyster [*Ostrea angassi* or *sinuata*].
1770 Rock Oyster [*Saxostrea commercialis*].
1770 Mangrove Oyster [*Crassostrea glomerata*].
1770 Large Muscle [Mussel, *Modiolus* sp.].
1770 Pearl fishery envisaged.
1770 Hammer Oyster, *Malleus albus.*
1770 *Trochus perspectivus* [*Architectonica perspective*, the Perspective Sundial Shell].
1770 Large Cockle, *Chama* [= Giant Clam, '*Tridacna gigas*'].
1770 Black Hercules' Club [*Pyrazus ebeninus*].
1770 [Warrener, *Subninella undulata*].
1770 [Sydney Turban Shell, *Ninella torquata*].
1770 Coach Road Whelk [so-called in the Leverian Museum = Cartrut Shell, *Dicathais orbita*].
1770 Ear Shell [or Abalone, *Notohaliotis ruber*].
1770 Spondylus [= Thorny Oyster, *Spondylus ducalis*].
1770 Top Shell, Trochus [= *Trochus niloticus*].
1770 Persian Crown Shell [= Baler Shell, *Melo diadema*].
1770 Turban Shell, *Turbo undulatus.*
1770 Duck's Bill Patella [*Scutus*? or a limpet].
1770 [Sydney Cockle], *Anadara trapezia.*
1770 Mussel, *Mytilus obscurus.*
1770 [Hairy Mussel], *Trichomya hirsuta.*
1770 [Noddiwink], *Nodilittorina tuberculata.*
1770 [Conniewink], *Bembicium melanostoma.*
1770 [Bubble Shell], *Bullaria botanica.*
1770 [Australwink], *Austrocochlea obtusa.*
1770 Shells in Banks' Collection which may have been collected during the *Endeavour* voyage (based on McMichael, MS., 1970) — as below and additional to above:
1770 *Septifer bilocularis*
1770 [Boring Mussell], *Lithophaga teres.*
1770 [Pearl Shell], *Pinctada vulgaris.*
1770 [Razor Shell], *Pinna muricata.*
1770 [Shell], *Batissa triquetra* (or *violacea*)
1770 [Shell], *Codakia tigerina.*
1770 [Basket Cockle], *Corbis fimbriata.*
1770 [Various Shells], *Lioconcha castrensis.*
1770 *Lioconcha varians.*
1770 *Gafrarium scriptum.*
1770 *Gafrarium pectinatum.*
1770 *Gafrarium tumidium.*
1770 *Antigona* or *Periglypta puerpera.*
1770 *Antigona* or *Periglypta reticulata.*
1770 *Chione marica.*
1770 *Paphia philippinarum.*
1770 *Asaphis deflorata.*
1770 *Contumax nodulosum.*
1770 *Cerithium morum.*
1770 *Cerithium echinatum.*
1770 *Cerithium aluco.*
1770 *Cerithium vertagus.*
1770 *Cerithium sinense obeliscum.*
1770 *Cerithium asper.*
1770 [Various Cowries], *Ovula ovum.*
1770 *Calpurnus verrucosus.*
1770 *Pustularia cicercula.*
1770 *Pustularia globulus.*
1770 *Pustularia childreni.*
1770 *Cypraea staphylaea.*
1770 *Cypraea facifer.*
1770 *Cypraea nucleus.*
1770 *Cypraea helvola.*
1770 *Cypraea poraria.*
1770 *Cypraea erosa.*
1770 *Cypraea annulus.*
1770 *Cypraea moneta.*
1770 *Cypraea onyx.*
1770 *Cypraea errones.*
1770 *Cypraea caurica.*
1770 *Cypraea punctata.*
1770 *Cypraea asellus.*
1770 *Cypraea clandestina.*
1770 *Cypraea humphreyii.*
1770 *Cypraea ziczac.*
1770 *Cypraea hirundo.*
1770 *Cypraea chinensis.*
1770 *Cypraea teres.*
1770 *Cypraea cribraria.*
1770 *Cypraea isabella.*
1770 *Cypraea testudinaria.*
1770 *Cypraea argus.*
1770 *Cypraea talpa.*
1770 *Cypraea arabica.*
1770 [Cowry], *Cypraea maculifera.*

1770 [Cowry], *Cypraea histrio.*
1770 [Cowry], *Cypraea mauritiana.*
1770 [Tiger Cowry], *Cypraea tigris.*
1770 [Cowry], *Cypraea lynx.*
1770 [Cowry], *Cypraea vitellus.*
1770 [Cowry], *Cypraea carneola.*
1770 [Various Shells], *Ranularia pyrum.*
1770 *Monoplex parthenopeum australasiae.*
1770 *Cymatium chlorostoma.*
1770 *Distorsio anus.*
1770 *Bursa granifera* or *granularis.*
1770 *Bursa rubecula.*
1770 [Fig Shell], *Ficus ficus.*
1770 [Various Shells], *Murex monodon* or *Euphylum cornucervi?*
1770 *Murex adustus.*
1770 *Murex torrefactus.*
1770 *Murex ternispina.*
1770 *Haustellum haustellum.*
1770 *Cronia amygdala.*
1770 *Phos senticosus.*
1770 [False Trumpet Shell], *Syrinx aruanus.*
1770 [Various Shells], *Latirus polugonus.*
1770 *Latirus nodatus* (?= *L. polygonus*).
1770 *Peristernia nassatula.*
1770 *Fasciolaria filamentosa.*
1770 *Fusinus colus.*
1770 *Fusinus tuberculatus.*
1770 [Rose-petal Bubble Shell], *Hydatina physis.*
1770 [Cone Shell], *Conus catus.*
1770 [Cone Shell], *Conus coronatus.*
1770 [Cone Shell], *Conus distans.*
1770 [Cone Shell], *Conus eburneus.*
1770 [Cone Shell], *Conus ebraeus.*
1770 [Cone Shell], *Conus figulinus.*
1770 [Cone Shell], *Conus flavidus.*
1770 [Cone Shell], *Conus generalis.*
1770 [Cone Shell], *Conus lividus.*
1770 [Cone Shell], *Conus quercinus.*
1770 [Cone Shell], *Conus nussatella.*
1770 [Cone Shell], *Conus magus.*
1770 [Cone Shell], *Conus marmoreus.*
1770 [Cone Shell], *Conus pulicarius.*
1770 [Cone Shell], *Conus textilus.*
1770 [Cone Shell], *Conus virgo.*
1770 [Cone Shell], *Conus vermiculatus.*
1770? [Volute], *Cymbiolacca pulchra.*
1772 Wing Shell, *Pinna.*
1772 Scallop [*Notovola meridionalis*].
1772 Chama or Heart Cockle.
1772 Cone shells, rouleaux [Fam. Conidae].
1772 Olives.
1772 Cornets.
1777 Stinking Laplysia or Sea Hare [*Aplysia tasmanica*].

Ascidians

1770 Salps, *Dagysa gemma* and *D. cornuta* = Thalia democratica.
1770 Salp, *Dagysa strumosa* [= *Tethyum vagina*].
1770 Sea Squirt [Probably *Cynthia praeputialis*].

Insects

1770 Small butterfly between New Zealand and Australia.
1770 Mosquito [*Aedes* and/or *Culex*].
1770 Green Ant [*Oecophylla smaragdina virescens*].
1770 'Caterpilar...like wrathful militia' [Larvae of *Limacodid* moth].
1770 Cynips which fertilizes figs.
1770 Termites [*Microcerotermes turneri*].
1770 Black Ants in pith of tree [*Colobopsis* and *Tetraponera* spp.].
1770 Butterflies over 3 or 4 acres [*Danais melissa hamata*].
1770 Pupa from which butterfly emerged [*Euploea sylvester*].
1770 Fly, Culex of Parkinson [Sandfly].
1770 Ants nesting in epiphyte plant.
1770 Insects, miscellaneous. The insects of the *Endeavour* voyage were named by Fabricius and a list of 221 species is given in A. Musgrave's *Bibliography of Australian Entomology*, 1932, p. 86.
1773 Tasmanian Ant [= Bulldog Ant or Inchman, *Myrmecia esuriens* or *M. forficata*].
1777 Lice on natives.
1777 Maggots, flies.
1777 Knatt [Gnatt].
1777 Grasshoppers.
1777 Moths
1777 Dragon Flies [*Aeschna brevistyla* and *Libellula* sp.].
1777 Gadflies.
1777 Camel flies.

Crustacea

1770 Megalopa larva of a crab, *Cancer erythroptalmus* = *Cancer cyapophthalmus.*
1770 Crab, *Portunus pelagicus.*
1770 Crab, *Portunus sanguinolentus.*
1770 Crab, *Matuta* sp. (fide Whitehead, 1969, p. 177).
1770 Barnacles [*Lepas* or perhaps *Uperotis clava*].
1773 Tasmanian Crayfish [*Jasus verreauxi* or perhaps *Astacopsis franklinii*].

Other Arthropoda

1770 Scorpions, probably from Endeavour River district.
1770 Centapees or Centumpees [Centipedes, probably from the Endeavour River area].
1777 Spiders, several sorts from Tasmania.
1777 Tasmanian Scorpion [*Cercophonius squama*].

Echinodermata

1770 Sea Eggs, off Endeavour River [echinoderm].
1772 Starfish.
1772 Sea Urchin.
1777 Sea Stars [*Patiriella*].

Worms

1770 *Doris complanata*, from between Australia and New Zealand (not strictly Australian) [A planarian worm].

Coelenterata

1770 *Medusa pelagica* [Jellyfish, *Pelagia* sp.].
1770 *Medusa radiata* [Jellyfish, *Aequoria forskali*].
1770 *Holothuria obtusata* [Portuguese Man-o'-war, *Physalia utriculus*].
1770 *Phyllodoce velella* [= By the wind Sailor, *Velella velella*].
1770 Beautiful corallines of all colours and figures (Parkinson) and coral in hull of *Endeavour.*
1770 Organ Pipe Coral, *Tubipora musica.*
1777 'Medusa's Heads'

Porifera

1777 Sponges, *Spongia dichotoma.*

7

Ethnography

Encounters with Aborigines, 1606–1756

In the 150 years from 1606, European discoverers and explorers made at least ten contacts with Aborigines on the northern, western and southern coasts of Australia. Most of these contacts were with small groups, whose numbers probably never exceeded 100. Most of the Dutch mariners made brief observations of the Aborigines. Dampier was the most literate and scientifically minded of the European observers, and his descriptions are accordingly more detailed and extensive. Despite their being permeated with assumptions of cultural superiority, these earliest descriptions still offer some valuable ethnographic insights.

Although these explorers assumed that Australia and New Guinea were geographically linked, they did distinguish differences between Aborigines and Papuans in physique and behaviour. They knew Papuans by their race name, derived from the language of the Moluccans, of the nearby Spice Islands, who knew them as Os Papuas — meaning frizzle-haired'. The Aborigines, VOC explorers conceded, were not as 'cunning, bold and evil-natured' as the New Guineans. Papuans took many Dutch lives; Aborigines were known to have taken only one Dutch life, in 1606. The total number of Aborigines killed by Europeans is not known.

Carstenz, who wrote the first European description of the Aborigines on the north coast in 1623, also described Papuans he encountered on his expedition. Of the first-met Papuans he wrote:

On going a short distance into the wood, we also saw twenty or more small huts made of dry grass, the said huts being so small and cramped that a man could hardly get into them on all fours, from which we could sufficiently conclude that the natives here must be of small stature, poor and wretched, we afterwards tried to penetrate somewhat farther into the wood, in order to ascertain the nature and situation of the country, when on our coming upon a piece of brushwood, blacks sprang out of it and began to let fly their arrows at us with great fury and loud shouts, by which a carpenter was wounded in the belly and an assistant in the leg: we were all of us hard pressed, upon which we fired three or four muskets at them killing one of the blacks stone-dead, which utterly took away their courage; they dragged the dead man into the wood. (Heeres, 30)

On the 26 [March 1623] the weather was good, the wind N.N.W., course held S.E. by E. along the land in five fathom. In the forenoon 4 small canoes put off from the land and followed us; we waited for them to come alongside, and found they were manned with 25 blacks, who had nothing with them except their arms; they called out and made signs for us to come ashore; we then threw out to them some small pieces of iron and strings of beads, at which they showed great satisfaction; they paid little or no attention to the gold, silver, copper, nutmeg and cloves which we showed them, though they were quite ready to accept these articles as presents. Their canoes are very skilfully made out of one piece

> of wood, some of them being so large that they will hold 20 and even more blacks. Their paddles are long, and they used them standing or sitting; the men are black, tall and well-built, with coarse and strong limbs, and curly hair, like the Caffirs, some of them wearing it tied to the neck in a knot, and others letting it fall down loose to the waist. They have hardly any beards; some of them have two, others three holes through the nose, in which they wear fangs or teeth of hogs or sword-fishes. They are stark-naked and have their privities enclosed in a conch-shell, fastened to the waist with a bit of string; they wear no rings of gold, silver, copper, tin or iron on their persons, but adorn themselves with rings made of tortoise-shell or terturago, from which it may be inferred that their land yields no metals or wood of any value. (Heeres, 32)

Carstensz had his first meeting with Aborigines on 18 April in the vicinity of the Mitchell River, on the lower west coast of Cape York Peninsula, and other meetings up and down the coast followed. His impressions were:

> These natives are coal-black, with lean bodies and stark-naked, having twisted baskets or nets round their heads; in hair and figure they are like the blacks of the Coromandel coast, but they seem to be less cunning, bold and evil-natured than the blacks at the western extremity of Nova Guinia;
>
> On the 19th…when the men were engaged in cutting wood, a large number of blacks upwards of 200 came upon them, and tried every means to surprise and overcome them, so that our men were compelled to fire two shots, upon which the blacks fled, one of their number having been hit and having fallen; our men then proceeded some what farther up the country, where they found several weapons, of which they took some along with them by way of curiosities. During their march they observed in various places great quantities of human bones, from which it may be safely concluded that the coast of Nova Guinia [i.e. Cape York] are man-eaters who do not spare each other when driven by hunger. (Heeres, 36–7)
>
> The natives are in general utter barbarians, all resembling each other in shape and features, coal-black, and with twisted nets wound round their heads and necks for keeping their food in; so far as we could make out, they chiefly live on certain evil-smelling roots which they dig out of the earth. We infer that during the eastern monsoon they live mainly on the beach, since we have there seen numerous small huts made of dry grass; we also saw great numbers of dogs, herons and curlews, and other wild fowl, together with plenty of excellent fish, easily caught with a seine-net; they are utterly unacquainted with gold, silver, tin, iron, lead and copper, nor do they know anything about nutmegs, cloves and pepper, all of which spices we repeatedly showed them without their evincing any signs of recognising or valuing the same; from all which together with the rest of our observations it may be safely concluded that they are poor and abject wretches, caring mainly for bits of iron and strings of beads. Their weapons are shields, assagays, and callaways, of the length of 1½ fathom, made of light wood and cane, some with fish-bones and others with human bones fastened to their tips; they are very expert in throwing the said weapons by means of a piece of wood, half a fathom in length, with a small hook tied to it in front, which they place upon the tip of the callagay or assagay. (Heeres, 41–2)

As the instructions to Carstensz show, the VOC foresaw that it might be useful to have Aborigines as interpreters for trade:

> In places where you meet with natives, you will either by adroit management or by other means endeavour to get hold of a number of full-grown persons, or better still, of boys and girls, to the end that the latter may be brought up here and be turned to useful purpose in the said quarters when occasion shall serve. (Heeres, 31)

At this time, Europeans did not consider taking captives reprehensible. In 1606, the year of the *Duyfken*'s voyage, Torres captured 20 Papuans on the southern coast of New Guinea, probably hoping that they would learn Spanish, become Christians, and then help convert their fellows. In 1623,

Carstensz also pursued this policy, offering the boats' crews ten pieces-of-eight for each Aborigine taken. Not surprisingly, the Aborigines resisted capture, and violence was the result. The Dutch crews shot three Aborigines on three of their encounters with them. One who was wounded and taken captive at Port Musgrave died on the way to a boat. In his head net they found a piece of metal which almost certainly came from the encounter with the *Duyfken* seventeen years earlier. Carstensz recalled that the Aborigines had gained some knowledge of muskets 'to their great damage' on that occasion.

This is how Carstensz captured two Aborigines to take to Batavia. The first one:

> when the boats returned, the skipper reported that as soon as the party had landed a great mob of BLACKS, some with arms and some without, had come up to them, and were so bold and free as to touch the men's muskets and try to take them off their shoulders, and in fact, wanted to take everything they thought they might have use for. These being kept interested with iron and beads, an opportunity was espied, and one of them was seized by a string which he had round his neck and taken on board the boat. The others who were on the beach made a great hubbub and outcry, but those who were concealed in the bush remained there.

The second one:

> When we had got into the pinnace again, the blacks emerged with their arms from the wood at two different points; by showing them bits of iron and strings of beads we kept them on the beach, until we had come near them, upon which one of them who had lost his weapon, was by the skipper seized round the waist, while at the same time the quartermaster put a noose round his neck, by which he was dragged to the pinnace; the other blacks seeing this, tried to rescue their captured brother by furiously assailing us with their assagays; in defending ourselves we shot one of them, after which the others took flight, upon which we returned on board without further delay...We cannot...give any account of their customs and ceremonies, nor did we learn anything about the thickness of the population, since we had few or no opportunities for inquiring into these matters; meanwhile I hope that with God's help Your Worships will in time get information touching these points from the black we have captured. (Heeres, 40)

Europeans first saw Aborigines in Western Australia on the north-west coast in 1628 from the merchantman *Vianen* in the vicinity of Roebourne. The ship's journal referred to 'barren and dangerous coasts...and exceedingly savage, black, barbarian inhabitants' (Heeres, 54). The next year Pelsaert saw Aborigines on the coast between Geraldton and North-West Cape. Of a search for water while making his way to Batavia, he recorded:

> They also saw four men, who came creeping on hands and feet, to get near our people, then our men unseen by them out of a low place to the high came close, they sprang up and ran away at full speed...They were black men, quite naked, having no covering. (Sharp, 61)

Of his only other encounter, Pelsaert wrote: 'Here we saw also 8 black men, who each had a stick in the hand, and approached about a musket-shot of us, then as we went toward them, they ran away, and we could not make them stay, until we could come to them' (Sharp, 62).

What kind of contact was had by the two mutineers whom Pelsaert later marooned is unknown.

Where Aborigines are concerned, the records of the European explorers are almost silent for the next 60 years.

By contrast, Tasman received instructions for his 1642 expedition to the Pacific to be most respectful and tolerant of natives. These read:

> [You] shall use great care at all places in landing with small craft, because it is apparent, the Southlands are peopled with very rough wild people, for which reason [you] must always be well armed and carefully on guard, since in all parts of the world, it has been found by experience, no barbarous people are to be trusted, because they usually think, that the people who appear so exceedingly strange and unexpected come only to take over their lands,

which (because of carelessness and easy trust) has caused many a treacherous murder in the discovery of America. For which reason the barbarous people whom [you] may meet and come to speech with, [you] shall make contact with properly and amicably, small affronts of thievery, or other things, which they might visit on our people, [you] shall let pass unmarked, in order not to cause any enmity towards us by punishing them, but by showing of good countenances, attract them to us, so that [you] may the better find out, in what circumstances they and their lands are, and whether anything useful is to be got or done there.

Of the nature of the lands, what fruits and livestock be there, what sort of structure of houses, the form and appearance of the inhabitants, their clothing, weapons, customs, manners, food, livelihood, religion, government, war and other notable things, particularly whether [they] are good or ill-natured, [you] shall as time allows, duly try to observe, showing them various samples of the goods, given for this purpose, in order to find out what wares and materials they have, and what [they] want of ours in return, all which [you] shall keenly observe, properly draw and correctly describe, keeping for this purpose a full, and suitably extensive journal, in which all your encounters are completely noted, in order therewith on your return, to be able to make appropriate report to us.

If [you] visit any land populated with civilized people (as [is] not likely), [you] shall take more account of them, than of the wild savages, trying to get in conversation and acquaintance with the leaders and subjects, informing them, [you] come there to trade, showing the samples of the wares, given for this purpose, as [you] shall be able to see in invoice, duly observing what they esteem, and to what goods they are most attracted, particularly finding out what wares are among them, likewise about gold and silver, and if [it] is in valued regard by them, representing yourself to be not eager for it, in order to keep them unaware of the value of the same, and if [they] should give you gold or silver in any bartering, [you] must conduct yourself as if [you] did not value this specie, showing copper, spelter, and lead, as if these minerals were with us of greater value.

All insolence and hostility of the crew towards the discovered peoples, [you] will carefully prevent, and take care no harm is done to them in their houses, gardens, craft, property or women &c. Likewise no inhabitants brought away from their land against their will, but if any are somewhat willingly inclined thereto, [you] may then duly bring these hither. (Tasman, 36–7)

In the journal of his 1642 voyage, Tasman did allude to seemingly giant humans at his landing place in Tasmania, Blackman's Bay, about 50 kilometres from Hobart, but he and his men did not actually see any of them. In three days there, Tasman's men reported:

> That they had heard some sound of men, also playing as if by a horn or small gom [a gong], which was not far from them; but they had not managed to see anyone.
>
> That [they] had seen 2 trees about 2 to 2½ fathoms thick 60 to 65 feet high under the Boughs, in which trees gashed with flints and the bark was peeled off (thereby to climb up and gather the birdnests) in shape of Steps Each being fully 5 feet from one another So that they presumed, here to be Very tall people or that these Same by some means must know how to climb up said trees, in one tree these carved Steps appeared, So fresh and green, as if the same was cut not four days before. (Tasman, 110)

Modern authorities think that the Dutch were misled by certain signs of human activity. N.J.B. Plomley points out that Aboriginal women developed the practice of climbing trees:

> in quest of the possum by means of the grass rope. This is a dangerous way of climbing trees and is effected first by bruising the bark with a stone so as to form a notch. In this they place their foot and then, embracing the tree with the grass rope and at the same time laying hold of the ends in each hand, they proceed to ascend, shifting the bark by a jerk and notching the bark for their feet as they advance. Some of the notches are wide apart and the traveller in his

> journey through the bush will frequently see trees thus notched, which have been climbed by the natives in quest of the possum, their native food.

And Peter Chapman thinks that they may also have been confused by the way eucalypts burn from the inside out, so as to conclude that the trees had been set alight at greater than normal human height — consider Tasman's comment that 'in various spots and places, in the wood [they] also have seen some smokes; so that here without doubt people, who must be of unusual height' (Tasman, 111).

Presumably, Tasman did encounter Aborigines on the northern and north-western coasts of Australia during his 1644 voyage, but as his journal is lost we have no details. In 1658 Jacob Pieterszoon Peereboom, skipper of the *Elburg* (a community name), touched at Geographe Bay on the south-west coast of Western Australia, to report that at Cape Leeuwin they found:

> three black men, hung with skins like those at the [Cape of Good Hope] with whom, however, they could not come to parley. On the spot where the blacks had been sitting, our men found a burning fire, near which there lay a number of assagays together with three small hammers, consisting of a wooden handle to one end of which a hard pebble was fastened by means of a wax or gum, the whole strong and heavy enough to knock out a man's brains. [These were kodj axes; the gum was from the Black Boy tree (*Xanthorrhoea preissii*) which has an aromatic smell.] A little further inward they came upon a number of huts, without any persons in them, and in various spots they found rills of fresh water, and here and there large quantities of the wax or gum aforesaid, of which we beg leave to hand you a small sample herewith, together with one of the said hammers, the wax or gum being of a red colour, and emitting an agreeable smell after being rubbed for some time. (Heeres, 81)

De Vlamingh's expedition in 1696–97 was the last Dutch contact with Aborigines on the west coast. De Vlamingh had with him two Malay interpreters 'familiar with many languages', whom it was hoped might be able to learn of the whereabouts of castaways from Aborigines. A report by Nicolaas Witsen, based on journals of crewmen, is more informative about the Aborigines than de Vlamingh's journal. Witsen wrote:

> Our people had seen but twelve of the natives, all as black as pitch, and stark naked, so terrified, that it was impossible to bring them to conversation, or a meeting: They lodge themselves as the Hottentots, in pavilions of small branches of trees. By night our people saw fires all over the country; but when they drew near, the natives were fled. The coast is very low, but the country far from the sea is high…
>
> [Our people] they made their way inland over a distance of a few miles, saw a body of water and some dilapidated huts, not unlike those which the Hottentots make at the Cape, and the footprints of people both young and old, but of an ordinary shape, which they have compared with their own feet and measured, they belonging to barefoot people…
>
> The huts were only two to three feet high, made of stakes or crooked sticks on top of or against which some tree branches or brushwood had been placed, with an opening in one side in front of which the inhabitants commonly have a fire going, wherefore smoke is seen rising up everywhere by day, and fire by night. In these simple huts some tree bark was found which was soft, which seemed to serve for lying on when asleep.

The journal of one of the mariners who was on this voyage speaks of these huts as follows:

> the huts in the South Land between thirty-one and twenty degrees in Hollandia Nova are very sober, covered with rushes of a kind, the posts are tree branches let into the ground with one end, and at the other end fitted together on top. In these huts there are holes in the ground like the Hottentots at the Cape of Good Hope have, in which they lie down to sleep: in the year 1697 fishbones were found in some of these huts and a leathern bag put together with straw or dried rushes: once at twenty-seven degrees southern latitude skipper Vlamingh saw five huts close together, about one hour's distance

from the beach, one of which was made of clay with a roof sloping down on two sides. About the huts hot coals or burning wood were seen with fish lying on or near to it to be cooked, and also some fish of which someone had eaten and had left the bones, so that the people must have recently left it...

It seems that the fires are lit near the huts according to how the wind blows, and that they place the opening according to it, which indicates that at night it is quite cold in this region, so that the fire is necessary for these naked people, except that it also serves them to drive off the flies and mosquitoes which vex the people terribly, as our Dutchmen have learnt from experience...

When he had gone inland about eight or ten miles along the banks of the Salt River discovered by him and named after me, he discovered a high mountain range and saw that a great many footprints, both of grown-up people and of children, pointed in that direction, and he also thought to see much smoke below that mountain range, so that there will probably be a great accumulation of people there at the foot: he considered stepping in that direction, but bearing in mind that they were already eight or ten miles inland and that the ships were lying at anchor rather far out into sea at an insecure roadstead and being worried that they might be surrounded by a great crowd of people, he retreated, although many in his company would have ventured the approach, as they reported to me orally, confident in their firearms and the timid nature of the inhabitants who people this coast.

It is singular that although one sees so much smoke rising up by day everywhere in this Land of Eendracht or Hollandia Nova, and fires at night—where there are hearths there are settled people—so few people are in fact seen, it seems that fear made them flee at the least sight or hearing of foreign folk and that they are fleet of foot and and know how to hide in the forest. In very many places trees were seen which had been cut down, some put across one another crosswise and set on fire, the cause whereof our mariners could not fathom, perhaps also being caused since the South Landers frequently light fires and set themselves down to rest under and against the trees which then catch fire.

Holes were also found dug, which indicated that people had recently been staying there so that to all appearances this seacoast is inhabited by nothing but savage naked people, the most settled people possibly living inland, of whom we have gained no knowledge so far, although we had given the order that some natives should be conveyed here either by purchase or voluntarily, in order to learn the Dutch language so as to give an account of everything, but this has failed and we remain in the same obscurity as before, not knowing where so many Dutchmen who have been wrecked here earlier have ended up, whether they have been killed or perhaps transported deep into the land and still alive: the interior of this land has never yet been visited by any Christian, but in all probability all the inhabitants will be equally black and savage, taking after those from whom they are held to have sprung for the greater part, to wit the peoples of Nova Guinea, Moluccas, etc...

When a hole is dug, sweetish water is found first, but upon digging more deeply it is salty water, which is worthy of surprise, and leaves one in ignorance of where the people there obtain drinking water: wherefore there is no profit in calling at this coast. (Schilder, 216–22)

Dampier, who came to the King Sound region in 1688, provides the best description of the Aborigines in the seventeenth century. The first European known to fraternise with them, he wrote:

> The Inhabitants of this Country are the miserablest People in the World. The *Hodmadods* of *Monomatapa* though a nasty People, yet for Wealth are Gentlemen to these; who have no Houses, and skin Garments, Sheep, Poultry, and Fruits of the Earth, Ostrich Eggs, &c. as the *Hodmadods* have: And setting aside their Humane Shape, they differ but little from Brutes. They are tall, strait-bodied, and thin, with small long Limbs. They have great Heads, round Foreheads, and great Brows. Their Eye-lids are always half closed, to keep the Flies out of their Eyes; they being so troublesome here, that no fanning will keep them from coming to

one's Face; and without the Assistance of both Hands to keep them off, they will creep into one's Nostrils, and Mouth too, if the Lips are not shut very close: so that from their Infancy being thus annoyed with these Insects, they do never open their Eyes as other People: And therefore they cannot see far, unless they hold up their Heads, as if they were looking at somewhat over them.

They have great Bottle-Noses, pretty full Lips, and wide Mouths. The two Fore-teeth of their Upper-jaw are wanting in all of them, Men and Women, old and young; whether they draw them out, I know not: Neither have they any Beards. They are long-visaged, and of a very unpleasing Aspect, having no one graceful Feature in their Faces. Their Hair is black, short and curl'd, like that of the Negroes: and not long and lank like the common *Indians*. The colour of their Skins, both of their Faces and the rest of their Body, is Coal-black, like that of the Negroes of *Guinea*.

They have no sort of Cloaths, but a piece of the Rind of a Tree tied like a Girdle about their Waists, and a handful of long Grass, or three or four small green Boughs full of Leaves, thrust under their Girdle, to cover their Nakedness.

They have no Houses, but lie in the open Air without any covering; the Earth being their Bed, and the Heaven their Canopy. Whether they cohabit one Man to one Woman, or promiscuously, I know not; but they do live in Companies, 20 or 30 Men, Women, and Children together. Their only Food is a small sort of Fish, which they get by making Wares of Stone [weirs, i.e. stone fish traps] across little Coves or Branches of the Sea; every Tide bringing in the small Fish, and there leaving them for a Prey to these People, who constantly attend there to search for them at Low-water. This small Fry I take to be the top of their Fishery: They have no Instruments to catch great Fish, should they come; and such seldom stay to be left behind at Low-water: Nor could we catch any Fish with our Hooks and Lines all the while we lay there. In other Places at Low-water they seek for Cockles, Muscles, and Periwincles: Of these Shell-fish there are fewer still; so that their chiefest dependance is upon what the Sea leaves in their Wares; which, be it much or little they gather up, and march to the Places of their Abode. There the old People that are not able to stir abroad by reason of their Age, and the tender Infants, wait their return; and what Providence has bestowed on them, they presently broil on the Coals, and eat it in common. Sometimes they get as many Fish as makes them a plentiful Banquet; and at other times they scarce get every one a taste: But be it little or much that they get, every one has his part, as well as the young and tender, the old and feeble, who are not able to go abroad, as the strong and lusty. When they have eaten they lie down till the next Low-water, and then all that are able march out, be it Night or Day, rain or shine, 'tis all one; they must attend the Wares, or else they must fast: For the Earth affords them no Food at all. There is neither Herb, Root, Pulse nor any sort of Grain for them to eat, that we saw; nor any sort of Bird or Beast that they can catch, having no Instruments wherewithal to do so.

I did not perceive that they did worship any thing. These poor Creatures have a sort of weapon to defend their Ware, or fight with their Enemies, if they have any that will interfere with their poor Fishery. They did at first endeavour with their Weapons to frighten us, who lying ashore deterr'd them from one of their Fishing-places. Some of them had wooden Swords, others had a sort of Lances. The Sword is a long strait Pole sharp at one end, and hardened afterwards by heat. I saw no Iron, nor any other sort of Metal: therefore it is probable they use Stone-Hatchets, as some *Indians* in *America* do.

How they get their Fire I know not; but probably as *Indians* do, out of Wood: I have seen the *Indians* of *Bon-Airy* [an island off the coast of Venezuela] do it, and have myself tried the Experiment: They take a flat piece of Wood that is Pretty soft, and make a small dent in one side of it, then they take another hard round Stick, about the bigness of one's little Finger, and sharpening it at one end like a Pencil, they put that sharp end in the hole or dent of the flat soft piece, and then rubbing or twirling the hard piece between the Palms of their Hands, they drill the soft piece till it smoaks, and at last takes Fire.

These People speak somewhat thro' the Throat; but we could not understand one word that they said. We anchored, as I said before, *January* the 5th, and seeing Men walking on the Shore, we presently sent a Canoa to get some Acquaintance with them: for we were in hopes to get some Provision among them. But the Inhabitants, seeing our Boat coming, run away and hid themselves. We searched afterwards three Days in hopes to find their Houses; but found none: yet we saw many places where they had made Fires. At last, being out of hopes to find their Habitations, we searched no farther; but left a great many Toys ashore, in such places where we thought that they would come. In all our search we found no Water, but old Wells on the sandy Bays.

At last we went over to the Islands, and there we found a great many of the Natives: I do believe there were 40 on one Island, Men, Women, and Children. The Men at our first coming ashore threatned us with their Lances and Swords; but they were frighted by firing one Gun, which we fired purposely to scare them. The Island was so small that they could not hide themselves: but they were much disordered at our Landing, especially the Women and Children: for we went directly to their Camp. The lustiest of the Women snatching up their Infants ran away howling, and the little Children run after squeaking and bawling; but the Men stood still. Some of the Women, and such People as could not go from us, lay still by a Fire, making a doleful noise, as if we had been coming to devour them: but when they saw we did not intend to harm them, they were pretty quiet, and the rest that fled from us at our first coming returned again. This their place of Dwelling was only a Fire, with a few Boughs before it, set up on that side the Winds was of.

After we had been here a little while, the Men began to be familiar, and we cloathed some of them, designing to have had some service of them for it: but we found some Wells of Water here, and intended to carry 2 or 3 Barrels of it abroad. But it being somewhat troublesome to carry to the Canoas, we thought to have been made these Men to have carry'd it for us, and therefore we gave them some old Cloaths; to one an old pair of Breeches, to another a ragged Shirt, to the third a Jacket that was scarce worth owning; which yet would have been very acceptable at some places where we had been, and so we thought they might have been with these People. We put them on them, thinking that this finery would have brought them to work heartily for us; and our Water being filled in small long Barrels, about six Gallons in each, which were made purposely to carry Water in, we brought these our new Servants to the Wells, and put a Barrel on each of their Shoulders for them to carry to the Canoa. But all the signs we could make were to no purpose, for they stood like Statues, without motion, but grinn'd like so many Monkeys, staring one upon another: For these poor Creatures seem not accustomed to carry Burthens; and I believe that one of our Ship-boys of 10 Years old, would carry as much as one of them. So we were forced to carry our Water our selves, and they very fairly put the Cloaths off again, and laid them down, as if Cloaths were only to work in. I did not perceive that they had any great liking to them at first, neither did they seem to admire any thing that we had.

At another time our Canoa being among these Islands seeking for Game, espy'd a drove of these Men swimming from one Island to another; for they have no Boats, Canoas, or Bark-logs. They took up Four of them, and brought them aboard; two of them were middle aged, the other two were young men about 18 or 20 Years old. To these we gave boiled Rice, and with it Turtle and Manatee [Dugong] boiled. They did greedily devour what we gave them, but took no notice of the Ship, or any thing in it, and when they were set on Land again, they ran away as fast as they could. At our first coming, before we were acquainted with them, or they with us, a Company of them who liv'd on the Main, came just against our Ship, and standing on a pretty high Bank, threatned us with their Swords and Lances, by shaking them at us: At last the Captain ordered the Drum to be beaten, which was done of a sudden with much vigour, purposely to scare the poor Creatures. They hearing the noise, ran

> away as fast as they could drive; and when they ran away in haste, they would cry *Gurry, Gurry*, speaking deep in the Throat. Those Inhabitants also that live on the Main, would always run away from us; yet we took several of them. For, as I have always observed, they had such bad Eyes, that they could not see us till we came close to them. We did always give them Victuals, and let them go again, but the Islanders, after our first time of being among them, did not stir for us. (Dampier, 1968, 312–16)

Although Dampier bought and took a slave to England from his buccaneering voyage, he does not mention having any intention of taking Aborigines captives on either of his voyages to New Holland. His instructions for his 1699 voyage told him to bring home natives 'provided they shall be willing to come along'. On this second expedition he had a number of violent encounters with Aborigines at Lagrange Bay, south of Broome. Once, he fired a gun to frighten them; and on a second occasion, in a struggle, wounded one. Dampier added little to his first description of the Aborigines as a consequence of this visit:

> While we were at work there came 9 or 10 of the Natives to a small Hill a little way from us, and stood there manacing and threatning of us, and making a great Noise. At last one of them came towards us, and the rest followed at a distance. I went out to meet him, and came within 50 Yards of him, making to him all the Signs of Peace and Friendship I could; but then he ran away, neither would they any of them stay for us to come nigh them; for we tried two or three Times. At last I took two Men with me, and went in the Afternoon along by the Sea-side, purposely to catch one of them, if I could, of whom I might learn where they got their fresh Water. There were 10 or 12 of the Natives a little way off, who seeing us three going away from the rest of our Men, followed us at a distance. I thought they would follow us: But there being for a while a Sand-bank between us and them, that they could not then see us, we made a halt, and hid our selves in a bending of the Sand-bank. They knew we must be thereabouts, and being 3 or 4 times our Number, thought to seize us. So they dispers'd themselves, some going to the Sea-shore, and others beating about the Sand-hills. We knew by what Rendounter we had had with them in the Morning that we could easily out-run them. So a nimble young Man that was with me, seeing some of them near, ran towards them; and they for some time, ran away before him. But he soon over-taking them, they faced about and fought him. He had a Cutlass, and they had wooden Lances; with which, being many of them, they were too hard for him. When he first ran towards them I chas'd two more that were by the Shore: But fearing how it might be with my young Man, I turnd'd back quickly, and went up to the top of a Sandhill, whence I saw him near me, closely engag'd with them. Upon their seeing me, one of them threw a Lance at me, that narrowly miss'd me. I discharg'd my Gun to scare them, but avoided shooting any of them; till finding the young Man in great danger from them, and my self in some; and that tho' the Gun had a little frighted them at first, yet they had soon learnt to despise it, tossing up their Hands, and crying Pooh, Pooh, Pooh; and coming on afresh with a great Noise, I thought it high time to charge again, and shoot one of them, which I did. The rest, seeing him fall, made a stand again; and my young Man took the Opportunity to disengage himself, and come off to me; my other Man also was with me, who had done nothing all this while, having come out unarm'd; and I return'd back with my Men, designing to attempt the Natives no farther, being very sorry for what had happened already. They took up their wounded Companion; and my young Man, who had been struck through the Cheek by one of their Lances, was afraid it had been poison'd: But I did not think that likely. His Wound was very painful to him, being made with a blunt Weapon: But he soon recover'd of it.
>
> Among the N. Hollanders, whom we were thus engag'd, there was one who by his Appearance and Carriage, as well in the Morning as this Afternoon, seem'd to be the Chief of them, and a kind of Prince or Captain among them. He was a young brisk Man, not very tall, nor so personable as some of the rest, tho' more active and couragious. He was

painted (which none of the rest were at all) with a Circle of white Paste or Pigment (a sort of Lime, as we thought) about his Eyes, and a white streak down his Nose from his Forehead to the tip of it. And his Breast and some part of his Arms were also made white with the same Paint; not for Beauty or Ornament, one would think, but as some wild Indian Warriors are said to do, he seem'd thereby to design the looking more Terrible; this his Painting adding very much to his natural Deformity; for they all of them have the most unpleasant Looks and the worst Features of any people that ever I saw, tho' I have seen great variety of Savages. (Dampier, 1906, 438–40)

The anthropologist A.A. Abbie assesses Dampier's ethnography in this way:

> His 'Hodmadods' are the Hottentots of South Africa and the mention of ostrich eggs probably refers to the Hottentot custom of storing water in empty ostrich egg-shells; the Aborigines, after all, had plenty of emu eggs, which Dampier evidently did not see, but I have never heard that they stored water in them. The 'Wares of Stone' constitute the first record of Aboriginal fish traps while the 'piece of Wood shaped somewhat like a Cutlass' is almost certainly a curved throwing-stick. The sea-mammal that Dampier calls a 'Manatee' must have been a dugong; both are sirenians but the manatee — better known, perhaps, as the 'sea-cow' — occurs on tropical Atlantic shores while the dugong is found on the coasts around the Indian Ocean.
>
> He made some mistakes as might be expected from the limited area covered during his brief visit: Aboriginal skin colour is not coal-black — though in 1623 Carstensz and van Colster had described it as pitch-black; over the greater part of the continent skin colour is chocolate but in the far north and in the 'Western Desert' the colour is darker than elsewhere. Aboriginal hair is not frizzled like that of the Negro — it will be noted that Dampier found it 'short and curled' in 1688 and 'frizled' in 1699; in any tribe anywhere on the continent, hair types range from completely straight to quite deeply curled and our observations suggest that the curly form is more common in the north: this, together with the Aboriginal custom of cutting the hair to make hairstring, might well have produced the short curled hair Dampier mentions. Also, but very uncommonly, Aborigines have quite thick lips, so Dampier's first impression of a negroid people was not altogether unreasonable.
>
> Banks later questioned Dampier's veracity — as a former buccaneer Dampier was suspect anyway — over the matter of missing teeth, since Banks did not observe this in the Endeavour River Aborigines though he had failed to notice that the Botany Bay people did remove front teeth. We now know that the practice of removing teeth is not universal among the Aborigines, and there is no reason to doubt that Dampier recorded as accurately for the north-west as Banks did for the north-east.
>
> Dampier saw no evidence that the Aborigines had boats, houses or food other than seafood, but was wrong in inferring that this was a universal condition in Australia. Also, had he seen the Tierra del Fuegians as Darwin saw them in 1834, he might have revised his opinion that the Aborigines 'are the miserablest People in the World'; as he himself reports, they showed great humanity towards the weaker members of the tribe in the matter of food distribution, more, probably, than would have been found in any European community of that day. On the other hand his guess about stone hatchets and the fire drill was a particularly happy one — for the north of the continent, anyway.
>
> Taken by and large, Dampier's initial account of the Aborigines is an excellent first approximation and he is certainly entitled to much more credit than he usually receives.

In the eighteenth century Dutch explorers had only two meetings with Aborigines, both on northern coasts. In 1705 an expedition of three ships was at Coburg Peninsula and Melville and Bathurst Islands. Skipper Martin van Delft, of the *Vossenbosch* (a castle's name), under-steersman Andries Roseboom, of the *Waijer*, and Pieter Fredericks, captain of a *Pattsjallang*, a large Malayan vessel, noted an exception to the nakedness of the Aborigines: women who had children with them wore a 'slight covering of leaves...over their middle'. In one encounter they shot a man who appeared to them to be a chief. Nevertheless, the Aborigines fraternised with them:

> The women are tall and slim, with very large mouth and small eyes; the head of both sexes is curly, like that of the Papuan islanders, and a yellow or red ointment, prepared with turtle fat, seems to be used as an ornament. The nature of these tribes is foul and treacherous, as was apparent at the last moment, when our people were on the point of departing. Eight islanders attacked and wounded two sailors, with the hope of seizing upon their clothes, and that after having conversed with these men for weeks, eaten and drunk with them, visited them on board, and being allowed to examine everything to their great admiration, after having received presents, and also on their part regaled our people with fish and crabs. Besides this, their bad disposition came to light in the case of the man who had been previously wounded by our party as before mentioned; when he afterwards was assisted and bandaged, and had every possible attention shown him by our men, he tore the linen to pieces and threw it away into a corner; notwithstanding that at other times these natives appeared particularly greedy after linen, knives, beads and such toys.
>
> They however possess nothing which is of value themselves, and have neither iron nor anything like mineral ore or metal, but only a stone which is ground and made to serve as a hatchet. They have no habitations, either houses or huts; and feed on fish, which they catch with harpoons of wood, and also by means of nets, putting out to sea in small canoes, made of the bark of trees, which are in themselves so fragile, that it is necessary to strengthen them with cross-beams.
>
> Some of them had marks on their body, apparently cut or carved, which, as it seemed to our people, were looked upon them as a kind of ornament. They eat sparingly and moderately, whereby they grow up always active and nimble; their diet seems to consist of fish, and a few roots and vegetables, but no birds or wild animals of any kind are used as food, for though animal food exists, and was found by our men in abundance, the natives appeared to be indifferent to it.
>
> According to the notes of the captain of the sloop *Waijer*, from the 14th of June, about five hundred people with women and children, were met and one occasion about two miles inland; at night also they were descried sitting round several fires among the bushes; nothing, however, was seen in their possession of any value. Our men might also easily have taken and brought to Batavia with them two or three of the natives who daily came on board but the skipper of the *Vossenbosch*, following out his instructions to the letter, would not allow them to be taken without their full consent, either by falsehood or fraud, and as no one understood their language, nothing was to be done in the matter; consequently they remained in their own country.
>
> ...the inhabitants were so stupid that they attempted to tow the patsjallang, while lying at anchor, with three little canoes, but seeing that no progress was made, they tried to effect their object by tugging at the anchor. This also proving ineffectual, they returned to the shore. (Major, 169–70)

Then, in 1756, Lieutenant Jean Etienne Gonzal of the *Rijder*, with a second ship explored the western side of Cape York. His report to the VOC again mentions violence, with an Aborigine being wounded. It also describes Aborigines' first experience with European alcohol and the taking of two captives. Gonzal wrote of the encounter on Cape York:

> The persons...returned...accompanied by a number of females who had their privities covered with a kind of small mats. The natives then all of them sat down on the beach near our men, who made signs to them that they were seeking fresh water; upon which the natives got up and signified to our men their willingness to show them the places where water was obtainable. Nor were our men deceived, for after walking on along the beach for some time, they were conducted to a pleasant valley with fine trees such as those above described. This seemed to be the dwelling-place of the natives, for our men saw here more women and

children and also a number of primitive dwellings, merely consisting of sheltered places under the trees partly covered in with bark. The water which they found here, welled up out of the earth in pits dug by human hands. After having inspected the whole place, they went back to the beach, where they found the two praus in which the natives had previously approached the ship. As our men were seated on the beach, nineteen natives came up to them, all of them with bodies daubed over with red; when the said natives were by our men treated to some arrack [an ardent spirit concocted in the East from juices of coco and other palms] with sugar, they began to make merry, and even struck up a kind of chant, at the conclusion of which they retired to the wood again.

In the morning of 27 [May] our men went ashore again for the purpose of attempting to get hold of one or two natives, but did not succeed in doing so that day, because they landed too late to lure the natives to the beach. Early in the morning of 28 [May] they again landed in order to execute their plan; on their arrival the natives came up to them dancing and singing [probably Europeans' first experience of a corroboree], sat down close to them, laid aside their so-called assagays or weapons, and again enjoyed the liquor with which our men plied them. While they were thus making merry, our men seized hold of two of them, upon which the others jumped to their feet, snatched up their assagays and began to throw them at our people without, however, wounding any one; except that the ship's clerk, who in flying tried to seize one of the natives round the body, was in the scuffle slightly wounded in the hand; upon this, our men fired a volley, wounding one of the natives, who thereupon all of them fled into the bush. Our people then tried to drag to the boat the two men they had got hold of, but as they were tying their arms and legs together, one of them by frantic biting and tearing contrived to get loose and effect his escape. Shortly after upwards of fifty natives again made their appearance, throwing assagays, but they also took to their heels, when our people let off another volley of musketry, after which our men succeeded in carrying off their one prisoner to the boat. (Heeres, 94-6)

Then, he tells how they obtained their second captive:

> a canoe...came paddling up to them, containing two men who made signs for them to come ashore; and when with great difficulty they had got ashore through the surf, the two natives of the canoe had already fled into the bush; shortly after, however, eleven men and five females again came running up to them, armed with the assaygays hereinbefore described, who directly tried to take our men's hats off their heads, and on being prevented from doing so, forthwith prepared to throw their weapons; but when our men fired a shot, they all fled except a youth, whom our people carried on board along with the canoe aforesaid, this man being the younger of the two natives brought hither. (Heeres, 97)

In the first 150 years of contact between Europeans and Aborigines one Dutch sailor is known to have been killed, in 1606. Europeans are known to have killed or wounded six Aborigines, and to have captured four. The fate of the captives is unknown.

Encounters with Aborigines, 1770–1777

The eighteenth-century explorers' close adherence to the advice offered by Lord Morton and the Royal Society produced ethnographic descriptions of the Aborigines that were significantly more detailed than those given earlier by the Dutch navigators and by Dampier.

Cook saw the first sign of habitation, smoke, in the vicinity of Mt Dromedary on 22 April 1770, the third day of sailing north after sighting the eastern Australian coast. The next day, a week before landing at Botany Bay, he saw Aborigines on the shore near Brush Island, north of Bateman's Bay. He wrote in his journal: '[we] were so near the Shore as to distinguish several people upon the Sea beach.

Sydney Parkinson, 'Two of the Natives of New Holland, Advancing to Combat'. Plate xviii of *A Journal of a Voyage to the South Seas...*, 1773. (Facsimile edition, Libraries Board of South Australia, 1972.)

They appear'd to be of a very dark or black Colour but whether this was the real colour of their skins or the Clothes they might have on I know not'. Some days later he 'saw the smook of fire in several places near the sea beach' (Cook, I, 301, 303).

On the ninth day he made his first attempt to communicate with the Aborigines near Bulli:

> we saw several people a Shore four of whome were carrying a small boat or canoe which we imagined they were going to put into the water in order to come off to us but in this we were mistaken. Being now not above two Miles from the Shore Mr Banks Dr Solander Tupia and my self put off in the yawl and pull'd in for the land to a place where we saw four or five of the natives who took to the woods as we approached the Shore, which disapointed us in the expectation we had of getting a near view of them if not to speak to them; but our disappointment was heighten'd when we found that we no where could effect a landing by reason of the great surff which beat everywhere upon the shore. We saw hauld up on the beach 3 or 4 small Canoes which to us appear'd not much unlike the small ones of New Zeland. (Cook, I, 304)

Banks was also a close observer of the approach to Botany Bay and entry into it the next day:

> 28 [April]. The land this morn appeard Cliffy and barren without wood. An opening appearing like a harbour was seen and we stood directly in for it. A small smoak arising from a very barren place directed our glasses that way and we soon saw about 10 people, who on our approach left the fire and retird to a little emminence where they could conveniently see the ship; soon after this two Canoes carrying 2 men each landed on the beach under them, the men hauld up their boats and went to their fellows upon the hill. Our boat which had been sent ahead to sound now approachd the place and they all retird higher up on the hill; we saw however that at the beach or landing place one man at least was hid among some rocks who never that we could see left that place. Our boat proceeded along shore and the Indians followd her at a distance. When she came back the officer who was in her told me that in a cove a little within the harbour they came down to the beach and invited our people to land by many signs and words which he did not at all understand; all however were armd with long pikes and a wooden weapon made something like a short scymetar [a spear and probably a woomera, a spear thrower]. During this time a few of the Indians who had not followd the boat remaind on the rocks opposite the ship, threatening and menacing with their pikes and swords [probably boomerangs] — two in particular who were painted with white, their faces seemingly only dusted over with it [pipe clay], their bodies painted with broad strokes drawn over their breasts and backs resembling much a soldiers cross belts, and their legs and thighs also with such like broad strokes drawn round them which imitated broad garters or bracelets. Each of these held in his hand a wooden weapon about 2½ feet long, in shape much resembling a scymeter; the blades of these lookd whitish and some thought shining insomuch that they were almost of opinion that they were made of some kind of metal, but myself thought they were no more than wood smeard over with the same white pigment with which they paint their bodies. These two seemd to talk earnestly together, at times brandishing their crooked weapons at us as in token of defiance. By noon we were within the mouth of the inlet which appeard to be very good. Under the South head of it were four small canoes; in each of these was one man who held in his hand a long pole with which he struck fish, venturing with his little imbarkation almost into the surf. (Banks, II, 53)

Evidently, the sight of the *Endeavour*, massively larger than any Aboriginal canoe, did not seem to alarm some Aborigines:

> These people seemed to be totaly engag'd in what they were about; the ship passed within a quarter of a mile of them and yet they scarce lifted their eyes from their employment; I was almost inclind to think that attentive to their business and deafnd by the noise of the surf they neither saw nor heard her go past. At 1 we came to an anchor abreast a small village

consisting of about 6 or 8 houses. Soon after this an old woman followed by three children came out of the wood; she carried several peices of stick and the children also had their burthens; when she came to the houses 3 more smaller children came out of one of them to meet her. She often looked at the ship but expressd neither surprise nor concern. Soon after this she lighted a fire and the four Canoes came in from fishing; the people landed, hauld up their boats and began to dress their dinner to all appearances totaly unmovd at us, tho' we were within little more than ½ a mile of them. Of all these people we had seen so distinctly through our glasses we had not been able to observe the least signs of Cloathing; myself to the best of my judgement plainly discernd that the woman did not copy our mother Eve even in the fig leaf. (Banks, II, 54)

Cook and Banks encountered Aborigines on five days during their stay at Botany Bay. Banks described the first occasion as follows:

> After dinner the boats were mann'd and we set out from the ship intending to land at the place where we saw these people, hoping that as they regarded the ships coming in to the bay so little they would as little regard our landing. We were in this however mistaken, for as soon as we approachd the rocks two of the men came down upon them, each armd with a lance of about 10 feet long and a short stick which he seemd to handle as if it was a machine to throw the lance. They calld to us very loud in a harsh sounding Language of which neither us or Tupia understood a word, shaking their lances and menacing, in all appearance resolvd to dispute our landing to the utmost tho they were but two and we 30 or 40 at least. In this manner we parleyd with them for about a quarter of an hour, they waving to us to be gone, we again

The Artist of the Chief Mourner, 'Australian Aborigines in bark canoes. April 1770'. Pencil and watercolour. (British Library, London.)

signing that we wanted water and that we meant them no harm. They remaind resolute so a musquet was fird over them, the Effect of which was that the Youngest of the two dropd a bundle of lances on the rock at the instant in which he heard the report; he however snatchd them up again and both renewd their threats and opposition. A Musquet loaded with small shot was now fird at the Eldest of the two who was about 40 yards from the boat; it struck him on the legs but he minded it very little so another was immediately fird at him; on this he ran up to the house about 100 yards distant and soon returnd with a sheild. [Shields were seen only at Botany Bay. Parkinson described 'a shield, of an oval figure, painted white in the middle, with two holes in it to see through' (p. 134).] In the mean time we had landed on the rock. He immediately threw a lance at us and the young man another which fell among the thickest of us but hurt nobody; 2 more musquets with small shot were then fird at them on which the Eldest threw one more lance and then ran away as did the other. We went up to the houses, in one of which we found the children hid behind the sheild and a peice of bark in one of the houses. We were conscious from the distance the people had been from us when we fird that the shot could have done them no material harm; we therefore resolvd to leave the children on the spot without even opening their shelter. We therefore threw into the house to them some beads, ribbands, cloths &c as presents and went away. We however thought it no improper measure to take away with us all the lances which we could find about the houses, amounting in number to forty or fifty. They were of various lenghs, from 15 to 6 feet in lengh; both those which were thrown at us and all we found except one had 4 prongs headed with very sharp fish bones, which were besmeard with a greenish colourd gum that at first gave me some suspicions of Poison. The people were blacker than any we have seen in the Voyage tho by no means negroes; their beards were thick and bushy and they seemd to have a redundancy of hair upon those parts of the body where it commonly grows; the hair of their heads was bushy and thick but by no means wooley like that of a Negro; they were of a common size, lean and seemd active and nimble; their voices were coarse and strong. Upon examining the lances we had taken from them we found that the very most of them had been usd in striking fish, at least we concluded so from sea weed which was found stuck in among the four prongs. — Having taken the resolution before mentioned we returnd to the ship in order to get rid of our load of lances, and having done that went to that place at the mouth of the harbour where we had seen the people in the morn; here however we found nobody. — At night many moving lights were seen in different parts of the bay such as we had been usd to see at the Islands; from hence we supposd that the people here strike fish in the same manner. (Banks, II, 55)

Thus ended these Aborigines' first encounter with Europeans. In the Europeans it produced caution. After describing how he fired a warning shot, Cook said: 'they both made off, but not in such haste but what we might have taken one, but Mr Banks being of opinion that the darts were poisoned, made me cautious how I advanced into the woods' (Cook, I, 305).

Cook was not wanton in the use of firearms and no Aborigines were seriously hurt at Botany Bay or Endeavour River. Generally he respected the Aborigines' rights and restrained his crew from interfering with them. He always allowed them to make the first move. Still, in a situation where neither side understood the other's language, there was always the possibility of serious misunderstanding. Parkinson recorded that at the landing Aborigines 'often [cried] to us, *Warra warra wai*' and when a shot wounded one of them they 'shout[ed] for assistance calling *Halu, halu mae*; that is (as we afterwards learned), Come hither' (Parkinson, 134). He did not give a meaning for the first call but eighteen years later the First Fleet crew heard similar sounding words which they learnt meant 'go away'.

Over the next five days the Aborigines and the *Endeavour*'s crew went about their business, occasionally challenging and retreating from each other. Cook wrote of four futile attempts to communicate. This is how he described the first:

> As soon as the wooders and waterers were come on board to dinner 10 or 12 of the natives came to the watering place and took away there canoes that lay there but did not offer to touch any one of our Casks that had been left ashore; and in the after noon 16 or 18 of them came boldly up to within 100 yards of our people at the watering place and there made a stand. Mr. Hicks who was the officer ashore did all in his power to intice them to him by offering them presents &c but it was to no purpose, all they seem'd to want was for us to be gone. After staying a short time they went away. They were all arm'd with darts and wooden swords, the darts have each four prongs, and pointed with fish bones, those we have seen seem to be intended more for strikeing fish than offensive weapons; neither are they poisoned as we at first thought. (Cook, I, 306)

The second:

> In the PM ten of the natives again Viseted the watering place. I, being on board at this time went emmidiately ashore but before I got there they were going away, I follow'd them alone and unarm'd some distance along shore but they would not stop untill they got farther off than I choose to trust my self; these were arm'd in the same manner as those that came yesterday...This morning a party of us went ashore to some hutts not far from the watering place where some of the natives are daly seen, here we left several articles such as Cloth, Looking glasses, Combs, Beads Nails &c. (Cook, I, 306–7)

The third:

> In the morning I had sent Mr Gore with a boat up to the head of the bay to dridge for oysters; in his return to the ship he and another person came by land and met with these people, who follow'd him at the distance of 19 or 20 yards; when ever Mr Gore made a Stand and fac'd them they stood also, and not withstanding they were all arm'd they never offer'd to attack him, but after he had parted from them and they were met by Dr Monkhouse and one or two more who upon makeing a sham retreat they throw'd 3 darts after them, after which they began to retire. Dr Solander, I, and Tupia made all the haste we could after them but could by neither words or actions, prevail upon them to come near us. Mr Gore saw some up the bay who by signs invited him ashore which he prudantly declined. (Cook, I, 308)

The fourth:

> One of the Midshipmen met with a very old man and woman and two small Children; they were close to the water side where several more were in their canoes gathering shell fish and he being alone was afraid to make any stay with the two old people least he should be discovred by those in the Canoes. He gave them a bird he had shott which they would not touch neither did they speak one word but seem'd to be much frighten'd, they were quite naked even the woman had nothing to cover her nuditie. Dr Monkhouse and a nother man being [in] the woods not far from the watering place discovered six more of the natives who at first seemd to wait his coming but as he was going up to them had a dart thrown at him out of a tree which narrowly escaped him, as soon as the fellow had thrown the dart he descended the tree and made off and with him all the rest. (Cook, I, 309–10)

Cook wrote brief first impressions of the Botany Bay Aborigines:

> On the Sand and Mud banks are Oysters, Muscles, Cockles &c which I beleive are the cheif support of the inhabitants, who go into shoald water with their little Canoes and pick them out of the sand and Mud with their hands and sometimes roast and eat them in the Canoe, having often a fire for that purpose as I suppose, for I know no other it can be for. The Natives do not appear to be numberous neither do they seem to live in large bodies but dispers'd in small parties along by the water side; those I saw were about as tall as Europeans, of a very dark brown colour but not black nor had they wooly frizled hair, but black and lank much like ours. No sort of cloathing or ornaments were ever seen by any of us upon any one of them or in or about any of their hutts, from which I conclude that they never wear any. Some we saw that had their faces and bodies painted with a sort

Anonymous, 'Aborigines fishing, cooking and eating in canoes'. Ink , wash and watercolour, undated (but after the 1788 settlement). (Banks' papers, Vol. 15, f. 10; Mitchell Library, State Library of New South Wales.)

> of white paint or Pigment. Altho I have said that shell fish is their chief support yet they catch other sorts of fish some of which we found roasting on the fire the first time we landed, some of these they strike with gigs and others they catch with hook and line; we have seen them strike fish with gigs & hooks and liners were found in their hutts. Sting rays I believe they do not eat because I never saw the least remains of one near any of their hutts or fire places. However we could know but very little of their customs as we never were able to form any connections with them, they had not so much as touch'd the things we had left in their hutts on purpose for them to take away. (Cook, I, 312)

Banks did not record details of his first impressions, but of the fifth day of their stay he said that he was 'now quite void of fear as our neighbours have turned out such rank cowards' (II, 59).

In 43 days from Botany Bay to Cooktown the people of the *Endeavour* seem to have had no contact with Aborigines. Cook scarcely mentioned them; Banks made seven references. Banks saw 20 on the shore near the Queensland border, who seemed 'intirely unmovd by the neighbourhood of so remarkable an object as a ship must necessarily to be people who have never seen one' (63). Another group showed the first sign of interest in the ship. Aborigines were seen at three of the four landing places; some of them shouted at the ship. Two men and a woman had a canoe with an outrigger at Whitsunday Passage, 'which made us hope that the people were something improvd as their boat was far preferable to the bark Canoes of Stingrays bay [i.e. Botany Bay]' (Banks, II, 75). Banks wondered about the purpose of the fires the Aborigines evidently lit. Now it seems likely that they were signalling the presence of the ship to others.

The *Endeavour*'s 48 day delay for repairs at Endeavour River gave Cook and Banks the best opportunity they had to observe the Aborigines closely — to meet them individually, to exchange gifts, to learn something of their language. The Aborigines had their camp across the river opposite the careening ship. What the Europeans took to be an 'unacceptable timidity' deferred a meeting for seventeen days. When they did make a cautious approach to the ship, it was to fraternise rather than to attack. Parkinson's comment was that 'though of a diminutive size, [the natives] ran very swiftly, and were very merry and facetious' (Parkinson, 146). Over twelve consecutive days, eight meetings occurred; during only one was there conflict. Thereafter, the Aborigines' reserve returned until the ship left a fortnight later. This is how Banks recorded the meetings:

10 [July]. Four Indians appeard on the opposite shore; they had with them a Canoe made of wood with an outrigger in which two of them embarkd and came towards the ship but stop'd at the distance of a long Musquet shot, talking much and very loud to us. We hollowd to them and waving made them all the signs we could to come nearer; by degrees they venturd almost insensibly nearer and nearer till they were quite along side, often holding up their Lances as if to shew us that if we usd them ill they had weapons and would return our attack. Cloth, Nails, Paper, &c &c. was given to them all which they took and put into the canoe without shewing the least signs of satisfaction: at last a small fish was by accident thrown to them on

Anonymous, 'A family of New South Wales'. Ink, wash and watercolour, undated (but from 1788). (Banks' papers, Vol. 15, f. 12; Mitchell Library, State Library of New South Wales.)

which they expressd the greatest joy imaginable, and instantly putting off from the ship made signs that they would bring over their comrades, which they very soon did and all four landed near us, each carrying in his hand 2 Lances and his stick to throw them with. Tupia went towards [them]; they stood all in a row in the attitude of throwing their Lances; he made signs that they should lay them down and come forward without them; this they immediately did and sat down with him upon the ground. We then came up to them and made them presents of Beads, Cloth &c. which they took and soon became very easy, only Jealous if any one attempted to go between them and their arms. At dinner time we made signs to them to come to us and eat but they refusd; we left them and they going into their Canoe padled back to where they came from.

11. Indians came over again today, 2 that were with us yesterday and two new ones who our old acquaintaince introduc'd to us by their names, one of which was Yaparico. Tho we did not yesterday Observe it they all had the Septum or inner part of the nose bord through with a very large hole, in which one of them had stuck the bone of a bird as thick as a mans finger and 5 or 6 inches long, an ornament no doubt tho to us it appeard rather an uncouth one. They brought with them a fish which they gave to us in return I suppose for the fish we had given them yesterday. Their stay was but short for some of our gentlemen being rather too curious in examining their canoe they went directly to it and pushing it off went away without saying a word.

12. Indians came again today and venturd down to Tupias Tent, where they were so well pleasd with their reception that three staid while the fourth went with the Canoe to fetch two new ones; they introduc'd their strangers (which they always made a point of doing) by name and had some fish given them. They receivd it with indifference, signd to our people to cook it for them which was done, and they eat part and gave the rest to my Bitch. They staid the most part of the morning but never venturd to go above 20 yards from their canoe. The ribbands by which we had tied medals round their necks the first day we saw them were coverd with smoak; I suppose they lay much in the smoak to keep off the Musquetos. They are a very small people or at least this tribe consisted of very small people, in general about 5 feet 6 in hight and very slender; one we measurd 5 feet 2 and another 5 feet 9, but he was far taller than any of his fellows; I do not know by what deception we were to a man of opinion, when we saw them run on the sand about ¼ of a mile from us, that they were taller and larger than we were. Their colour was nearest to that of chocolate, not that their skins were so dark but the smoak and dirt with which they were all casd over, which I suppose servd them instead of Cloths, made them of that colour. Their hair was strait in some and curld in others; they always wore it croppd close round their heads; it was of the same consistence with our hair, by no means wooly or curld like that of Negroes. Their eyes were in many lively and their teeth even and good; of them they had compleat setts, by no means wanting two of their fore teeth as Dampiers New Hollanders did. They were all of them clean limn'd, active and nimble. Cloaths they had none, not the least rag, those parts which nature willingly conceals being exposd to view compleatly uncoverd; yet when they stood still they would often or almost allways with their hand or something they held in it hide them in some measure at least, seemingly doing that as if by instinct. They Painted themselves with white and red, the first in lines and barrs on different Parts of their bodies, the other in large patches. Their ornaments were few: necklaces prettyly enough made of shells, bracelets wore round the upper part of their arms, consisting of strings lapd round with other stringst as what we Call gymp in England, a string no thicker than a packthread tied round their bodies which was sometimes made of human hair, a peice of Bark tied over their forehead, and the preposterous bone in their noses which I have before mentiond were all that we observd. One had indeed one of his Ears bord, the hole being big enough to put a thumb through, but this was peculiar to that one man and him I never saw wear in it any ornament. Their language was totaly different

> from that of the Islanders; it sounded more like English in its degree of harshness tho it could not be calld harsh neither. They almost continualy made use of the word *Chircau*, which we conceivd to be a term of Admiration as they still usd it when ever they saw any thing new; also Cherr, tut tut tut tut tut, which probably have the same signification. Their Canoe was not above 10 feet long and very narrow built, with an outrigger fitted much like those at the Islands only far inferior; they in shallow waters set her on with poles, in deep paddled her with paddles about 4 feet long; she just carried 4 people so that the 6 who visited us today were obligd to make 2 embarkations. Their Lances were much like those we had seen in Botany bay, only they were all of them single pointed, and some pointed with the stings of sting-rays and bearded with two or three beards of the same, which made them indeed a terrible weapon; the board or stick with which they flung them was also made in a neater manner.
>
> After having staid with us the greatest part of the morning they went away as they came. While they staid 2 more and a young woman made their appearance upon the Beach; she was to the utmost that we could see with our glasses as naked as the men. (Banks, II, 91–3)

(The subject of the medals or the type is not known. Before Cook left Tahiti he gave a Tahitian a few medals as testimony of his discovery, probably of the island of Huahine, and a small pewter plate inscribed with the words 'His Britannic Maj. Ship Endeavour, Lieut Cook Commander 16th July 1769'.)

The next day, 'Two Indians came in their Canoe to the ship, staid by her a very short time and then went along shore striking fish' (Banks, II, 93). Banks did not then mention the Aborigines for three days. This was probably partly because one of the crew had at last shot a specimen of what had been referred to as 'the animal'. This was their first close view of a kangaroo.

> 17 [July]. Tupia who was over the water by himself saw 3 Indians, who gave him a kind of longish roots about as thick as a mans finger and of a very good taste. On his return the Captn Dr Solander and myself went over in hopes to see them and renew our connections; we met with four in a canoe who soon after came ashore and came to us without any signs of fear. After receiving the beads &c that we had given them they went away; we attempted to follow them hoping that they would lead us to their fellows where we might have an opportunity of seeing their Women; they however by signs made us understand that they did not desire our company. (Banks, II, 95)

No references were made to approaches to Aboriginal women at any other stage of the voyage. After his return to England Banks, in a letter to an acquaintance, said the men 'were not uncivil, tho' very timorous and Jealous of their Sooty Wives' (Banks, II, 327).

Venturing aboard the *Endeavour* so emboldened the Aborigines that they became uncommonly assertive:

> 18 [July]. Indians were over with us today and seemd to have lost all fear of us and became quite familiar; one of them at our desire threw his Lance which was about 8 feet in Lengh — it flew with a degree of swiftness and steadyness that realy surprizd me, never being above 4 feet from the ground and stuck deep in at the distance of 50 paces. After this they venturd on board the ship and soon became our very good freinds, so the Captn and me left them to the care of those who staid on board.
>
> 19 [July]. Ten Indians visited us today and brought with them a larger quantity of Lances than they had every done before, these they laid up in a tree leaving a man and a boy taking care of them and came on board the ship. They soon let us know their errand which was by some means or other to get one of our Turtle of which we had 8 or 9 laying upon the decks. They first by signs askd for One and on being refusd shewd great marks of Resentment; one who had askd me on my refusal stamping with his foot pushd me from him with a countenance full of disdain and applyd to some one else; as however they met with no encouragement in this they laid hold of a turtle and hauld him forwards towards the side of the ship where their canoe lay. It however was soon taken from them and replacd. They nevertheless repeated the expiriment 2 or 3 times and after meeting with

so many repulses all in an instant leapd into their Canoe and went ashore where I had got before them Just ready to set out plant gathering; they seizd their arms in an instant, and taking fire from under a pitch kettle which was boiling they began to set fire to the grass to windward of the few things we had left ashore with surprizing dexterity and quickness; the grass which was 4 or 5 feet high and as dry as stubble burnt with vast fury. A Tent of mine which had been put up for Tupia when he was sick was the only thing of any consequence in the way of it so I leapd into a boat to fetch some people from the ship in order to save it, and quickly returning hauld it down to the beach Just time enough. The Captn in the meantime followd the Indians to prevent their burning our Linnen and the Seine which lay on the grass just where they were gone. He had no musquet with him so soon returnd to fetch one for no threats or signs would make them desist. Mine was ashore and another loaded with shot, so we ran as fast as possible towards them and came just time enough to save the Seine by firing at an Indian who had already fird the grass in two places just to windward of it; on the shot striking him, tho he was full 40 yards from the Captn who fird, he dropd his fire and ran nimbly to his comrades who all ran off pretty fast. The Captn then loaded his musquet with a ball and fird it into the Mangroves abreast of where they ran to shew them that they were not yet out of our reach, they ran on quickning their pace on hearing the Ball and we soon lost sight of them; we then returnd to the Seine where the people who were ashore had got the fire under. We now thought we were free'd from these troublesome people but we soon heard their voices returning on which, anxious for some people who were washing that way, we ran towards them; on seeing us come with our musquets they again retird leasurely after an old man had venturd quite to us and said something which we could not understand. We followd for near a mile, then meeting with some rocks from whence we might observe their motions we sat down and they did so too about 100 yards from us. The little old man now came forward to us carrying in his hand a lance without a point. He halted several times and as he stood employd himself in collecting the moisture from under his arm pit with his finger which he every time drew through his mouth. We beckond to him to come: he then spoke to the others who all laid their lances against a tree and leaving them came forwards likewise and soon came quite to us. They had with them it seems 3 strangers who wanted to see the ship but the man who was shot at and the boy were gone, so our troop now consisted of 11. The Strangers were presented to us by name and we gave them such trinkets as we had about us; then we all proceeded towards the ship, they making signs as they came along that they would not set fire to the grass again and we distributing musquet balls among them and by our signs explaining their effect. When they came abreast of the ship they sat down but could not be prevaild upon to come on board, so after a little time we left them to their contemplations; they stayd about two hours and then departed.

We had great reason to thank our good Fortune that this accident happned so late in our stay, not a week before this our powder which was put ashore when first we came in had been taken on board, and that very morning only the store tent and that in which the sick had livd were got on board. I had little Idea of the fury with which the grass burnt in this hot climate, nor of the dificulty of extinguishing it when once lighted: this accident will however be a sufficient warning for us if ever we should again pitch tents in such a climate to burn Every thing round us before we begin. (Banks, II, 95–7)

Despite the apparent reconciliation, the Aborigines did not come to the ship again. For two days, Banks wondered what had happened to them; then he heard the last of them:

> 22 [July]...One of our people who had been sent out to gather Indian Kale straying from his party met with three indians, two men and a boy, he came upon them as they sat down among some long grass on a sudden and before he was aware of it. At first he was much afraid and offerd them his knife, the only thing he had which he thought might be acceptable to

> them; they took it and after handing it from one to another return'd it to him. They kept him about half an hour behaving most civily to him, only satisfying their curiosity in examining his body, which done they made him signs that he might go away which he did very well pleasd. They had hanging on a tree by them, he said, a quarter of the wild animal and a cocatoo; but how they had been clever enough to take these animals is almost beyond my conception, as both of them are most shy especialy the Cocatoos. (Banks, II, 98)

Cook had written much less about the Aborigines, not only because he was probably less interested in them than Banks, but also because he was preoccupied with repairs to the ship and his party's uncertain future. However, he did praise their civility, noting that they allowed the straggler 'to go away without offering the least insult, and perceiving that he did not go right for the ship they directed him which way to go' (Cook, I, 363).

Thirty days later at Possession Island in Torres Strait, nine natives with spears and a bow and arrows at first confronted the Europeans, but then did not oppose their landing and walked slowly away. Their having bows and arrows shows that these people were Melanesians, for of all the inhabitants of all the continents, only Australia's Aborigines did not use these weapons.

In his general account of New South Wales, Banks presented an ethnography of the Aborigines, which, while still with large gaps and mistakes, went significantly beyond that offered by Dampier. (We should also remember that the cultures of east coast Aborigines differed significantly from that of those Dampier saw.) This is the opening of what he termed 'Some account of that part of New Holland now called New South Wales':

> I much wishd indeed to have had better opportunities of seeing and observing the people, as they differ so much from the account that Dampier (the only man I know of who has seen them besides us) has given of them. He indeed saw them on a part of the coast very distant from where we were and consequently the people might be different; but I should rather conclude them to be the same, chiefly from having observd an universal conformity in such of their customs as came under my observation in the several places we landed upon during the run of [ ] leagues along the coast. Dampier in general seems to be a faithfull relater, but in the voyage in which he touchd on the coast of New Holland he was in a ship of Pyrates, possibly himself not a little tainted by their idle examples: he might have kept no written Journal of any thing more than the navigation of the ship and when upon coming home he was sollicited to publish an account of his voyage have referrd to his memory for many particulars relating to people &c. These Indians when coverd with their filth which I beleive they never wash of are, if not coal black, very near it: as negroes then he might well esteem them and add the wooly hair and want of two fore teeth in consequence of the similitude in complexion between these and the natives of Africa; but from whatever cause it might arise, certain it is that Dampier either was mistaken very much in his account or else that he saw a very different race of people from those we have seen. (Banks, II, 111–12)

Banks did not speculate on the origins of the Aborigines but contrasted their lack of cultivation with other natives. He continued:

> This immense tract of Land, the largest known which does not bear the name of a continent, as it is considerably larger than all Europe, is thinly inhabited even to admiration, at least that part of it that we saw: we never but once saw so many as thirty Indians together and that was a family, Men women and children, assembled upon a rock to see the ship pass by. At Sting-Rays bay where they evidently came down to fight us several times they never could muster above 14 or 15 fighting men, indeed in other places they generaly ran away from us, from whence it might be concluded that there were greater numbers than we saw, but their houses and sheds in the woods which we never faild to find convincd us of the smallness of their parties. We saw indeed only the sea coast: what the immense tract of inland countrey may produce is to us totaly unknown: we may have liberty to conjecture however that they are totaly

uninhabited. The Sea has I beleive been universaly found to be the cheif source of supplys to Indians ignorant of the arts of cultivation: the wild produce of the Land alone seems scarce able to support them at all seasons, at least I do not remember to have read of any inland nation who did not cultivate the ground more or less, even the North Americans who were so well versd in hunting sowd their Maize. But should a people live inland who supported themselves by cultivation these inhabitants of the sea coast must certainly have learn'd to imitate them in some degree at least, otherwise their reason must be supposd to hold a rank little superior to that of monkies.

Whatever may be the reason of this want of People is dificult to guess, unless perhaps the Barreness of the Soil and scarcity of fresh water; but why mankind should not increase here as fast as in other places unless their small tribes have frequent wars in which many are destroyd; they were indeed generaly furnished with plenty of weapons whose points of the stings of Sting-Rays seemd intended against nothing but their own species, from whence such an inference might easily be drawn.

That their customs were nearly the same throughout the whole lengh of the coast along which we saild I should think very probable. Tho we had Connections with them only at one place yet we saw them either with our eyes or glasses many times, and at Sting Rays bay had some experience of their manners; their Colour, arms, method of using them, were the same as we afterwards had a nearer view of; they likewise in the same manner went naked, and painted themselves, their houses were the same, they notchd large trees in the same manner and even the bags they carried their furniture in were of exactly the same manufacture, something between netting and Knitting which I had no where else seen in the intermediate places. Our glasses might deceive us in many things but their colour and want of cloths we certainly did see and wherever we came ashore the houses and sheds, places where they had dressd victuals with heated stones, and trees notchd for the convenience of climbing them sufficiently evincd them to be the same people.

The tribe with which we had connections consisted of 21 people, 12 men 7 women a boy and a girl, so many at least we saw and there might be more, especialy women, who we did not see. The men were remarkably short and slender built in proportion; the tallest we measurd was 5 feet 9, the shortest 5-2; their medium hight seemd to be about five feet six, as the tall man appeard more disproportioned in size from his fellows than the short one. What their absolute colour is is difficult to say, they were so completely coverd with dirt, which seemd to have stuck to their hides from the day of their birth without their once having attemptd to remove it; I tryd indeed by spitting upon my finger and rubbing but alterd the colour very little, which as nearly as might be resembled that of Chocolate. The beards of several were bushy and thick; their hair which as well as their beards was black they wore croppd close round their ears; in some it was lank as a Europeans, in others a little crispd as is common in the South sea Islands but in none of them at all resembling the wool of Negroes. They had also all their fore teeth; in which two things they differ cheifly from those seen by Dampier, supposing him not to be mistaken. As for colour they would undoubtedly be calld blacks by any one not usd to consider attentively the colours of different Nations; myself should never have thought of such distinctions had I not seen the effect of Sun and wind upon the natives of the South sea Islands, where many of the Better sort of people who keep themselves close at home are nearly as white as Europeans, while the poorer sort, obligd in their business of fishing &c. to expose their naked bodies to all the inclemancies of the Climate, have some among them but little lighter than the New Hollanders. They were all to a man lean and clean limnd and seemd to be very light and active; their countenances were not without some expression tho I cannot charge them with much, their voices in general shrill and effeminate.

Of Cloths they had not the least part but naked as ever our general father was before his fall, they seemd no more conscious of their nakedness than if they had not been the children of Parents who eat the fruit of the tree of knowledge. Whether this want of what most nations look upon as absolutely necessary proceeds from idleness or want of invention is difficult to say; in the article of ornaments however, useless as they are, neither has the one hinderd them from contriving nor the other from making them. Of these the cheif and that on which they seem to set the greatest value is a bone about 5 or 6 inches in lengh and as thick as a mans finger, which they thrust into a hole bord through that part which divides the nostrils so that it sticks across their face, making in the eyes of Europeans a most ludicrous appearance, tho no doubt they esteem even this as an addition to their beauty which they purchasd with hourly inconvenience; for when this bone was in its place, or as our seamen termd it their spritsail yard was riggd across, it compleatly stop'd up both nostrils so that they spoke in the nose in a manner one should think scarce intelligible. Besides these extrordinary bones they had necklaces made of shells neatly enough cut and strung together, bracelets also if one may call by that name 4 or 5 ring[s] of small cord wore round the upper part of the arm, also a belt or string tied round the waist about as thick as worsted yarn, which last was frequently made of either human hair or that of the Beast calld by them Kangooroo. Besides these they paint themselves with the colours of red and white: the red they commonly lay on in broad patches on their shoulders or breasts; the white in stripes some of which were narrow and confind to small parts of their body, others were broad and carried with some degree of taste across their bodies, round their legs and arms &c; they also lay it on in circles round their eyes and in patches in different parts of their faces. The red they usd seemd to be red ocre but what the white was we could not find out; it was heavy and close graind almost as white lead and had a saponaceos feel, possibly it might be a kind of Steatites [kaolin]. We lamented not being able to procure a bit to examine. These people seemd to have no Idea of traffick nor could we teach them; indeed it seemd that we had no one thing on which they set a value equal to induce them to Part with the smallest trifle; except one fish which weighd about ½ a pound that they brought as a kind of token of peace no one in the ship I beleive procurd from them the smallest article. They readily receivd the things we gave them but never would understand our signs when we askd for returns. This however must not be forgot, that whatever opportunities they had they never once attempted to take any thing in a clandestine manner; whatever they wanted they openly askd for and in almost all cases bore the refusal if they met with one with much indifference, except Turtles.

Dirty as these people are they seem to be intirely free from Lice, a circumstance rarely observd among the most cleanly Indians, and which here is the more remarkable as their hair was generaly Matted and filthy enough. In all of them indeed it was very thin and seemd as if seldom disturbd with the Combing even of their fingers, much less to have any oil or grease put into it; nor did the custom of oiling their bodies, so common among most uncivilizd nations, seem to have the least footing here.

On their bodies we observd very few marks of cutaneous disorders as scurf, scars of sores &c. Their spare thin bodies indicate a temperance in eating, the consequence either of necessity or inclination, equaly productive of health particularly in this respect. On the fleshy parts of their arms and thighs and some of their sides were large scars in regular lines, which by their breadth and the convexity with which they had heald shewd plainly that they had been made by deep cuts of some blunt instrument, a shell perhaps or the edge of a broken stone. These as far as we could understand by the Signs they made use of were the marks of their Lamentations for the deceasd, in honour to whose memory or to shew the excess of their greif they had in this manner wept for in blood. [They were marks of initiation into adulthood.]

For Food they seem to depend very much tho not intirely upon the Sea. Fish of all kinds, Turtle and even crabs they strike with their Lances very dextrously. These are generaly bearded with broad beards and their points smeard over with a kind of hard resin which makes them peirce a hard body far easier than they would do without it. In the southern parts these fish spears had 4 prongs and besides the resin were pointed with the sharp bone of a fish; to the Northward again their spears had only one point; yet both I beleive struck fish with equal dexterity. For the Northern ones I can witness who several times saw them through a glass throw their Spear from 10 to 20 yards and generaly succeed; to the Southward again the plenty of Fish bones we saw near their fires provd them to be no indifferent artists.

For striking of Turtle they use a peg of wood well bearded and about a foot long: this fastens into a socket of a stiff of light wood as thick as a mans wrist and 8 or 9 feet long, besides which they are tied together by a loose line of 3 or 4 fathoms in lengh. The use of this must undoubtedly be that when the Turtle is struck the staff flies off from the peg and serves for a float to shew them where the Turtle is, as well as assists to tire him till they can with their canoes overtake and haul him in. That they throw this Dart with great force we had occasion to observe while we lay in Endeavours river, where a turtle which we killd had one of them intirely buried in its body just across its breast; it seemd to have enterd at the soft place where the fore fins work but not the least outward mark of the wound remaind.

Besides these things we saw near their fire places plentifull remains of lobsters, shell fish of all kinds, and to the Southward the skins of those Sea animals which from their property of spouting out water when touchd are commonly calld sea squirts. These last, howsoever disgustfull they may seem to an European palate, we found to contain under a coat as tough as leather a substance like the guts of a shell fish, in taste tho not equal to an oyster yet by no means to be despisd by a man who is hungrey.

Of Land animals they probably eat every kind that they can kill which probably does not amount to any large number, every species being here shy and cautious in a high degree. The only vegetables we saw them use were Yams of 2 sorts, the one long and like a finger the other round and coverd with stringy roots, both sorts very small but sweet; they were so scarce where we were that we never could find the plants that producd them, tho we often saw the places where they had been dug up by the Indians very newly. It is very probable that the Dry season which was at its hight when we were there had destroyd the leaves of the plants so that we had no guides, while the Indians knowing well the stalks might find them easily. Whether they knew or ever made use of the Coccos [i.e. taro] I cannot tell; the immence sharpness of every part of this vegetable before it is dressd makes it probable that any people who have not learnd the uses of it from others may remain for ever ignorant of them. Near their fires were great abundance of the shells of a kind of fruit resembling a Pine apple very much in appearance, tho in taste disagreable enough; it is common to all the East Indies and calld by the Dutch there *Pyn appel Boomen* (*pandanus*); as also those of the fruits of a low Palm calld by the Dutch *Moeskruidige Calappus* (*Cycas circinalis*) which they certainly eat, tho they are so unwholesome that some of our people who tho forewarnd depending upon their example eat one or 2 of were violently affected by them both upwards and downwards, and our hogs whose constitutions we thought might be as strong as those of the Indians literaly dyed after having eat them. It is probable however that these people have some method of Preparing them by which their poisonous quality is destroyd, as the inhabitants of the East Indian Isles are said to do by boiling them and steeping them 24 hours in water, then drying them and using them to thicken broth; from whence it should seem that the poisonous quality lays intirely in the Juices, as it does in the roots of the Mandihocca or Cassada of the West Indies and that when thouroughly cleard of them the pulp remain[in]g may be a wholesome and nutritious food.

Their victuals they generaly dress by broiling or toasting them upon the coals, so we judg'd by the remains we saw; they knew however the method of baking or stewing with hot stones and sometimes practis'd it, as we now and then saw the pits and burnd stones which had been made use of for that purpose.

We observd that some tho but few held

constantly in their mouths the leaves of an herb which they chewd as a European does tobacca or an East Indian Betele. What sort of plant it was we had not an opportunity of learning as we never saw any thing but the chaws which they took from their mouths to shew us; it might be of the Betele kind and so far as we could judge from the fragments was so, but whatever it was it was usd without any addition and seemd to have no kind of effect upon either the teeth or lips of those who usd it.

Naked as these people are when abroad they are scarce at all better defended from the injuries of the weather when at home, if that name can with propriety be given to their homes — as I beleive they never make any stay in them but wandering like the Arabs from place to place set them up whenever they meet with one where sufficient supplys of food are to be met with, and as soon as these are exhausted remove to another leaving the houses behind, which are framd with less art or rather less industry than any habitations of human beings probably that the world can shew.

At Sting-Rays Bay, where they were the best, each was capable of containing within it 4 or 5 people but not one of all these could in any direction extend himself his whole lengh; for hight he might just set upright, but if inclind to sleep must coil himself in some crooked position as the dimensions were in no direction long enough to hold him otherwise. They were built in the form of an oven of pliable rods about as thick as a mans finger, the Ends of which were stuck into the ground and the whole coverd with Palm leaves and broad peices of Bark; the door was a pretty large hole at one end, opposite to which by the ashes there seemd to be a fire kept pretty constantly to the Northward. Again where the warmth of the climate made houses less necessary they were in proportion still more slight; a house there was nothing but a hollow shelter about 3 or 4 feet deep built like the former and like them coverd with bark; one side of this was intirely open which was always that which was sheltered from the course of the prevailing wind, and opposite to this door was always a heap of ashes, the remains of a fire probably more necessary to defend them from Mosquetos than cold. In these it is probable that they only sought to defend their heads and the upper part of their bodies from the Draught of air, trusting their feet to the care of the fire, and so small they were that even in this manner not above 3 or 4 people could possibly croud into one of them. But small as the trouble of erecting such houses must be they did not always do it; we saw many places in the woods where they had slept with no other shelter than a few bushes and grass a foot or two high to shade them from the wind; this probably is their custom while they travel from place to place and sleep upon the road in situations where they do not mean to make any stay.

The only Furniture belonging to these houses, that we saw at least, was oblong vessels of Bark made by the simple contrivance of tying up the two ends of a longish peice with a withe which not being cut off serves for a handle, these we imagind serv'd for the purpose of Water Buckets to fetch water from the springs which may sometimes be distant. We have reason to suppose that when they travel these are carried by the women from place to place; indeed the few opportunities we had of seeing the women they were generaly employd in some laborious occupation as fetching wood, gathering shell fish &c.

The men again maybe constantly carry their arms in their hands, 3 or 4 lances in one and the machine with which they throw them in the other; these serve them in the double capacity of defending them from their enemies and striking any animal or fish that they may meet with. Besides these each has a small bag about the size of a moderate Cabbage net which hangs loose upon his back fas[t]ned to a small string which passes over the crown of his head; this seems to contain all their worldly treasures, each man hardly more than might be containd in the crown of a hat — a lump or two of Paint, some fish hooks and lines, shells to make them of, Points of Darts and resin and their usual ornaments were the general contents...

Tools among them we saw almost none, indeed having no arts which require any it is not to be expected that they should have many. A stone made sharp at the edge and a wooden mallet were the only ones we saw that had been formd by art; the use of these we supposd to be in making the notches in the bark of high trees by which they climb them for purposes unknown to us, and for cutting and perhaps driving wedges to take of the bark which they must have in large peices for making Canoes, Sheilds and water buckets and also for covering their houses. Besides these they use shells and corals to scrape the points of their darts, and polish them with the leaves of a kind of wild Fig tree (*Ficus Radulo*) which bites upon wood almost as keenly as our European shave grass usd by the Joiners. Their fish hooks are made of shell very neatly and some exceedingly small; their lines are also well twisted and they have them from the size of a half inch rope to almost the fineness of a hair made of some vegetable. Of Netting they seem to be quite ignorant but make their bags, the only thing of the kind we saw among them, by laying the threads loop within loop something in the way of knitting only very coarse and open, in the same manner as I have seen ladies make purses in England. That they had no sharp instruments among them we venturd to guess from the circumstance of an old man who came to us one day with a beard rather larger than his fellows; the next day he came again, his beard was then almost croppd close to his chin and upon examination we found the ends of the hairs all burnd so that he had certainly singd it off. Their manner of Hunting and taking wild animals we had no opportunity of seeing: we only guessd that the notches which they had every where cut in the Bark of large trees, which certainly servd to make climbing more easy to them, might be intended for the ascending these trees in order either to watch for any animal who unwarily passing under them they might peirce with their darts, or for the taking birds who at night might Roost in them. We guessd also that the fires which we saw so frequently as we passd along shore, extending over a large tract of countrey and by which we could constantly trace the passage of the Indians who went from us in Endeavours river up into the countrey, were intended in some way or other for the taking of the animal calld by them *Kanguru*, which we found to be so much afraid of fire that we could hardly force it with our dogs to go over places newly burnt. They get fire very expeditiously with two peices of stick very readily and nimbly: the one must be round and 8 or nine inches long and both it and the other should be dry and soft; the round one they sharpen a little at one end and pressing it upon the other turn it round with the palms of their hands just as Europeans do a chocolate mill, often shifting their hands up and running them down quick to make the pressure as hard as possible; in this manner they will get fire in less than 2 minutes and when once posessd, of the smallest spark increase [it] in a manner truely wonderfull. We often admird to see a man run along shore who seemd to carry no one thing in his hand and yet as he ran along, just stooping down every 50 or 100 yards, smoak and fire were seen among the drift wood and dirt at that place almost the instant he had left it. This we afterwards found was done cheifly by the infinite readyness with which every kind of rubbish, sticks, witherd leaves or dry grass already almost dryd to tinder by the heat of the sun and dryness of the season would take fire: he took for instance when he set off a small bit of fire and wrapping it up in dry grass ran on, this soon blazd, he then layd it down on the most convenient place for his purpose that he could find and taking up a small part of it wrappd that in·part of the dry rubbish in which he had layd it, in this manner proceeding as long as he thought proper.

Their Weapons, offensive at least, were precisely the same where ever we saw them except that at the very last view we had of the countrey we saw through our glasses a man who carried a Bow and arrows; in this we might but I beleive we were not mistaken. They consisted of one only species, a Pike or Lance from 8 to 14 feet in lengh: this they threw short distances with their hands and for longer, 40 or more yards, with an instrument made for the purpose. The upper part of these Lances were made either of Cane or the stalk of a plant something resembling a Bullrush which was very streight and light: the point again was made of very heavy and hard wood, the whole artfully balancd for throwing tho very clumsily made in two, three or four joints, at each of which the parts were let into each other and besides being tied round the Joint was smeard over very thick with their Resin which made it larger and more clumsey than any other part. The points were of several sorts: those which we concluded to be intended against men were indeed most cruel weapons: they were all single pointed either with the stings of sting-rays, a large one of which servd for the point, and three or 4 smaller tied the contrary way made barbs: or simply of wood made very sharp and smeard thick over with resin into which was stuck many broken bits of sharp shells, so that if such a weapon pierced a man it was many to one that it could not be drawn out without leaving several of those unwelcome guests in his flesh, certain to make the wound ten times more dificult to cure than it otherwise would be. The others which we supposd to be usd merely for striking fish, birds &c had generaly simple points of wood or if they were barbd it was with only one splinter of wood. The instrument with which they threw them was a plain stick or peice of wood 2 and ½ or 3 feet in lengh, at one end of which was a small knob or hook and near the other a kind of cross peice to hinder it from slipping out of their hands. With this contrivance, simple as it is and ill fitted for the purpose, they threw the lances 40 or more yards with a swiftness and steadyness truley surprizing; the knob being hookd into a small dent made in the top of the lance they held over their shoulder and shaking it an instant as balancing threw it with the greatest ease imaginable. The neatest of these throwing sticks that we saw were made of hard reddish wood polishl[d] and shining; their sides were flat and about 2 inches in breadth and the handle or part to keep it from dropping out of the hand coverd with thin layers of polishd bone very white; these I beleive to be the things which many of our people were deceivd by imagining them to be wooden swords, Clubs &c. according to the direction in which they happned to see them. Defensive weapons we saw only in Sting-Rays bay and there only a single instance — a man who attempted to oppose our Landing came down to the Beach with a sheild of an oblong shape about 3 feet long and 1½ broad made of the bark of a tree; this he left behind when he ran away and we found upon taking it up that it plainly had been piercd through with a single pointed lance near the center. That such sheilds were frequently usd in that neighbourhood we had however sufficient proof, often seeing upon trees the places from whence they had been cut and sometimes the sheilds themselves cut out but not yet taken off from the tree; the edges of the bark only being a little raisd with wedges; which shews that these people certainly know how much thicker and stronger bark becomes by being sufferd to remain upon the tree some time after it is cut round.

That they are a very pusilanimous people we had reason to suppose from every part of their conduct in every place where we were except Sting Rays bay, and there only the instance of the two people who opposd the Landing of our two boats full of men for near a quarter of an hour and were not to be drove away till several times wounded with small shot, which we were obligd to do as at that time we suspected their Lances to be poisned from the quantity of gum which was about their points; but upon every other occasion both there and every where else they behavd alike, shunning us and giving up any part of the countrey which we landed upon at once: and that they use stratagems in war we learnt by the instance in Sting-rays bay where our Surgeon with another man walking in the woods met 8 Indians; they stood still but directed another who was up in a tree how and when he should throw a Lance at them, which he did and on its not taking effect they all ran away as fast as possible.

Their Canoes were the only things in which we saw a manifest difference between the Southern and the Northern people. Those to the Southward were little better contrivd or executed than their Houses: a peice of Bark tied together in Pleats at the ends and kept extended in the middle by small bows of wood was the whole embarkation, which carried one or two, nay we once saw three people, who movd it along in shallow water by setting [punting] with long poles; and in deeper by padling with padles about 18 inches long, one of which they held in each hand. In the middle of these Canoes was generaly a small fire upon a heap of sea weed, for what purpose intended we did not learn except perhaps to give the fisherman an opportunity of Eating fish in perfection by broiling it the moment it is taken.

To the Northward again their canoes tho exceeding bad were far superior to these. They were small but regularly hollowd out of the trunk of a tree and fitted with an outrigger to prevent them from oversetting; in these they had paddles large enough to require both hands to work them. Of this sort we saw only _____ and had an opportunity of examining only one of them which might be about 10 or 11 feet long but was immensely narrow; the sides of the tree were left in their natural state untouch'd by tools but at each [end?] they had cut off from the under part and left part of the upper side overhanging; the inside also was not ill hollowd and the sides tolerably thin. What burthen it was capable of carrying we had many times an opportunity to see: 3 people or at most 4 were as many as dare venture in it and if any more wanted to come over the river, which in that place was about a half a mile broad, one of these would carry back the Canoe and fetch them.

This was the only peice of workmanship which I saw among the New Hollanders that seemd to require tools. How they had hollowd her out or cut the ends I cannot guess but upon the whole the work was not ill done; Indian patience might do a great deal with shells &c. without the use of stone axes, which if they had had they would probably have used to form her outside as well as inside. That such a canoe takes them up much time and trouble in the making may be concluded from our seeing so few, and still more from the moral certainty which we have that the Tribe which visited [us] and consisted to our knowledge of 21 people and may be of several more had only one such belonging to them. How tedious must it be for these people to be ferried over a river a mile or two wide by threes and fours at a time: how well therefore worth the pains for them to stock themselves better with boats if they could do it!

I am inclind to beleive that besides these Canoes the Northern People know and make use of the Bark one of the South, and that from having seen one of the small paddles left by them upon a small Island where they had been fishing for Turtles; it lay upon a heap of Turtle shells and bones, Trophies of the good living they had had when there, and which it lay a broken staff of a Turtle pegg and a rotten line, tools which had been worn out I suppose in the service of Catching them. We had great reason to beleive that at some season of the year the weather is much more moderate than we found it, otherwise the Indians never could have venturd in any canoes that we saw half so far from the main Land as Islands were on which we saw evident marks of their having been, such as decayd houses, fires, the before mentiond Turtle bones &c. May be at this more moderate time they may make and use such Canoes, and when the Blustering season comes on may convert the bark of which they were made to the purposes of covering houses, making Water buckets &c. &c. well knowing that when the next season returns they will not want a supply of bark to rebuild their vessels. Another reason we have to imagine that such a moderate season exists, and that the Winds are then upon the Eastern board as we found them, is that whatever Indian houses or sleeping places we saw on these Islands were built upon the summits of small hills if there were any, or if not, in places where no bushes or wood could intercept the course of the wind, and their shelter was always turnd to the Eastward. On the main again, their houses were universaly built in valleys, or under the shelter of trees which might defend them from the very winds which in the Islands they exposd themselves to.

Of their Language I can say very little. Our acquaintance with them was of so short a duration that none of us attempted to use a single word of it to them, consequently the list of words I have given could be got no other manner than by signs enquiring of them what in their Language signified such a thing, a method obnoxious to many mistakes: for instance a man holds in his hand a stone and asks the name of [it]: the Indian may return him for answer either the real name of a stone, one of the properties of it as hardness, roughness, smoothness &c, one of its uses or the name peculiar to some particular species of stone, which name the enquirer immediately sets down as that of a stone. To avoid however as much as Possible this inconvenience Myself and 2 or 3 more got from them as many words as we could, and having noted down those which we though[t] from circumstances we were not mistaken in we compard our lists; those in which all the lists agreed, or rather were contradicted by none, we thought our selves moraly certain not to be mistaken in. Of these my list cheefly consists, some only being added that were in only one list such as from the ease with which signs might be contrivd to ask them were thought little less certain than the others.

Wageegee	the head
Meanang	Fire
Morye	the hair
Walba	a stone
Melcea	the ears
Yowall	Sand
Yembe	the Lips
Gurka	a Rope
Bonjoo	the Nose
Bama	a man
Unjar	the tongue
Poinja	a male turtle
Wallar	the Beard
Mameingo	a female
Doomboo	the Neck
Maragan	a Canoe
Cayo	the Nipples
Pelenyo	to Paddle
Toolpoor	the Navel
Takai	Set down
Mangal	the Hands
Mierbarrar	smooth
Coman	the thighs
Garmbe	Blood
Pongo	the Knees
Yocou	Wood
Edamal	the Feet
Tapool	bone in nose
Kniorror	the Heel
Charngala	a Bag
Chumal	the Sole
Chongarn	the ancle
Kulke	the Nails
Gallan	the Sun
Cherr *Cherco* *Yarcaw* *Tut tut tut tut*	(expressions maybe of admiration which they continualy usd while in company with us)

They very often use the article Ge which seems to answer to our English 'a' as Ge Gurka a rope. (Banks, II, 122–37)

Though less extensive than Banks', Cook's ethnographic description of the Aborigines is in some ways the more enquiring. Intrigued by the differences in material culture and food resources—in particular by the use of outrigger wooden canoes from the Whitsundays northward and the absence of coconuts—Cook wondered about the origins of the Aborigines:

> When one considers the Proximity of this Country with New-Guiney, New-Britain and several other Islands which produce Cocoa-Nutts and many other fruits proper for the Support of Man, it seems strange that they should not long ago have been transplanted here; by its not being done it should seem that the Natives of this Country have no Commerce with their neighbours the New-Guinians, it is very probable that they are a different people and speake a different Language; for the advantage of such who want to clear up this point I shall add a short Vocabulary of a few words in the New-Holland Language which we learnt when in Endeavour River. (Cook, I, 396–7)

Then, in a general comment that owed much less to Enlightenment theories of nature and man than has usually been supposed, Cook went far beyond the views common at the time, when he wrote, with an obvious allusion to Dampier:

> From what I have said of the Natives of New-Holland they may appear to some to be the most wretched people upon Earth, but in reality they are far more happier than we Europeans; being wholy unacquainted not only with the

superfluous but the necessary Conveniencies so much sought after in Europe, they are happy in not knowing the use of them. They live in a Tranquillity which is not disturb'd by the Inequality of Condition: The Earth and sea of their own accord furnishes them with all things necessary for life, they covet not Magnificent Houses, Houshold-stuff &c, they live in a warm and fine Climate and enjoy a very wholsome Air, so that they have very little need of Clothing and this they seem to be fully sencible of, for many to whome we gave Cloth &c to, left it carlessly upon the Sea beach and in the woods as a thing they had no manner of use for. In short they seem'd to set no Value upon any thing we gave them, nor would they ever part with any thing of their own for any one article we could offer them; this in my opinion argues that they think themselves provided with all the necessarys of Life and that they have no superfluities. (Cook, I, 399)

It is interesting to compare Banks' sentiments on this head. From the beginning, the pair had discussed in detail what they had seen, and for his journal entries Cook had often borrowed from those of his younger, better-read companion. By this point of the voyage, however, Cook had become confident enough to trust his own judgments more, and he had accordingly grown less reliant on Banks. Now, it was Banks whose view was the more conventional, the more abstract, the less empirical:

> Thus live these I had almost said happy people, content with little nay almost nothing, Far enough removd from the anxieties attending upon riches, or even the possession of what we Europeans call common necessaries: anxieties intended maybe by Providence to counter-balance the pleasure arising from the Posession of wishd for attainments, consequently increasing with increasing wealth, and in some measure keeping up the balance of hapiness between the rich and the poor. From them appear how small are the real wants of human nature, which we Europeans have increasd to an excess which would certainly appear incredible to these people could they be told it. Nor shall we cease to increase them as long as Luxuries can be invented and riches found for the purchase of them; and how soon these Luxuries degenerate into necessaries may be sufficiently evincd by the universal use of strong liquors, Tobacco, spices, Tea &c. &c. In this instance again providence seems to act the part of a leveler, doing much towards putting all ranks into an equal state of wants and consequently of real poverty: the Great and Magnificent want as much and may be more than the midling: they again in proportion more than the inferior: each rank still looking higher than his station but confining itself to a certain point above which it knows not how to wish, not knowing at least perfectly what is there enjoyd. (Banks, II, 130)

There were also some brief contacts between Europeans and the Aborigines of Tasmania in the 1770s. In 1772 Marion du Fresne came to Blackman's Bay where Tasman had heard but not seen Aborigines in 1642. He was the first European to try to show the Aborigines that white-skinned people shared a common humanity with black-skinned people. Two volunteers from the crews went ashore naked and, in contrast with the mainlanders who met Cook at Botany Bay, the Tasmanians tolerated them.

An officer with the ships, Lieutenant Julien-Marie Crozet, described the meeting:

> When we anchored, in 22 fathoms, on a grey, sandy bottom, we put the boats to sea [and] were not long in noticing about 30 men who were assembled on the shore. This part of New Holland promised us much with the beauty of the landscape which presented our view. The fires and smoke which we had seen day and night, heralded a very densely populated country.
>
> The following day the yawls and longboats were sent ashore armed. Some of the officers, soldiers, and sailors landed on the shore without any opposition. The natives showed themselves gracious, gathered wood and made a kind of pile. They then presented the new arrivals with some dry lighted branches and appeared to invite them to set fire to the pile. We were ignorant of the meaning of this ceremony, and we lit the pile. The savages did not appear at all astonished; they remained around us without

making either any friendly or hostile demonstrations They had with them their women and children. The men as well as the women were of an ordinary height, black, with woolly hair, and all were equally naked, men and women. Some of the women carried their children on their backs, attached with a rush cord. The men were all armed with pointed staves and with several stones, which appeared to us to be edged — similar to iron axe-heads.

We noticed that these savages had generally small eyes of a bilious colour, full mouths, very white teeth, and flattened noses; their hair, like the 'wool' of Kaffirs, was tied in rolled knots and powdered with red ochre. The men have small natural parts and are not circumcised. Several among them had a kind of cut encrusted on the skin of the chest. They appeared to us generally thin, fairly well-built, broad chested [and with] shoulders thrown back. Their language seemed to us very harsh and they appeared to draw their sounds from the bottom of the throat.

We attempted to win them over with little presents: they rejected with disdain all that we offered, even iron, mirrors, handkerchiefs, and pieces of cloth. They were shown chickens and ducks, brought from the vessel, to make them understand that we wished to buy the like from them. They took these animals, which showed that they were unfamiliar with them and threw them away with a choleric air.

We had been examining these savages for about an hour when M. Marion landed. One savage left the group and presented him, as the others had, with a firebrand to light a small pile of wood. The captain, imagining this was a ceremony necessary to prove that he had come with pacific intentions, did not hesitate to light the pile, but immediately it seemed that this was quite to the contrary, and that the acceptance of the brand was an acceptance of defiance, or a declaration of war.

As soon as the pile was lighted, the savages withdrew hastily onto a hillock, from which they threw a shower of stones, by which M. Marion, as well as an officer who was with him, was wounded. We immediately fired several shots and everyone re-embarked. The yawls and longboats coasted a distance with the intention of disembarking in the middle of the bay — in a place we had sighted where there was no high ground from which the landing party would be troubled. Then the savages sent their women and children into the woods and followed the boats along the shore. When we wished to disembark they opposed our landing. One of them uttered a fearful cry, and the whole troupe immediately threw their pointed sticks at us, as a result, a black domestic was wounded in the leg. The wound was not serious, and the ease with which it healed proved that these wooden javelins were not poisoned. As soon as they had thrown their javelins we responded with a fusillade which wounded several, and killed one. They immediately fled into the woods, howling fearfully; in theif flight they carried those who, being wounded, could not follow them. Fifteen men armed with muskets followed them, and found at the entry to the forest one of the savages dying from the gunshot wound he had received. This man was five feet three inches high, and had his chest slashed like the Kaffirs of Mozambique; he seemed black, but on washing him we found that his natural colour was reddish, and that it was only smoke and dirt which made him look so dark. (Duyker, 1992, 24–6)

Lieutenant Le Dez gave further details of this incident:

7 March

This morning we manned three boats to go and reconnoitre the country and M. Marion wanted to go ashore himself in his boat with M. Duclesmeur. He had given orders to the officers who commanded the two longboats that one was to take the right and the other the left of a very beautiful sandy cove where we had seen men the day before; they were to make for the shore about a league away from him and then, running along it as closely as they could, they were to come and meet him in the middle of this cove, noting carefully on the way if there were any rivers or freshwater streams and the most suitable place to land. The Diemenlanders, seeing us coming, came to the water's edge, where they lit a fire and gathered round it to wait for us. When the first boat was within earshot (it was the boat with the two captains in it), they said a lot of things to us as if we could understand them, adding several gestures which did not appear to invite us ashore. We kept on going and went close to the land to find out how many of them there were, their demeanour and the quality of their weapons. They followed the boat on several turns, waiting for the two other boats and looking for the place where the undertow was the least strong. There were around 40 of them, completely naked, and the only weapons they had were several long spears and a few stones which they held in their hands. At that moment one of the longboats arrived. They watched it come without showing the least sign of fright.

M. Marion, seeing that they did not appear very dangerous and very much wanting to commence, made two sailors undress and go ashore, unarmed, carrying with them some small presents such as mirrors, necklaces etc. The Diemenlanders, seeing them acting thus, put their spears on the ground and with several gestures which marked their joy and contentment, came leaping to meet them, singing and clapping their hands. Our sailors reached the shore; they [the Aborigines] presented them with fire and then, as if to recognise this good welcome, [the sailors] handed out the trinkets they had brought. The thing that impressed them the most was the mirror. They did not cease looking at themselves in it and grabbing it from one another. After these first impulses, they gestured to the boats to go towards the end of the cove and they themselves followed on land. Our sailors made their way with them — they were two big boys, well-built and very white. The Diemenlanders could not leave looking at them and touching them; often they stopped to do this and on each occasion there were new expressions of astonishment and a lot of talk between them.

At the end of the cove where it was hardly easier to land, with slippery rocks washed by a strong sea and dominated by other rocks which the Diemenlanders climbed on to, Messrs Marion, Duclesmeur and a few other people went towards them. They distributed a few more small presents, many caresses and tried to make them understand that they wanted to be their friends. We seemed very pleased with each other. M. Marion even gave a signal, which he had prearranged, to let those on board know that these people were gentle and sociable. They were envious of everything they saw, particularly anything brilliant or of a striking colour and if we had let them have their way we would soon have been dressed Diemensland-style, just like them. They seemed quite prepared to trade but they had nothing but their spears, which did not interest us at all. One put his hand on the musket of one of our gentlemen and even attempted to snatch it from him. The latter did the same with his spears. The Diemenlander gave them willingly, but seeing that the other was not letting him have the musket, he very calmly took them back. We presented them with different things, including bread (we ate in front of them, making signs for them to do the same; they tasted it and threw the rest back in our faces with a kind of disdain); water (we tried to make them understand we were looking for some; they drank a little, threw away the rest and kept the bottle); and a nail (they scarcely looked at it). We showed them a live hen and a live duck. They took them with a certain indifference and snatching the hen from one another they had soon torn it to pieces. The duck provided them with amusement for a long time: they threw it into the sea and threw their spears at it. Our third boat arrived then and, whether they had already made the decision to attack us or whether they did not want to let any more people approach them, they made signs for it not to come nearer, threatening them with their spears and talking very excitedly among themselves. The people in the boat then took up their muskets; their bayonets were fixed and the sight of them increased the Diemenlanders' distrust and pushed them to attack us. We could see them getting more and more excited, so M. Marion began to withdraw quietly with the people who were with him.

Up until then the Diemenlanders had been content to shout at us and threaten us with their spears. M. Marion, who did not want to hurt them or even frighten them, went to re-embark with his men. They seized this moment to hurl several spears and a hail of stones at us, one of which fell on M. Marion's shoulder and another on M. Duclesmeur's leg. We responded with a volley fired in the air so to speak. Terror made them withdraw, but a moment later they reappeared without showing the least fear. As this place was in no way advantageous for us, we all re-embarked to go to the other end of the cove where it was much easier to land, since there was only mild surf. They followed us along the beach; some of them even came knee-deep into the water to threaten us, others chased the duck in front of them and threw their spears at it, no doubt to make us see their skill and the effect of their weapons, in which they succeeded very badly. When we had arrived at the place where we intended to land, they prepared to oppose us without seeming afraid of our muskets which they believed only made noise. They threw a lot of spears at us, but always very clumsily. One man was wounded in the leg and the tip broke off and remained [in the wound], so we then fired a more serious volley. Several fell down instantly, but forthwith got up again and they all ran away, leaving us masters of the beach and of the whole bay, where we have not seen them since. We chased them for about a league all round; we heard them calling out in the woods several times without being able to find them. We found one who was dead, pierced by two balls, at a place two musket-shot's range from where we had fired the volley. This was a young man of about twenty; five feet three or four inches tall; his hair was black, woolly and very hard, and in the front was powdered with a red dust. He had very little beard, his face and his body were blackened; on his chest he had several little scars or black marks in a crescent shape. After having made a good visit of the cove, where we found no fresh water at all, our boats came back on board about 5 o'clock in the evening. (Duyker, 1992, 31–3)

N.J.B. Plomley thinks Marion was not attacked for infringement of ceremony, but rather that the numbers landing frightened the Aborigines. They gave the firebrand to Marion, just as the seamen who swam ashore earlier to help the landings from the boats were handed firebrands, according to their custom of receiving strangers.

Crozet then recorded subsequent events:

After the flight of the savages, M. Marion despatched two well-armed detachments, with officers, to look for fresh water and timber suitable for re-masting the *Castries*. The detachments surveyed two leagues inland without meeting with either inhabitants, fresh water, or timber suitable for making the masts.

We remained six days at Frederick Henry Bay, during which time we did not cease to make searches for fresh water — in vain. The land here is sandy like that at the Cape of Good Hope; it is covered with heath and small trees, most of which we found stripped of bark by the savages, who make use of it for cooking their shellfish. We found traces of fire everyhere; the ground seemed covered with ashes. In the midst of these trees stripped of their bark and mostly burnt at the foot, we noticed a species of pine a little less tall than ours, which appeared well preserved — probably because the savages gained something useful from it, and did not maltreat it as they did other trees. It seemed to us that in going further away from the sea and penetrating the interior, we should find in the valleys these same pines of a height and thickness sufficient to be used in masting ships.

In the areas which had not been burnt, the soil was covered with grass and fern, similar to that of Europe, and also with sorrel and wood sorrel. There was little game, and we presumed that the fires made by the savages in this area had driven them inland. Our hunters encountered a tiger cat, and several holes in the ground, like a warren. They killed some crows similar to those in France; some blackbirds; thrushes; turtle doves; a parakeet, resembling a South American parrot with its plumage, and with a white beak. They killed all sorts of seabirds, above all pelicans, and a black bird with red beak and feet which Abel Tasman mentions in his journal.

The climate of this southern part of New Holland seemed very cold to us, although we

> were there at the end of summer; we could not understand how the savages could exist there in their naked state. What appeared more extraordinary to us was that we found no indication of houses, only some windbreaks, roughly formed with the branches of trees, and with traces of fires near these windbreaks. By the considerable piles of shells which we encountered from place to place, we judged that the usual food of these savages was mussels, pinna, scallops, cockles, and other similar shellfish. (Duyker, 1992, 26)

Like Tasman, Captain Tobias Furneaux, accompanying Cook's *Resolution* in the *Adventure*, did not see Tasmanian Aborigines during his five days' stay at Adventure Bay in 1773. However, he too reported signs of human habitation:

> While we lay here we saw several smokes and large Fires about Eight or ten miles in-shore to the Northward, but did not see any of the Natives, tho' they frequently come into this bay as there were several Wigwams or hutts, in which we found some bags and netts made of Grass, which I imagine they carry their provisions and other necessaries in. In one of them there was the stone they strike fire with and Tinder made of Bark, but of what tree could not find out. We found in one of their huts one of their spears, it was sharp at one end done I suppose with a shell or stone: Those things we brought away and left in the room of them, Medals, Gun flints and a few Nails, and an old empty barrel with the Iron hoops on it. They seem to be quite ignorant of every sort of Metal; the boughs of which their Huts are made are either broken or split and tied together with grass in a circular form the largest end stuck in the ground and the smaller parts meeting in a point at the top, and covered with Fern and bark, so poorly done that they will hardly keep out a showr of rain. In the middle is the fireplace surrounded with heaps of Mussel, pearl scallop and Cray-Fish shells, which I believe to be their chief food (tho' we could not find any of them). They lay on the ground on dry grass round their fire, and I believe they have no settled place of habitation, as their houses seem'd to be built but for a few days, but wander about in small parties from place to place in search of Food and are actuated by no other motive. We never found more than three or four huts in a place, capable of containing three or four persons each only; and what is remarkable never saw the least signs either of Canoe or boat, and it is generally thought they have none, and are altogether from what we can judge, a very Ignorant and wretched set of people, tho' natives of a country capable of producing every necessary of life, and a climate the finest in the world. We found not the least signs of any minerals or metals. (Cook, II, 735)

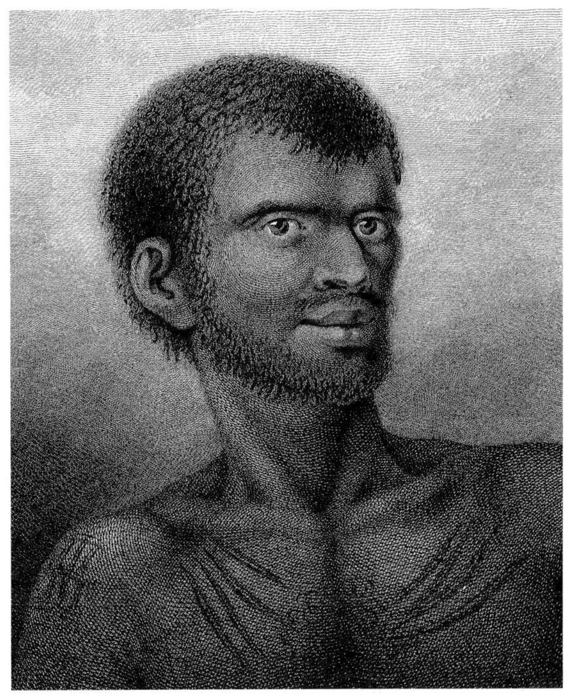

John Webber, 'A Man of Van Diemen's Land', 1784. (Mitchell Library, State Library of New South Wales.)

Cook's visit to Adventure Bay for five days in the *Resolution* in January 1777 produced extended ethnographic observations of the Tasmanians, who were friendly. Between them, Cook and his surgeon-naturalist, William Anderson, wrote about 3000 words. Cook's account was:

> In the afternoon we were agreeably surprised at the place where we were cuting Wood, with a Visit from some of the Natives, Eight men

and a boy: they came out of the Woods to us without shewing the least mark of fear and with the greatest confidence immaginable, for none of them had any weapons, except one who had in his hand a stick about 2 feet long and pointed at one end. They were quite naked & wore no ornaments, except the large punctures or ridges raised on the skin, some in straight and others in curved lines, might be reckoned as such: they were of the common stature but rather slender; their skin was black and also their hair, which was as woolly as any Native of Guinea, but they were not distinguished by remarkable thick lips nor flat noses, on the contrary their features were far from disagreeable; they had pretty good eyes and their teeth were tolerable even but very dirty; most of them had their hair and beards anointed with red ointment and some had their faces painted with the same composition. They differ in many respects from the Inhabitants of the more northern parts of this Country, nor do they seem to be that miserable people Dampier mentions to have seen on the western coast. They received every thing we gave them without the least appearence of satisfaction; some bread was given them but as soon as they understood it was to eat, they either return'd it or threw it away without so much as tasting it; and the same by fish either dress'd or undressed, but birds they kept & gave us to understand they would eat them. I shew'd them two Pigs I had brought a shore to leave in the woods, the instant they saw them they seized [them] by the ears like a dog and were for carrying them off immidiatily, with no other view as we could perceive but to kill them. As I wanted to know the use of the stick which one of them carried in his hand I made signs to them to shew me, and so far succeeded that one of them set up a mark at about 20 yards distance and threw at it, but did not seem to be a good marks man: Omai to shew them how much superior our weapons were to theirs, fired his musket at the Mark, on which they instantly ran into the woods not withstanding all we could do or say to prevent them: one of them was so frightened that he let drop an ax and two knives that were given him. From us they went to the Watering place where the Discoverys boat was taking in Water, the officer not knowing they had been with us nor what thier intent might be fired a musket in the air which sent them off as fast as their heels could carry them.

After they were gone I tooke the two Pigs a boar and a Sow, and carried them about a mile within the woods at the head of the bay and there left them by the side of a fresh Water brook. I did intend to have left also a young Bull & Cow, some sheep and Goats, and should have done it had I not been fully satisfied that the Natives would distroy them, as I am persuaided they will do the Pigs if ever they

Engraver, Johann Jacobe (1733–1797), 'Omai, a native of the island of Ulietea'. Mezzotint. Omai, a Pacific Islander, sailed to England with Furneaux in 1774 and was fêted in London by royalty, nobility, scientists and writers. He was sailing back to his home with Cook when the *Discovery* called at Van Diemen's Land. He went on from there to his homeland to astound the natives with gifts he had received — including a suit of armour, a horse and a cow. (Rex Nan Kivell Collection, National Library of Australia.)

Sir Joshua Reynolds, 'Omai of the Friendly Isles'. Pencil drawing. (Rex Nan Kivell Collection, National Library of Australia.)

meet with them; but as this is an animal that soon becomes wild and is fond of the thickest part of the woods, there is a great probability of their escaping, whereas the other Cattle must have been left in an open place where it would have been impossible for them to remain concealed many days.

WEDNESDAY 29*th.* The Morning was ushered in with a dead Calm which continued all the day and effectually prevented our sailing; I therefore sent the grass Cutters over to the East point of the bay, where I was told there was some good grass, and the Wooding party to the usual place: with this party I went my self, as several of the Natives were at this time stroling along the shore. We had not be[en] long landed before about twenty of them men and boys joined us without expressing the least fear or distrust, some of them were the same as had been with us the day before, but the greatest part were strangers. There was one who was much deformed, being humpbacked, he was not less distinguishable by his wit and humour, which he shewed on all occasions and we regreted much that we could not understand him for their language was wholy unintilligible to us: it is different from that spoken by the inhabitants of the more Northern parts of this Country, which is not extraordinary sence they differ in many other respects. Some of these men wore loose round the neck 3 or 4 folds of small Cord which was made of the fur of some animal, and others wore a narrow slip of the Kanguroo skin tied round the ankle; these were all the ornaments I saw any of them wear.

I gave each of them a string of Beads and a Medal, which I thought they received with some satisfaction. They seem'd to set no value on Iron or Iron tools nor did they seem to know the use of fish hooks; yet we cannot suppose but that people who inhabit a Sea Coast must have ways and means to catch fish, altho we did not see it, nor did we see a Canoe or any Vessel in which they could go upon the water. Either fish is plenty with them or they do not eat it for they absolutely rejected all we offered them, but I think the first the most probable: it was evedent that shel fish made a part of their food by the many heaps of Muscle shels we saw in different parts near the shore and about some deserted habitations near the head of the bay. These were little Shades or hovels built of sticks and covered with bark; we also saw evedent signs of them some times takeing up their aboad the trunks of large trees, which had been hollowed out by fire most probable for this very purpose. In or near all these habitations, and where ever there was a heap of shells there remained the marks of fire, an indubitable sign that they do not eat their food raw.

After staying about an hour with the Wooding party and the Natives and finding that the latter was not likely to give the former any disturbance, I left them and went over to the party that were cutting grass and found they had met with a fine patch. After lading the boats I left that party and return'd on board to dinner, where Mr King arrived soon after; from whom I learnt that soon after I had left him several Women and Children made there appearance, and were Interduced to him by some of the

Men; he made them all presents of such trifles as he had about him, and the Men gave them the most of what they had got from me. The Women wore a Kanguroo skin in the same shape as it came from the animal, tied over the shoulder and round the waist, but it was evidently intended for no other purpose than for the conveniency of carrying the child, for in all other respects they [are] as naked as the men, and as black, with hair of the same Colour & texture. Some had their heads wholy shaved, some only on one side, while others again shaved all the upper part and leaving a circle of hair round the head as is the custom with some Fryers. Many of the Children had fine features and were thought pretty, but the Women, especially those advanced in years, were thought otherways; Some of the Gentlemen belonging to the Discovery I was told, paid their addresses and made them large offers which were rejected with great disdain whether from a sence of Verture or for fear of displeasing the Men I shall not pretend to determine. This thing was certainly not very agreeable to the latter, for an elderly man as soon as he observed it, ordered all the Women & Children away, which they obeyed, but not without some of them shewing a little reluctancy. This conduct to Indian Women is highly blameable, as it creates a jealousy in the men that may be attended with fatal consequences, without answering any one purpose whatever, not even that of the lover obtaining the object of his wishes. I believe it has generally been found amongst uncivilized people that where the Women are easy of access, the Men are the first who offer them to strangers, and where this is not the case they are not easily come at, neither large presents nor privacy will induce them to violate the laws of chastity or custom. This observation I am sure will hold good throughout all parts of the South Sea where I have been, why then should

Anonymous, 'A New South Wales native stricking fish while his wife is employed fishing with hooks & lines in her canoe', 1788–92.

> men risk their own safety where nothing is to be obtained? (Cook, III, 54–6)

Anderson wrote:

> About four in the afternoon nine of the natives came unexpectedly to the place where our people were cutting wood. The foremost held something like a spear in his hand in a striking position, but one of the people making signs or waving something to him he drop'd it and advanc'd from the edge of the wood with three more after which the rest soon follow'd. They did not express that surprize which one might have expected from their seeing men so much unlike themselves, and things to which we were well assur'd they had been hitherto utter strangers, from whence it may reasonably be concluded they had been reconnoitring us from the wood this and the preceding day without having resolution to discover themselves. They soon became pretty familiar and after some knives and handkerchiefs had been given them they did not scruple to ask any thing they saw, yet did not seem disappointed on a refusal. One or two were detected endeavouring to pilfer but they by no means appear to be so dexterous in that respect as almost all the inhabitants of the south sea. Their attention seem'd to be more fixed on the people who cut the wood than any other object, and some of them attempted to saw in which they succeeded after a little time. We address'd them in two or three of the South sea Languages but they did not understand any of them, though they immediately repeated the word Kan'gooroo which was mentioned on seeing a piece of skin suppos'd to be of that animal, which is so nam'd by the natives whom Captn Cook met with in Botany Bay on the east Coast of New Holland in 17[70]. We desir'd one who had a blunt pointed stick in his hand about two feet long to throw it at some object that we might judge of their dexterity, but he hit several times very wide of the mark. We then put up a piece of wood and made signs we would fire at it with a musket but the report (notwithstanding they had heard several at a small distance) alarm'd them so much that several drop'd their knives and one a hatchet that was given them, and without being able to collect courage though they seem'd inclin'd to stay walk'd hastily up a path which led perhaps towards their habitation…
>
> …these Indians have little of that fierce or wild appearance common to people in their situation, but on the contrary seem mild and cheerfull without reserve or jealousy of strangers — a disposition almost constantly observ'd by Europeans amongst those who have never before had any intercourse with them. This however may arise from their having little to loss or care for…for as I have observ'd the more fruitfull or populous any country is the more likely are we to meet with opposition though with some exceptions. With respect to personal activity or genius we can say but little of either. They do not seem to posess the first in any remarkable degree, and as for the last they have to appearance less than even the half animated inhabitants of Terra del Fuego, who have not invention sufficient to make cloathing to defend themselves from the rigour of their climate though furnish'd with the materials. The small stick rudely pointed which we have already mentioned was the only thing we saw which requires any mechanical exertion, if we except some bits of Kangooras skin fix'd on their feet with thongs as amongst some labourers of other countrys, though it could not be learned whether these were in use as shoes or only to defend some sore on the feet. It must be owned, however, they are masters of some contrivance, in the manner of cutting their arms and bodies in lines of different lengths and directions, which are raised considerably above the surface of the skin, so that it is difficult to guess the method they use in executing this embroidery of their persons. Their not expressing that surprise which one might have expected from their seeing men so much unlike themselves, and things to which, we were well assured, they had been hitherto utter strangers — their indifference for our presents, and their general inattention, were sufficient proofs of their not possessing any acuteness of understanding.
>
> Their colour is a dull black, and not quite so deep as that of the African Negroes. It should seem, also, that they sometimes heightened their black colour, by smutting their bodies; as a mark

was left behind on any clean substance, such as white paper, when they handled it. Their hair, however, is perfectly woolly, and it is clotted or divided into small parcels, like that of the Hottentots, with the use of some sort of grass, mixed with a red paint or ochre, which they smear in great abundance over their heads. This practice, as some might imagine, has not the effect of changing their hair into the frizzling texture we observed; for, on examining the head of a boy, which appeared never to have been smeared, I found the hair to be of the same kind. Their noses, though not flat, are broad and full. The lower part of the face projects a good deal, as is the case of most Indians I have seen; so that a line let fall from the forehead, would cut off a much larger portion than it would in Europeans. Their eyes are of a middling size, with the white less clear than in us; and though not remarkably quick or piercing, such as give a frank, cheerful cast to the whole countenance. Their teeth are broad, but not equal, nor well set; and either from nature or from dirt, not of so true a white as is usual among people of a black colour. Their mouths are rather wide; but this appearance seems heightened by wearing their beards long, and clotted with paint, in the same manner as the hair on their heads. In other respects, they are well-proportioned; though the belly seems rather projecting. This may be owing to the want of compression there, which few nations do not use, more or less. The posture of which they seem fondest, is to stand with one side forward, or the upper part of the body gently reclined, and one hand grasping (across the back) the opposite arm, which hangs down by the projecting side. . .

What the ancient poets tell us of Fauns and Satyrs living in hollow trees, is here realised. Some wretched constructions of sticks, covered with bark, which do not even deserve the name of huts, were indeed found near the shore in the bay; but these seemed only to have been erected for temporary purposes; and many of their largest trees were converted into more comfortable habitations. These had their trunks hollowed out by fire, to the height of six or seven feet; and the hearths, made of clay, to contain the fire in the middle, leaving room for four or five persons to sit round it. At the same time, these places of shelter are durable; for they take care to leave one side of the tree sound, which is sufficient to keep it growing as luxuriantly as those which remain untouched. . .

The inhabitants of this place are, doubtless, from the same stock with those of the northern parts of New Holland. Though some of the circumstances mentioned by Dampier, relative to those he met with on the western coast of this country, such as their defective sight, and want of fore-teeth, are not found here; and though Hawkesworth's account of those met with by Captain Cook of the east side shows also that they differ in many respects, yet still. upon the whole, I am persuaded that distance of place, entire separation, diversity of climate, and length of time, all concurring to operate, will account for greater differences, both as to their persons and as to their customs, than really exist between our Van Diemen's Land natives, and those described by Dampier, and in Captain Cook's first Voyage. This is certain, that the figure of one of those seen in Endeavour River, and represented in Sidney Parkinson's Journal of that voyage, very much resembles our visitors in Adventure Bay. That there is not the like resemblance in their language, is a circumstance that need not create any difficulty. For though the agreement of the languages of people living distant from each other may be assumed as a strong argument for their having sprung from one common source, disagreement of language is by no means a proof of the contrary.

However, we must have a far more intimate acquaintance with the languages spoken here and in the more northern parts of New Holland, before we can be warranted to pronounce that they are totally different. Nay, we have good grounds for the opposite opinion; for we found that the animal called kangooroo at Endeavour River was known under the same name here; and I need not observe that it is scarcely possible to suppose that this was not transmitted from one another, but accidentally adopted by two nations, differing in language and extraction. Besides, as it seems very improbable that the Van Diemen's Land inhabitants should have ever lost the use of canoes or sailing vessels if they had been originally conveyed thither by sea, we must necessarily admit that they, as well as the kangooroo itself, have been stragglers by land from the more northern parts of the country. And if there by any force in this observation, while it traces the origin of the people, it will, at the same time, serve to fix another point, if Captain Cook and Captain Furneaux have not already decided it, that New Holland is nowhere totally divided by the sea into islands, as some have imagined.

As the New Hollanders seem all to be of the same extraction, so neither do I think there is anything peculiar in them. On the contrary, they much resemble many of the inhabitants whom I have seen at the islands Tanna and Manicola. Nay, there is even some foundation for hazarding a supposition that they may have originally come from the same place with all the inhabitants of the South Sea. For, of only about ten words which we could get from them, that which expresses cold differs little from that of New Zealand and Otaheite; the first being Mallareede, the second Makka'reede, and the third Ma'reede. The rest of our very scanty Van Diemen's Land Vocabulary is as follows:

Quadne,	A woman.
Eve'rai,	The eye.
Muidje,	The nose.
Lae'renne,	A small bird, a native of the woods here.
Ka'my,	The teeth, mouth, or tongue.
Koy'gee,	The ear.
No'onga,	Elevated scars on the body.
Teegera,	To eat
Toga'rago,	I must be gone, or I will go.

Their pronunciation is not disagreeable, but rather quick, though not more so than is that of the other nations of the South sea; and if we may depend upon the affinity of languages as a clue to discovering the origin of nations, I have no doubt but we shall find, on a diligent inquiry, and when opportunities offer to collect accurately a sufficient number of these words, and to compare them, that all the people from New Holland, eastward to Easter Island, have been derived from the same common root. (Cook, III, 784–8)

Cook was wrong in this speculation, but the way in which he arrived at it shows the growing understanding of how philology might reveal prehistory.

The English and French eighteenth-century descriptions of the east-coast and Tasmanian Aborigines mark the beginning of reliable ethnography. They also represent what knowledge the officers of the First Fleet arrived with in 1788.

8

Art and Artefacts

Seventeenth Century

Although there were some notable exceptions (such as during Johan Maurits van Nassau–Siegen's governorship of Dutch Brazil, 1637–44), seventeenth-century exploring expeditions did not usually have artists included for the purpose of making a visual record of the geography, flora, fauna and humans encountered. More often than not, visual records arose as an incidental consequence of the voyage, having been made by those with some skill at the drawing of coastal profiles, that practice which was a valuable aid to navigation.

This fact does much to explain the general paucity of visual records in the first phase of the European discovery of Australia. The multi-faceted William Dampier drew animals and plants not only from personal interest, but also with a sense of scientific description; and Willem de Vlamingh's 1696–97 expedition carried one artist who was to draw coastal profiles and other scenes of interest. Before this time, however, there are only scattered visual records — and some real puzzles.

The earliest depiction of what seems to be an Australian animal is that of a marsupial on the engraved title page of the 1597 edition of Gerard and Cornelis de Jode's *Specvlvm Orbis Terrae.* Though this depiction is imperfect, the animal is recognisable enough as a kangaroo. There is a second depiction of a marsupial, this time a wallaby, in Cornelis de Bruin's *Reizen over Moskovie, door Persie en Indie* (Amsterdam, 1714). In all probability, the Dutch acquired knowledge of these animals as a consequence of their contact with New Guinea and adjacent islands, which share fauna and flora with Australia. (De Bruyn's animal, for example, is a filander, a type of wallaby occurring on the Aru Islands.)

Diego Prado de Tovar, who accompanied Torres on his 1606 voyage, has left a number of drawings of Melanesians, some of them from islands in Torres Strait, but evidently not of Aborigines.

The first known depictions of an event in the early European discovery of Australia are a set of engravings showing the wreck of the *Batavia* on Houtman Abrolhos in 1629, and its bizarre aftermath. Published in Amsterdam in 1647, these crude illustrations show scenes of the shipwreck, mayhem, and the punishment of the mutineers.

Tasman sailed with instructions to construct a visual record of his discoveries; and one of his draughtsmen accordingly drew some 21 coastal profiles. Some of them have titles that now seem rather quaint — for example, 'A view of the coast when you are six miles from it'; 'A view of this land as you sail along it from Maria's Island to Schouten Island'. Interestingly, this artist did use some colour, and he also depicted the ships at sea. In New Zealand and Tonga, he drew some human scenes, but had no opportunity to do so in Tasmania, where the Dutch did not see Aborigines.

Entered on the ship's books as 'consoler of the sick', Victor Victorszoon was also the artist of de Vlamingh's expedition. He produced at least eighteen delicate watercoloured coastal profiles, fifteen of them of western Australia. He may also have been the artist responsible for three

Left: John Webber, portrait of Captain John Gore, oil on canvas. (Rex Nan Kivell Collection); National Library of Australia.)

Below left: 'Laughing kookaburra (*Dacelo novaeguineae*)'. This 'Grand martin-Pecheur de la Nouvelle Guinee' appears in plate 106 of Pierre Sonnerat's *Voyage à la Nouvelle Guinee* (1776). The caption wrongly ascribed this bird to New Guinea. In 1770 Joseph Banks had caught kookaburras in what was to be known as Australia. He gave this specimen to Sonnerat at the Cape of Good Hope that year. (Mitchell Library, State Library of New South Wales.)

Below right: Rainbow lorikeet (*Trichoglossus haematodus*) in P. Brown's *New Illustrations of Zoology* (1776). This bird, caught at Botany Bay, was Tupaia's pet. Tupaia died at Batavia, but the bird reached England aboard the *Endeavour* and was painted there by Brown. (Australian Museum.)

John Allcot, OBE, FRAS (1888–1973), *Roebuck*. Captain William Dampier's ship of the Royal Navy drops anchor in what was to be Shark's Bay on 6 August 1699. (Courtesy of the Australasian Pioneers' Club.)

Johannes van Keulen (1654–1715), 'Swartte Swaane drift op het Eyland Rottenest', *c.* 1726. Copper engraving, showing black swans near Rottnest Island. (Rex Nan Kivell Collection, NK2110; National Library of Australia.)

The 'Filander' (wallaby) was illustrated first in C. de Bruin, *Reizen over Moscovie door Persie en Indie,* 1714. (Mitchell Library, State Library of New South Wales.)

watercolours of Australian fishes, which are now lost. Again, one of his works may well have formed the basis of the engraving in Francois Valentijn's *Ouden Nieuw Oost–Indien* (Amsterdam, 1724-26), which shows de Vlamingh's crews capturing black swans at the mouth of the Swan River.

William Dampier produced more pictorial records of things Australian than all the VOC discoverers — as he wrote in *A Voyage to New Holland*:

> Having had in the Ship with me a Person skill'd in Drawing, I have by this means been enabled, for the greater Satisfaction of the Curious Reader, to present him with exact Cuts and Figures of several of the principal and most remarkable of those Birds, Beasts, Fishes and Plants, which are described in the following Narrative. (Dampier, 1906, 343)

The identity of Dampier's artist is unknown. Professor Bernard Smith has commented:

> seven sheets of drawings...are of direct interest to Australia. One contains nine coastal profiles and a chart of the Shark Bay area, one is of water birds found on the New Holland coast,

three are of plants found mainly in the same area, and two are of fishes. The drawings of birds, plants and fishes are the first authentic drawings of Australian natural history subjects and as such their historical importance is too obvious to require stressing. Those of the plants are much more skilled and professional in execution than those of the birds and fishes, from which it may well be supposed that they were drawn in England by a capable artist from the specimens which Dampier took home with him. But although the drawings of the birds and fishes are comparatively crude they are accurate enough for experts to identify.

The record is even sparser where artefacts are concerned. Tasman's crew are known to have acquired some stone adzes at Tonga in 1643, but as they had no contact with Aborigines in Tasmania, they had no opportunity of obtaining Australian items. And as there are no journals extant from the 1644 voyage, it is impossible to know if Tasman collected any items from northern Australia.

In 1658, Jacob Pieterszoon Peerboom acquired some stone axes at Geographe Bay in south-west Australia. One of these certainly reached Amsterdam, but its whereabouts are now unknown.

The situation is similar with Dampier. He is known to have collected two stone tools in New Guinea, which are now in a Cambridge museum, but the whereabouts of any artefacts he may have taken from Australia are unknown.

Eighteenth Century

While there is a handful of charts and drawings of Australian scenes from the other voyages of the period 1768–80, it is to Cook's *Endeavour* voyage that we must turn for what is incomparably the richest visual collection before 1788. Not only did Cook himself and his junior officers produce a series of charts and profiles of the eastern coast, but Sydney Parkinson and Herman Spöring, the draughtsmen/artists employed by Banks, also left many drawings of plants, and some of animals, fish and people.

Parkinson's principal task was to draw the plants collected by Banks and Solander. There are extant 276 finished and 676 unfinished works of this sort. However, particularly after Alexander Buchan's death at Tahiti in April 1769, Parkinson also extended his hand to zoological depictions (83 finished, 210 unfinished), and ethnographic and landscape subjects (*c.*140, in various states of completion). There are also extant 60 pencil drawings by Spöring, which include some Australian subjects. And there are a few works by other people on the voyage. The bulk of these drawings are in the Natural History Museum and the British Library in London.

The last decades have seen extensive, often sumptuous, publication of these works. The portfolio accompanying J.C. Beaglehole's editions of Cook's *Journals* (1969) reproduces the charts and coastal views, including nine attributed to Cook himself. More recently, there has been a more extensive edition of these works, accompanied by a scholarly apparatus: Andrew David, *et al.* (ed.) *The Charts and Coastal Views of Captain Cook's Voyages* (Hakluyt Society, London, 1988–).

A large selection of Parkinson's drawings was reproduced in D.J. Carr (ed.), *Sydney Parkinson: Artist of Cook's 'Endeavour' Voyage* (British Museum [Natural History] in association with the Australian National University Press, Canberra, 1983). Then, in 1985 there appeared the first volume of the splendid series edited by Bernard Smith and Rüdiger Joppien, *The Art of Captain Cook's Voyages* (Oxford University Press, Melbourne, 1985–87). Even more ambitious has been *Banks' Florilegium* (Alecto Historical Editions, London, 1980). On their return to London, Banks and Solander employed eighteen engravers over thirteen years to prepare plates from the specimens collected and drawings done on the circumnavigation. Some 738 of these plates, which require an unusual and complicated printing process were made, but never used. Now, after more than 200 years, the results are at last available to the public — though with the whole work costing over $100 000, the general public has had to limit its buying to selected individual items. The National Library of Australia and the major state libraries have acquired sets of what a spokesperson for the Smithsonian Institute in Washington has described as 'one of the world's great scientific and artistic treasures'.

It is from Parkinson that we have the first known

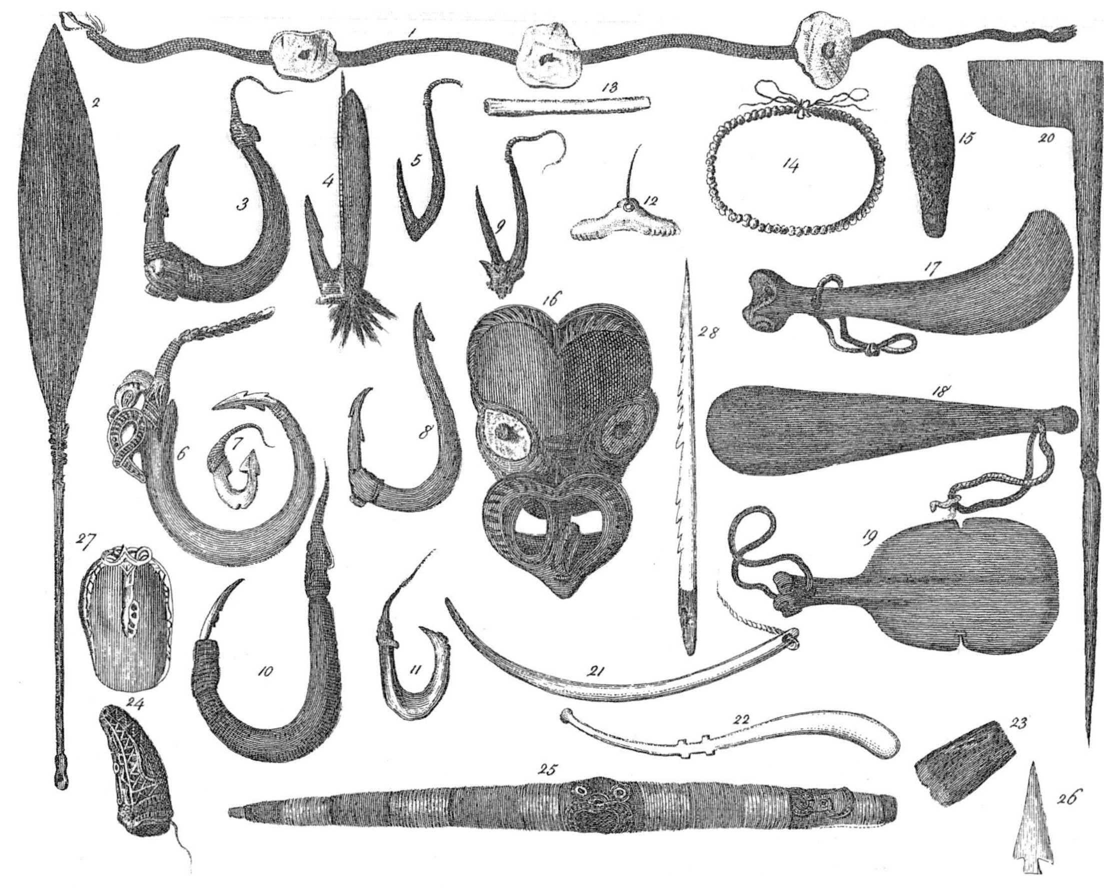

'Various kinds of Instruments Utensils &c, of the Inhabitants of New Zealand, with some Ornaments &c, of the people of Terra del Fuego & New Holland', S.H. Grimm, del.; T. Chambers Sc. Plate xxvi in Sydney Parkinson's *Journal of a Voyage to the South Seas.* (Facsimile edition, Libraries Board of South Australia, 1972.)

depictions of Aborigines. One of his sheets contains ten drawings, variously of an Aboriginal man and woman, a bark hut, bark canoes, and shields. It is uncertain whether these were done at Botany Bay or Endeavour River, but perhaps at the former location. A second group, done at Endeavour River, shows nests of white ants, a spear thrower, spear head, shields, a man wearing a European shirt and holding a spear, two huts, and a canoe with an Aborigine paddling. There is also the curious drawing by the person known as the Artist of the First Mourner (who may have been Banks himself), of Aborigines paddling and fishing from bark canoes.

There are comparatively few zoological drawings. Spöring has left six of fish, two of crabs and one of a cockatoo. There are two Parkinson sketches of kangaroos in flight; an unspecified mammal (probably a native cat); a banksia cockatoo; three fish; two turtles; crab lavae and a medusa; a type of jellyfish; and termite mounds. There are also three unfinished sketches by Parkinson of the hull of the *Endeavour* as it was being careened.

There is a handful of drawings and paintings done at a remove, from specimens brought from Australia. In England, the noted animal artist George Stubbs painted his famous kangaroo from Parkinson's sketches, and from the skin and skull of the animal shot at Endeavour River. It is possible that Stubbs also depicted a dingo from a skin, but this is uncertain. A few years later, Peter Brown published an engraving of a rainbow lorikeet in his *New Illustrations of Zoology* (London, 1776), the original drawing being of a bird captured at Botany Bay in 1770 and kept as a pet by Tupaia and then taken to England. In this same year, Pierre Sonnerat published an engraving of the kookaburra given to him by Banks at the Cape of Good Hope, in his fictitious *Voyage à la Nouvelle Guinée* (Paris, 1776).

Many of the original drawings done by Banks' artists were subsequently worked up by others to obtain the engravings published in accounts of the voyage — see, for example, 'Two of the Natives of New Holland, Advancing to Combat', plate 46 in Parkinson's *A Journal of a Voyage to the South Seas* (London, 1773, 1784); and the depiction of the *Endeavour* being repaired, plate 19 in John Hawkesworth, *An Account of the Voyages...for making Discoveries in the Southern Hemisphere* (London, 1773). Progressively, other versions reached a wide audience via the myriad summaries of the voyage in collections of voyages and travels and in geography books.

The officers of both French expeditions of 1772 charted the coasts they saw. Their logs and charts are variously in the Archives Nationales and the Bibliotheque Nationale, Paris. For the most part, these visual records remain unpublished.

During his brief stay at Tasmania in 1773, Tobias Furneaux and his officers produced charts of the southern and eastern coasts, and profiles of Adventure Bay. Furneaux also took two birds, a

Charles Praval, 'Portrait of an Australian Aborigine'. The Aborigine is shown wearing a shirt given to him by one of the *Endeavour*'s crew. (British Library, London.)

white goshawk and a crested penguin, to New Zealand where Johann Reinhold and Georg Forster, the naturalists on board the *Resolution*, described and drew them. In October 1774, Joseph Gilbert, the master of the *Resolution*, charted sections of Norfolk Island.

The next European visit to Adventure Bay, Tasmania, by Cook in 1777, produced a somewhat larger visual record. William Bligh drew a chart of the coast seen by the *Resolution* and *Adventure*, and William Ellis produced a 'View of the Fluted Cape, Van Diemen's Land, New Holland'. John Webber, the artist of the voyage, drew a number of studies of humans — of an Aboriginal man, and an Aboriginal woman carrying a child. He also sketched an opossum, a blue-tongue lizard and three birds — the superb blue wren, the yellow-winged honeyeater, and the striated pardalote. William Ellis, surgeon's mate, made more than 100 drawings of fish and Tasmanian birds and seabirds between Tasmania and New Zealand. Four of these drawings are coloured — the green rosella, the hooded dotterel, the black-faced cuckoo shrike and the superb blue wren. John Webber was also the artist of 'Cook's interview with Natives in Adventure Bay, Van Diemen's Land 24 January, 1777'.

These works are variously in the British Library, the Natural History Museum and Whitehall Library, Ministry of Defence, London; and in La Trobe Library, State Library of Victoria. They have been reproduced in the portfolio of charts accompanying Cook's *Journals*, and in the later volumes of *The Art of Cook's Voyages* and *The Charts and Coastal Views of Captain Cook's Voyages*.

The story concerning artefacts collected on these voyages is similar to that for the seventeenth-century voyages. Cook and Banks gathered numbers of what they knew as 'artificial curiosities' at Botany Bay and Endeavour River in 1770. We know they brought them back to England for, among other signs, John Miller drew a shield and a number of spears in 1771. The shield is likely that preserved in the British Museum's Department of Ethnography. However, of approximately 40 spears collected on the voyage, only a handful can now be located. A few items — for example, two boomerangs and two clubs — are in the Australian Museum in Sydney.

The records do not say whether Du Fresne and his officers collected any artefacts during their six days' stay at North Bay in 1772. However, the next year, Furneaux recorded how he:

> found some bags and netts made of Grass, which I imagine [the Aborigines] carry their provisions and other necessaries in. In one of them there was the stone they strike fire with and Tinder made of Bark, but of what tree could not find out. We found in one of their huts one of their spears, it was sharp at one end done I suppose with a shell or stone: Those things we brought away and left in room of them, Medals, Gun flints and a few Nails, and an old empty barrel with the Iron hoops on it. (Cook, II, 735)

Again, however, these items cannot be properly traced.

Part III

The Naming of Australian Places

1606–1756

Europeans named many conspicuous landmarks and other localities where they anchored or which they passed on the coastlines of continental Australia and Tasmania in the 171 years between 1606 and 1777. While many of these names are not now in use, 35 given by the Dutch navigators and William Dampier remain, as do dozens bestowed by James Cook and those who accompanied him. In the following calendar these names are listed in chronological order, together with details of the explorers, their ships, their descriptions, physical details and modern commemorations. All measurements and distances are approximate. It will be apparent that the calendar contains no Aboriginal place names. None of the explorers stayed long enough to learn more than a few Aboriginal words, and these did not include place names.

1606

Willem Jansz, explorer, of the *Duyfken* (Little Dove)

Cape Keer-Weer (Turn Again) is an indistinct promontory of tidal flats, 380 kilometres south of Cape York, on the western coast of Cape York Peninsula. Probably in March, Jansz turned back because he was short of food and water. A chart of his voyage included 320 kilometres of the Australian coast between Cape York and Cape Keer-Weer.

A VOC map published in 1622 showed seven places named on the chart, the first European ones bestowed in the country; only Cape Keer-Weer is still on maps. As the chart shows only one trace for his voyage up and down the coast, the order of the placing of names is not known. Jansz's landfall at Pennefather River is shown as R met het Bosch (River with Bush). He apparently anchored at Albatross Bay, now the site of the township and port of Weipa's bauxite industry, conducted by Comalco.

This illustration by Geoffrey C. Ingleton for *Heemskerck Shoals*, by Robert D. FitzGerald, was published by the Mountainside Press, 1949. It shows a Dutch leadsman with a lead line which tested the depth of water near coasts. (Mitchell Library, State Library of New South Wales.)

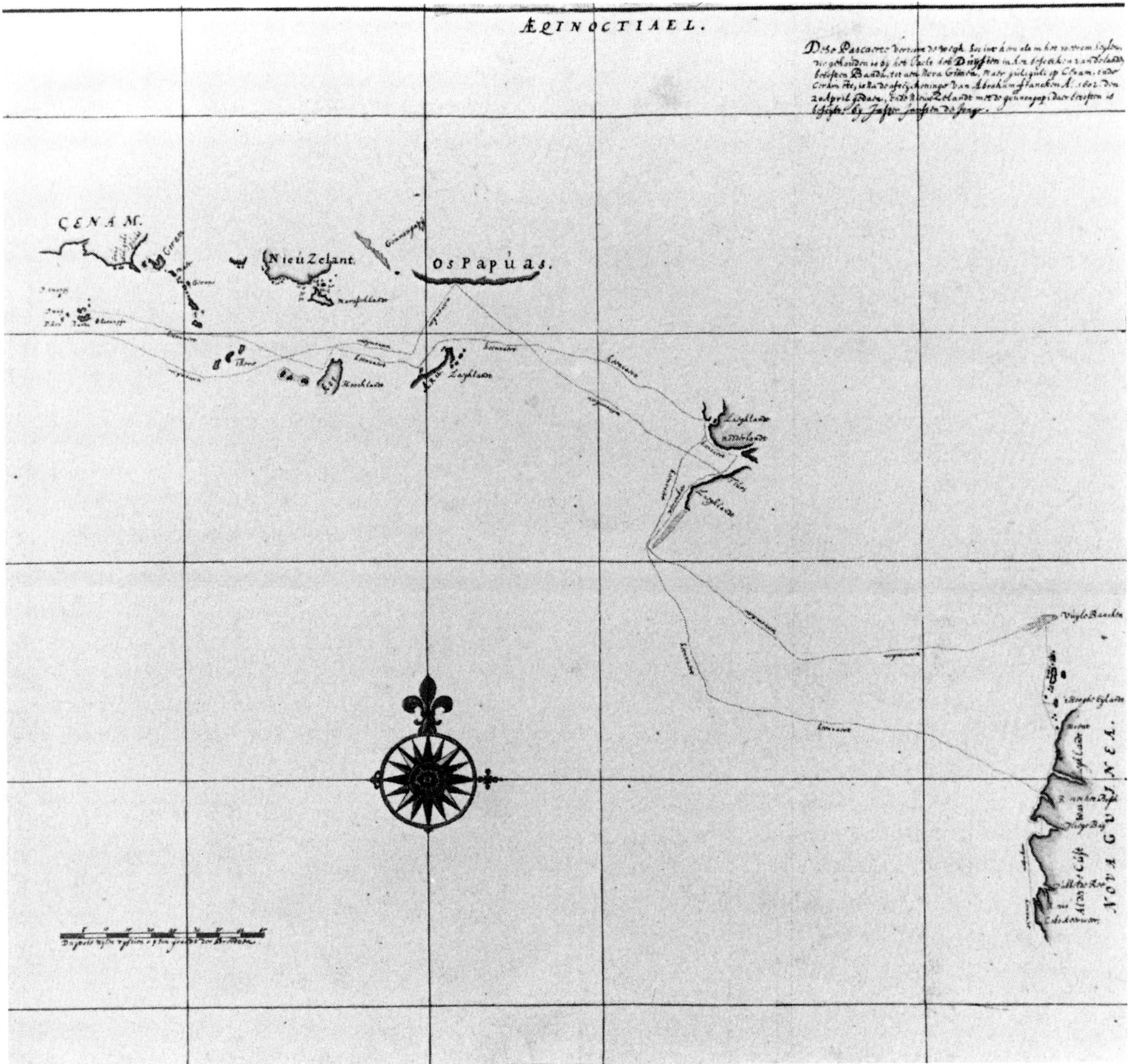

Chart of the *Duyfken*'s route 1605–06, from the *Van der Hem* atlas. (Osterreichische Nationalbibliothek, Vienna.)

His name for it, Vliege Bay (Fly Bay), may have come from bothersome flies or mosquitoes. Between here and Cape Keer-Weer names are Doublede Riv (Two Rivers) at the Archer and Watson Rivers and R Vis (Fish River), now the Dugally River.

On the northward course the *Duyfken* anchored and probably watered at Port Musgrave, north of his landfall. It is charted but not named. Port Musgrave is a natural harbour with an expanse of 8 kilometres for estuaries of rivers but regular use is not made of it. A boat went up the Wenlock River (one historian says 32 kilometres) and Aborigines killed one of the crew. Farther north names are: Moent, which is obscure and is now Crab Island; and 't Hooghe [high] Eyelandt, now Prince of Wales Island, west of Cape York and on the northern side of Endeavour Strait, Cook's passage through Torres Strait.

Matthew Flinders, noted hydrographer and navigator, commemorated Jansz's anchorage at Albatross Bay by naming the bay's northern headland Duyfken Point. John Forsyth, a Sydney historian, had a plaque recording Jansz's first known sighting of the continent placed at Duyfken Point.

Port Musgrave and Pennefather River have no memorials to his presence.

Jansz's log and journal are lost, although, as well as his chart, his experiences were known to later explorers. He was one of the most active of the VOC's mariners, landing at Exmouth Gulf on the west coast in 1618 as supercargo from the ship *Mauritius*and becoming a governor in the East Indies and an admiral.

Although Jansz's discovery of the continent is indisputable, no records of actual landings exist. It is inconceivable that he did not land. He was looking for Marco Polo's Beach, and its gold and other metals. He would certainly have landed to look for water. A boat went up the Wenlock River and certainly would have landed to show gold and metals to the Aborigines; and seventeen years later the next explorer in the vicinity, Carstenz, obtained a piece of metal from an Aboriginal, who presumably got it from the people on the *Duyfken.*

Historians, however, do not take landings for granted. In *Northmost Australia,* J.L. Jack takes an extreme stance that the crewman the Aborigines killed there 'may have been speared in the boat'.

1616

Dirk Hartog, of the merchantman *Eendracht* (Harmony)

Dirk Hartog Island is 77 kilometres long and up to 11 kilometres wide, lying along the north-western side of the entrance to Shark Bay on the central coast of Western Australia. Hartog landed at the northern extremity of the island, about 7 kilometres from West Point, the most westerly point on the continent. A globe published in Amsterdam in 1625 indicates the vicinity of Hartog's landfall by the European name given to part of the continent: Het Landt van Eendracht. It was the first name commonly used for the continent.

Hartog affixed an inscribed pewter plate to a post, now marked by a post known as Inscription Post, about 110 metres from Cape Inscription. The inscription reads:

> 1616
> On the 25th of October there arrived here the ship den Eendracht of Amsterdam; Supercargo Gilles Miebais of Leige; skipper Dirck Hartich of Amsterdam; she set sail again on 27th do. Subcargo [second merchant] Jan Stins; upper steersman [first mate] Pieter E. Doores of Bil. Dated 1616.

Eighty-one years later in 1697, another VOC mariner, Willem De Vlamingh, landed on the island which he named for Hartog. He was in command of three ships — *Geelvinck* (Yellow Finch), *Nüptang* (Little Nipper) and *Weseltje* (Small Weasel) — searching for a shipwreck and revising charts of the coast. De Vlamingh discovered Hartog's plate, took it away and put another pewter plate there commemorating both Hartog's visit and his own. The Hartog plate, the oldest European relic from Australia, eventually reached Amsterdam and is now in the Rijkskmuseum. De Vlamingh's plate, of 36 centimetres diameter, reads:

> 1697. On 4th of February 1697 arrived here the vessel Geelvinck of Amsterdam. Commander and skipper Willem de Vlamingh of Vlielandt; assistant, Joannes Bremer of Copenhagen; head steersman, Michil Bloem of Bremen. The hooker Nyptangh: skipper Gerrit Colaart of Amsterdam; assistant, Theodoris Heirmans' of the same place; head steersman, Gerrfidt Geritsen of Bremen. The galliot Het Wesseltje: master, Cornelis de Vlamingh of Vlielandt; steersman, Coert Gerritsen of Bremen. Our fleet set sail from here to continue exploring the Southern Land on the way to Batavia.

In 1801 a French explorer, Captain Hamelin of *Le Naturaliste,* saw de Vlamingh's plate half buried in sand and affixed it to a new post. He named the place Cape Inscription. In 1818 Louis de Saulces de Freycinet, who had been with Hamelin, returned there as commander of *L'Uranie.* Finding the plate still in the sand, he took it to the Royal Academy of Inscriptions and Belles Lettres in France. The de Vlamingh and Hamelin posts were removed in 1908 to the Western Australian Museum. They are now displayed at the Maritime Museum at Fremantle. De Vlamingh's post was callistris cypress from Rottnest Island.

Australians began seeking the de Vlamingh plate in 1938. It was believed lost but it turned up in a cupboard at the Museum of Paris in 1944. The plate came to the Western Australian Museum in 1950. In the 1950s the museum also sought the Hartog plate. It had to be content with a replica, as the Netherlands government declared that the plate was 'one of the most precious relics from the golden age of the Netherlands voyages of discovery'.

During Australia's sesquicentenary in 1938, the Commonwealth government put an inscribed tablet at Cape Inscription lighthouse, Dirk Hartog Island. The inscription on the tablet recounts the history of the locality and ends with these words: 'This memorial plate was placed here by the Commonwealth Government of Australia in 1938 to commemorate the first recorded landing of Europeans in Australia'.

Dirk Hartog Island is now used as a sheep station. The only other activity comes from occasional visits of fishermen and tourists.

1619

Frederick de Houtmann, of the merchantman *Dordrecht* (a commune's name)

Houtmann Abrolhos consists of three groups of islands — Wallabi, Easter and Pelsaert islands — and coral riders extending 80 kilometres in a north-westerly direction; they are 70 kilometres offshore from Geraldton, on the central west coast 425 kilometres north of Perth. Houtmann discovered them on 9 July. He marked his chart Abri voll olos, meaning in Portuguese 'Beware; keep eyes open'. A cartographer in 1627–28 gave the island groups their names. Guano and phosphate were once obtained from the islands. They are now the main base of the Western Australia lobster fishery of more than 350 boats, and home to some of the fishermen and their families. Air and boat tours are available.

1622

Unknown skipper of merchantman *Leeuwin* (Lioness)

Cape Leeuwin is the most south-westerly extremity of the continent. A cartographer charted it as Land van der Leeuwin in 1628. Flinders named the cape. The name Leeuwin survives but is seldom used. Cape Leeuwin is 325 kilometres south of Perth, adjoins the town of Augusta, and is in a national park.

1623

Jan Carstensz, explorer, of the *Pera* (a commune's name in Malaya)

Gulf of Carpentaria, a deep indentation on the northern coast, partly in Queensland and in the Northern Territory, is 400 kilometres wide at its mouth and recedes 550 kilometres southward to its head. Carstensz explored its eastern shore, which is the Cape York Peninsula, and named it for the VOC Governor-General, Pieter Carpentier, who sent him to explore it.

The gold Carstensz sought particularly was found in the 1870s at the Palmer River and Coen in the Cooktown region on the eastern side of the peninsula and in 1887 at Croydon, 180 kilometres inland from Karumba, the port of Normanton on the Norman River at the head of the Gulf. The region has cattle and prawning industries.

Staten River is 110 kilometres north of Karumba. Carstensz wrote:

> since according to resolution it was agreed to make the return journey [northward] from here we have had a wooden column, in the absence of stone, nailed to a tree, there being carved thereon the following words:
>
> In the year 1623 on April 24 there came two ships [the other was the *Arnhem*; skipper Willem Joosten van Coolsteerdt] sent by the High and Mighty States General! Accordingly the aforenamed river is entitled in the newly made chart the Staten river.

It was named for the Sates General, the Netherlands parliament.

Nassau River was named on 28 April for the house of Orange-Nassau. It is 160 kilometres north of Karumbah.

Coen River was named Dubbelde Ree by Jansz in 1606; Carstensz renamed it on 7 May for a Governor-General, Jan Pieterszoon Coen. It was renamed Archer in 1865 for the Archer family of Gracemere near Rockhampton, central Queensland.

Discoverers of gold in 1876 gave the name Coen to a tributary of the Archer. It is 80 kilometres south of Weipa.

Van Spoult Head, on the north-western coast of the top of Cape York, was named for the Governor of Ambon, Hermann van Sp(e)oult.

1623

Willem van Coolsteerdt, explorer, of the *Arnhem* (a commune's name)

Arnhem Land, on the western coast of the gulf, is 78 000 square kilometres in area. It was named originally as Arnhem Islands in error for the eastern extremity of Arnhem Land. The VOC referred to it as Arnhemsland. Van Coolsteerdt made the discovery on the way home to Batavia after parting from Carstensz. It is now the north-east corner of the Northern Territory and has been an Aboriginal reserve since 1931. A bauxite deposit is worked by Nabalco at the north-eastern extremity.

Cape Arnhem is a low grassy projection at the north-eastern extremity of Arnhem Land and the entrance to the Gulf. Van Coolsteerdt charted it as De Caep Hollandie.

1624

Unknown skipper of merchantman *Tortelduyf* (Turtle Dove)

Turtle Dove Shoal: The skipper sighted the shoal south of Houtmann Abrolhos. A cartographer charted it with the ship's name in 1628.

1627

Pieter Nuyts, a member of the council of India, and Francis Thijssen, skipper of the merchantman *Gulden Zeepard* (Golden Seahorse)

St Peter and **St Francis Islands** are the largest islands in Nuyts Archipelago, extending 65 kilometres in the Great Australian Bight. Nuyts and Thijssen named them after their patron saints. They sighted the continent on 26 January and sailed eastward in the Southern Ocean for 1600 kilometres from Cape Leeuwin to a point near Ceduna, a township to the west of Eyre Peninsula. They turned back at the archipelago of 30 islands which Flinders named for Nuyts in 1802.

St Peter Island, three kilometres off Cape Vivonne, is 33 square kilometres in area. It has been used for sheep farming.

St Francis, the second largest island in the archipelago, is 40 kilometres south-west of Cape Vivonne. Since 1888 it has been mined for guano and been used for sheep farming. A lighthouse is on the island. The port of Streaky Bay, in the locality, erected a memorial to Nuyts' ship's visit in 1927, its tercentenary.

Jonathan Swift, the Irish satirist who wrote *Gulliver's Travels* in 1726, placed Lilliput and Blufescu in the locality of Nuyts Archipelago. This placing was perhaps inspired by Purry's 1717 proposal for a Dutch colony in the area. Purry argued that it possessed the best climate in the world.

1636

Pieter Pieterszoon, explorer of the *Cleen* (new) *Amsterdam* and *Wessel* (weasel)

Van Diemen Gulf is formed by Coburg Island on the east coast, Melville Island on the west — at the top of the north-western coast of the Northern Territory. It is 65 kilometres wide and recedes to 120 kilometres. Pool's exploratory expedition was the first of three organised by Governor General van Diemen.

Wessel Islands is a group of islands extending 12 kilometres north-east from Napier Point in north-east Arnhem land. In 1622 Coolsteerdt named them the Speult Islands. Pool renamed them after one of his ships. The islands were renowned for Aboriginal rock paintings and have extensive deposits of bauxite.

1642

Abel Janszoon Tasman, explorer, of the *Heemskerck* (a commune's name) and *Zeehaen* (Sea Cock)

De Witt Island is one of several small, desolate islands in the Maatsuyker group, 16 kilometres south-east of South West Cape, Tasmania, and extending 20 kilometres southward. Tasman named it on 27 November. Fishermen know De Witt Island as 'Big Witch'. The name properly should be Witsen, a member of the VOC council at Batavia.

Maatsuyker Island is the most southerly of Australian lighthouses. It was named on 28 November, after another member of the council at Batavia.

Pedra Blanca is a rocky islet 24 kilometres off South-East Cape. The guano covering it reminded Tasman on 29 November of Pedra Blanca or White Rock, a Portuguese-named landmark off the coast of China.

Boreel Head: Tasman named an island off the south-east extremity of Bruny Island Boreel Island, after a member of the Batavia Council, but in 1773 Captain Tobias Furneaux, of the *Adventure*, who was on Captain Cook's second expedition, changed the name to The Fryers, now called The Friars. Boreel's name is preserved in a nearby headland.

Storm Bay: Tasman gave this name to a bay on the eastern side of South Bruny Island because he could not land there. It is now Adventure Bay. Furneaux gave it the name of his ship, and Tasman's name, Storm Bay, to D'Entrecasteaux Channel. The western side of Storm Bay is now the estuary of the Derwent River. It is 20 kilometres wide and recedes as far.

Tasman Island is a rocky, bare, rugged and flat-topped island at the south-eastern extremity of Tasman Peninsula and ten kilometres south-east of Port Arthur. It was named on 29 November.

Frederick Henry Bay was named on 1 December for the Stadtholder (Chief Magistrate) of the Netherlands. Tasman anchored 53 kilometres east of Hobart off Visscher Island in North Bay at Marion Bay's southern end.

His landing of eighteen men on 2 December was made 6 kilometres to the north-east in Frederick Henry Bay, an almost landlocked bay of 40 square kilometres connected with Marion Bay by a channel. In 1773 Furneaux transferred the name to an unconnected bay on the western side of Forestier Peninsula. Tasman's landing bay is now Blackman's Bay. On 3 December he had a flag planted on the north-western corner of Blackman's Bay to take possession of the country.

In 1923 the Royal Society of Tasmania placed an obelisk at Tasman's flag-planting site, about 8 kilometres from Dunalley and 58 kilometres from Hobart. A memorial at Dunalley commemorates the 300th anniversary of Tasman's presence. In 1953, the 300th anniversary of Tasman's birth, the Tasmanian government placed a plaque in the Groeingen village of Lutiegast where Tasman was born, 210 kilometres north of Amsterdam.

Maria's Island, 6 kilometres offshore and 24 kilometres north of Cape Frederick Hendrick, was named on 4 December for Van Diemen's wife, Maria Van Aelst. Its area is 100 square kilometres. The highest point is Bishop and Clerk, two huge rocks one above the other. The island is a national park 83 kilometres from Hobart. Darlington, an historic township at the northern end of the island, was a convict centre to 1850. It once had vineyards and silk and cement production industries, having commercial deposits of limestone.

Schouten Island is 34 square kilometres and situated 2 kilometres off the southern extremity of Freycinet Peninsula. It was named on 4 December for Justus Schouten, a member of the Batavia council. Once a whaling station, with coal and tin mines and sheep pasture, it is now part of Freycinet National Park and is uninhabited.

1644

Abel Tasman, explorer, *Limmen* (Limè), *Zeemeeu* (Seagull) and *Bracq* (a type of dog)

Van Diemen Inlet, on the east coast of the Gulf of Carpentaria, is a mouth of the Smithburne River and an outlet of the Gilbert River. Fifty kilometres north-east of the Norman River, it is more than a kilometre wide and recedes for 3 kilometres.

Caron River joins the Norman River at Normanton. Tasman's Caron River is the mouth of the Flinders River, south-west of Normanton. Franz Caron was a VOC executive.

Cape Van Diemen the north-east extremity of Mornington Island, is the largest island in the

Wellesley group of 22 offshore islands, south-western coast of the Gulf of Carpentaria. Mornington Island is about 65 kilometres long and 10–40 kilometres wide.

Cape Vanderlin, the northern extremity of Vanderlin Island, is the most easterly and largest of five inshore islands in the Sir Edward Pellew group, sheltering the entrance to the McArthur River, on the south-western coast of the Northern Territory. Cornelis Vanderlin was a member of the Batavia council.

Limmen Bight, a broad indentation on the south-eastern coast of Arnhem Land, extends 40 kilometres, recedes 16 kilometres and was named for Tasman's main ship. The Phelp, Roper and Limmen Bight rivers flow into it.

Maria Island is a small island 15 kilometres offshore in Limmen Bight.

Groote Eyelandt (Great Island) is a low-lying island, 35 kilometres east of Arnhem Land, 64 kilometres long from north to south and up to 64 kilometres wide, 630 kilometres east of Darwin. The island has a manganese mine operated by the Broken Hill Proprietary Ltd and a small township and a prawning industry.

Crocodile Islands are three islands and several islets in the Arafura Sea, 80 kilometres west of the Wessel Islands.

Cape Van Diemen is a narrow, low sandy point, the north-west extremity of Melville Island, off the north-west of the Northern Territory.

1658

Samuel Volkersen, of the merchantman, *Wackened Boey* (Vigilant Buoy)

Rottnest Island is 11 kilometres long, up to 3.5 kilometres wide and in sight of and 24 kilometres west of Perth. Houtmann saw it in 1619 but did not explore it. From the *Wackened Boey* which was searching for castaways and the *Vergulde Draeck* (Gilt Dragon), wrecked 80 kilometres north of Perth in 1656, an officer landed and explored the island. On 30 December 1696 de Vlamingh visited the island and saw no birds, only animals resembling large rats, hence his name for it — 'Rats Nest'. They were quokkas, the smallest of the scrub wallabies and about the size of a hare.

The island has many bays, sandy beaches and inland salt-water lakes. It was at various times a pilot station for the port of Fremantle, an Aboriginal reformatory, an internment camp, because of its strategic position a military establishment during World War II, and a source of salt. Its main lighthouse is the first Australian landmark for ships arriving via the Indian Ocean. The island is a popular tourist resort. Only a few residents are permitted to have cars; others walk or ride bicycles. A memorial tablet to de Vlamingh was placed there in 1935.

A legend about Rottnest Island as the Isle of Girls came from a French mistranslation of a narrative of de Vlamingh's expedition. The translator wrote he was approaching Mist-Eiland (Fog or Dung Island). The Dutch word *mist* (fog or dung) was misread as *meisji* (girls). On some maps the island was named Maidens' Isle. Carried away by enthusiasm for the idea, the translator continued:

> We perceived a very agreeable belt of trees, very thick and about half a league in extent. The trees were planted in line by the industry of man to form a park...I had great pleasure in admiring the island...HERE IT SEEMS THAT NATURE HAS SPARED NOTHING TO RENDER THIS ISLE DELIGHTFUL ABOVE ALL OTHERS THAT I HAVE EVER SEEN. It is very well disposed for the support of man having wood and stone and lime for building houses, and wanting only labourers to cultivate these fine plains where one finds salt in abundance while the coast swarms with fish. There one hears the chatter of the birds, which make these odorous woods resound with their sweet songs. Thus I believe that of so many people who seek to make themselves happy there would be many who would despise the fortune of our country to choose this, which would appear to them A TERRESTRIAL PARADISE.

1697

Willem de Vlamingh, explorer, with the *Geelvinck* (Finch), *Nijptangh* (Pincers) and *Weseltje* (Small Weasel).

Swan River: The expedition was at Rottnest Island and Swan River for a fortnight in 1696–97. On 4 January 86 soldiers and sailors went ashore on the mainland at what is now South Cottesloe. Apart from castaways from wrecks, the party was the largest known to have landed anywhere on the continent to this date. They were ashore on seven days and explored about 80 kilometres of the Swan River, later the site of Perth. The only discovery that interested them was black swans, the legendary bird of the ancients. They captured a number, bringing three to Batavia, which died before they could be sent to Holland.

De Vlamingh named the Swart Swanne (Black Swan) river. Nicolaas Witsen, principal director of VOC, Burgomaster of Amsterdam and one of the initiators of the expedition, commented favourably on an early report of the results, in which he said the charts showed a river (the Swan) named Witsen River. The discarding of his name prompted caustic comments in a letter he sent to a friend:

> there has not been done very much because the commander, too much addicted to drink, has indeed surveyed the coasts, but on land not visited much, nowhere stayed longer than three days, is against the instructions which I myself wrote and I ordered him to stay in each place for a long time. But he used too much of his time at the Cape with feasts and frolics, which grieves me, many of the people who made the voyage are already here but the skipper is expected this autumn.

Not surprisingly, de Vlamingh was not heard of again. Gerrit Collaert, skipper of the *Nijptangh*, finished up a rear admiral.

In 1974, on the 277th anniversary of the landing, a memorial was dedicated at South Cottesloe. It consists of four rectangular sculptured concrete shelters positioned closely to the points of the compass.

Red Bluff is a steep bluff, south of the resort town of Kalbarri and the Murchison River. It is about 600 kilometres north of Perth. De Vlamingh's chart reads: *Rode en Zeer kenbare hock* (red very notable corner). He saw it on 17 February.

1699

William Dampier, explorer, of the *Roebuck*

Shark Bay is a deep inlet 90 kilometres wide and receding 190 kilometres embracing the towns of Carnarvon, Shark Bay and Denman, about 800 kilometres north of Perth. Peron Peninsula divides it into branches, Hamelin Pool and Freycinet Estuary. It is protected on the north-west by Bernire and Dorre Islands, Dirk Hartog Island and a peninsula known as Edel Land, another survivor from VOC naming.

Dampier named the bay on 6 August:

> The Sea-fish that we saw here (for here was no River, Land or Pond of fresh Water to be seen) are chiefly Sharks. There are abundance of them in this particular Sound, and I therefore give it the Name of Shark's Bay...Of the sharks we caught a great many, which our men eat very savourily. Among them we caught one which was 11 Foot long...Its maw was like a leather Sack, very thick, and so tough that a sharp Knife could scarce cut it: In which we found the Head and Boans of a Hippopotomus; the hairy Lips of which were still sound and not putrified, and the Jaw was also firm, out of which we plucked a great many teeth.

(The shark had probably taken a dugong.) Dampier stayed at Shark Bay a week. Once a whaling and pearling base, it is now a tourist resort, has solar salt and gypsum industries and sheep stations.

Rosemary Island is 20 kilometres offshore in the Dampier Archipelago, north-western coast. This is evidently the only other place name Dampier bestowed. He did so on 22 August: 'I presently went ashore, and carried Shovels to dig for Water, but found none. There grow here 2 or 3 Sorts of Shrubs, one just like Rosemary; and therefore I call'd this Rosemary Island. It grew in great Plenty here, but had no Smell.'

The present Rosemary Island, which is not that originally named by Dampier, has a lighthouse. It is considered he gave the name to Lewis Island or another nearby.

Dampier is commemorated with a granite representation of a sea chest at Bedford Park, Broome, north-west coast, overlooking Roebuck Bay. This was provided by the Commonwealth government and the Western Australian Historical Society. The late John Masefield, Poet Laureate and an authority on Dampier, composed an oration for the society for the dedication of the memorial in 1938, Australia's sesquicentenary year. It included this couplet:

> We little guess which deed a future year
> May mark to mortals from our passing here.

1756

Stuurman (first mate) Lavienne Judowijk van Asschen, explorer, of the *Buijs* (a type of vessel)

Batavia River, the scene of Jansz's landing in 1606 at Port Musgrave, receives three rivers. Carstensz named the estuary Carpentier River and van Asschen named it Batavia. Jansz's boat went into the estuaries of the Ducie and Dulhunty rivers. The name Batavia was changed in 1939 to Wenlock to obviate confusion with an air strip there with Batavia, then the capital of Java.

1770

Victoria

James Cook, in the *Endeavour*

20 APRIL 1770

Point Hicks is a low granite promontory in East Gippsland, 60 kilometres from where the coast turns north. As first seen at 6 a.m. from a distance of 16 kilometres, it was merely a rise in the coastline where it dropped below the horizon to the westward. 'The Southernmost Point of land we had in sight...I have named...*Point Hicks* because Lieut. Hicks was the first who discover'd this land.'

There have been doubts about Cook's landfall. In 1843 an hydrographic surveyor renamed Point Hicks Cape Everard for Sir Everard Home who was then admiral on the Australian station. The name Point Hicks was given to Point Hicks Hill, 8 kilometres to the westward, because some authorities believed it was the land Cook first saw.

At a symposium on East Gippsland conducted by the Royal Society of Victoria in 1969, N.A. Wakefield quoted T.W. Fowler's conclusion that the position of Point Hicks in Cook's chart 'is in 50 fathoms of water and over 12 nautical miles from the nearest shore...The observation was faulty, the compass was in error or a bank of clouds was mistaken for land.' He shows the position on the chart as 19 kilometres westward of what is now accepted as Point Hicks.

In 1926 the Commonwealth Department of Navigation put an obelisk at Cape Everard with this inscription:

Lieutenant James Cook, R.N
of the Endeavour
First sighted Australia near the Point
which he named
Point Hicks
After Lieutenant Zachary Hicks
who first saw the Land
April 19 (Ship's Log Date)
April 20 (Calendar Date)
1770

On the 200th anniversary of the sighting, the government of Victoria restored the name Point Everard as a result of several committees' investigations. It declared the locality Captain James Cook National Park within Croajingalong National Park and commemorated it with a plaque.

Ram Head is 16 kilometres eastward of Point Hicks, where the coast begins to trend northward. It is in Croajingalong National Park. '[A] remarkable Point. [It] rises to a round hillick very much like the *Ram head* going into Plymouth Sound on which account I called it by the same name.' The name derives from an old high German word, *rama*, a post frame or barrier.

New South Wales

21 APRIL 1770

Cape Howe is a low point on the border of New South Wales and Victoria where the east coast begins. 'The Northernmost land in sight...[was] a small island [Gabo Island] lying close to a point...I have named *Cape Howe*.' Admiral Earl Howe was a Lord Commissioner of the Admiralty in 1768.

22 APRIL 1770

Mount Dromedary; **Cape Dromedary**. Mount Dromedary is 11 kilometres inland, near Tilba Tilba: 'we were a breast of a pretty high mountain laying near the shore which on account of its figure I named *Mount Dromedary*. The shore under the foot of this Mountain forms a point which I have named *Cape Dromedary*.'

Batemans Bay is 7 kilometres between heads and recedes as far. It is at the mouth of the Clyde River and is a resort for Canberra, 120 kilometres inland. 'An open Bay wherein lay three or 4 small Islands...seem'd to be but very little shelterd from the sea winds and yet it is the only likely anchoring place I have yet seen upon the Coast.' The bay was named on the chart for Captain Nathaniel Bateman, of the *Northumberland*, of which Cook was previously the master.

23 APRIL

Point Upright is the termination of a ridge of hills between Batemans Bay and Ulladulla: 'we were abreast of a Point of land which on account of its perpendicular clifts I call'd *Point Upright*.'

Pigeon House is 19 kilometres west of Ulladulla. 'A remarkable peaked hill laying inland the top of which look'd like a *Pigeon house* and occasioned my giving it that name.'

In this locality Cook wished to shelter behind an island about 200 metres offshore (Brush Island) but:

> we had a large hollow Sea from the SE rowling in upon the land which beat everywhere very high upon the Shore and this we have had ever sence we came upon the Coast...inland between Mount Dromedary and the Pigeon house are several pretty high Mountains [Budawang Range].

Cook drew a profile of the locality and drew the shape of the Pigeon House on the chart. A plaque was placed on the lookout there during the Bicentenary.

25 APRIL

Cape St George, the southern extremity of Jervis Bay, 140 kilometres south of Sydney. 'A point of land...I named *Cape St George* we having discover'd

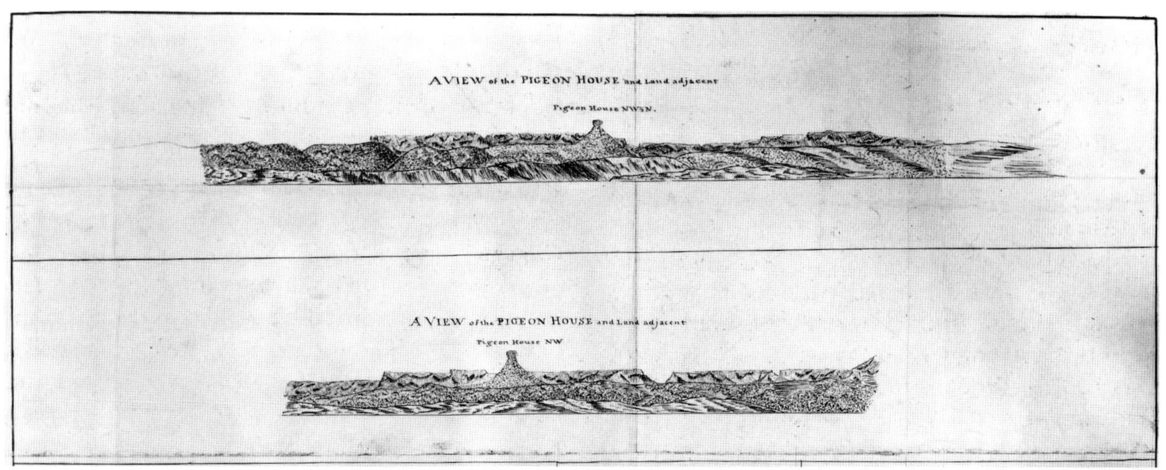

'A view of the Pigeon House and land adjacent', drawn by Cook, who sighted this landmark west of Ulladulla, New South Wales, on 27 April 1770. (British Library, London.)

it on that day. [He was writing of a day before the calendar.]' A total of 74 square kilometres of the locality is Commonwealth territory. This good harbour is now the Royal Australian Navy's principal base.

26 APRIL

Long Nose Point is the northern head of Jervis Bay.

> About 2 Leagues to the Northward of Cape St George the Shore seems to form a bay [Jervis Bay] which appeard to be shelterd from the NE winds but as we had the wind it was not in my power to look into it and the appearance was not favourable enough to induce me to lose time beating up to it. The north point of this bay on account of its figure I named *Long Nose.*

Red Point is composed of two hillocks, the higher one being known as Hill 60. It shelters the harbour of the iron and steel centre of Port Kembla. '8 Leagues to the northward of this [Long Nose Point] is a point which I called *Red point,* some of the land about it appeared of that colour...A little way in land to the NW of this point is a round hill the top of which look'd like the Crown of a hatt [Mt Kembla].'

30 APRIL

Botany Bay was Cook's first landing place on the continent, and the anchorage of the First Fleet before it sailed 16 kilometres up the coast to make a settlement at Sydney Cove, Port Jackson. It is now a region of metropolitan Sydney and a major port.

> At day light [29 April] in the morning we discoverd a Bay which appeard to be tollerably well shelterd from all winds into which I resolved to go with the Ship and with this view sent the Master with the Pinnace to sound the entrance while we kept turning with the ship haveing the wind right out...[April 30]. In the PM wind southerly and clear weather with which we stood into the bay and Anchor'd under the south shore about 2 Mile within the entrence in 6 fathoms water.

Cook's private log reads: 'At 3 p.m. anchor'd in 7 fathoms of water in a place which I called Sting-Ray Harbour'. His journal entry for 7 May reads: 'In the evening the Yawl return'd from fishing having caught two Sting rays weighing near 600 pounds. The great quantity of New Plants Mr Banks and Dr Solander collected in this place occasioned my giving it the name of *Botany Bay.*' He did not change the name Sting-Ray Harbour in his log; and while the change to Botany Bay in the journal was not contemporary, it had been made by 23 August, when Cook wrote his general description of New South Wales.

Cook wrote in his journal for 2 May: 'Last night Forby Sutherland seaman departed this life and in the AM his body was buried a shore at the watering place which occasioned my calling the south [inner] point of this Bay after his name'.

In his chart Cook named the north head of the bay Cape Banks and the outer southern head Point Solander (now Cape Solander).

The locality of the landing is now a reserve, Captain Cook's Landing Place Historic Site (324 ha). Its name, Kurnell, is either a corruption of an Aboriginal word *kundle* or *kundull* (wild carrot) or of the name of a land owner, Connell. There is a museum and several sites are distinguished: the *Endeavour*'s source of water; a monument to Cook at the landing place; a plaque on a rock from which Midshipman Isaac Smith, a cousin of Mrs Cook, was reportedly first ashore. (A family tradition was that Cook said: 'Isaac, you shall land first'.) There is also a memorial to Banks; a monument to Solander erected by Swedes in Australia; and a tablet which the Philosophical Society of Australasia (a forerunner of the Royal Society of New South Wales) placed at what is known as Inscription Point in 1822 for Cook and Banks as the 'Columbus and Maecenas [a Roman statesman and patron of literature] of their time'. It was the first memorial to them and is 7.5 metres above sea level opposite the spot where it was believed Cook first cast anchor.

In 1970 Queen Elizabeth II attended a re-enactment of the landing. The Commonwealth government's commemoration of the bicentenary included a water jet in Lake Burley Griffin; the addition of a plaque to the statue of Cook at Whitby, Yorkshire; the minting of a 50-cent coin, and the issuing of a series of six Australian and two Norfolk Island stamps.

Cook's favourable description of the harbour at

William Ellis, 'View of Adventure Bay, Van Diemen's Land, New Holland, 1777'. Watercolour and ink. The *Resolution* and *Discovery* are at anchor in the bay. (National Library of Australia.)

William Ellis, 'View of the Fluted Cape, Van Diemen's Land, New Holland, 1777'. (La Trobe Collection, State Library of Victoria.)

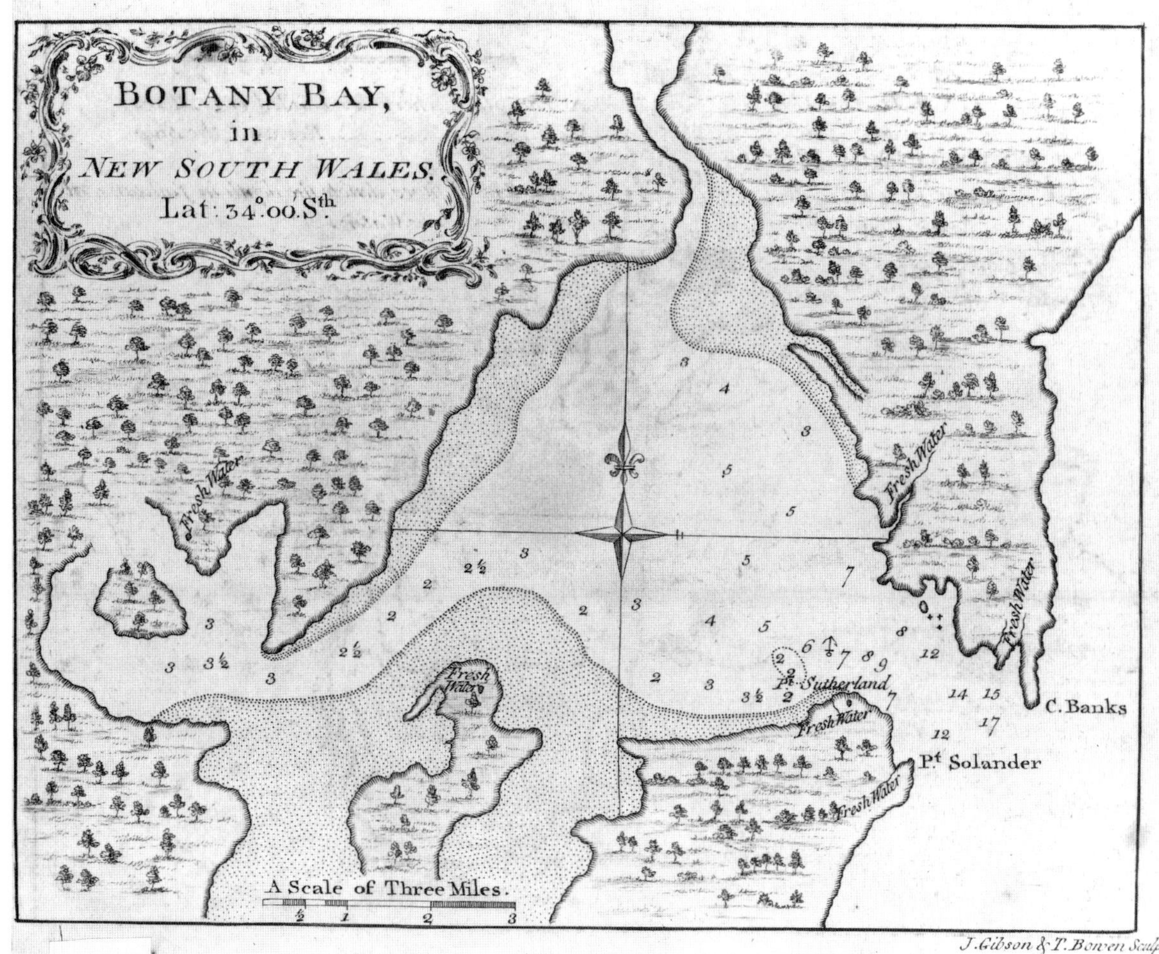

'A Sketch of Botany Bay in New South Wales'. A plan of the entrance of Endeavour River, New South Wales. Latitude 15. 26 South. This detailed plan shows where stores were landed, the *Endeavour* repaired, and where fish were caught. This place is now Cooktown, on the Endeavour River, Queensland. (*Historical Records of NSW.* Cook 1762–80. Facsimiles of Charts, 1893.)

Top left: Oswald L. Brett, 'Heemskerck Shoals — Nanuku Reef, N.E. Fiji, 6 February 1643'. Oil on canvas, 1973. Tasman's ships, the *Heemskerck* and *Zeehaen*, sailed from Van Diemen's Land for Batavia, finding their way through these dangerous reefs near Fiji. (Courtesy of Mrs Douglass C. Fonda, Jnr.)

Bottom left: Oswald L. Brett, 'HM Bark *Endeavour*, Lieut. James Cook, R. N. off Mount Warning, 16 May 1770'. From sketches made on the spot at sea. Oil on canvas, 1993. (Courtesy of Arthur Weller, CBE, Chairman of the HM Bark *Endeavour* Foundation.)

Botany Bay undoubtedly influenced the British government's choice of it for a settlement. On the day he sailed he wrote in his journal:

> It is Capacious safe and commodious, it may be known by the land on the Sea-coast which is of a pretty even and moderate height, rather higher than it is farther inland with steep rocky clifts next the Sea and looks like a long Island lying close under the Shore: the entrance of the harbour lies about the Middle of this land, in coming from the Southward it is discovrd before you are abreast of it which you cannot do in

coming from the northward; the entrance is little more than a Mile broad and lies in WNW. To sail into it keep the south shore on board untill within a small bare Island [Bare Island] which lies under the north shore, being within that Island the deepest Water is on that side, 7, 6 and five fathom a good way up. There is shoal'd water a good way off from the South Shore from the inner south point quite to the head of the harbour, but over towards north and NW shore is a channell of 12 or 14 feet water at low water 3 or 4 leagues up to a place where there is 3 & 4 fm but here I found very little fresh water. We anchord near the south shore about a Mile within the Entrance for the conveniency of sailing with a Southerly wind and the geting of fresh water but I afterwards found a very fine stream of fresh water on the north shore in the first sandy cove within the Island before which a Ship might lay almost land lock'd and wood for fual may be got every where.

Portrayed here after he became an admiral, Isaac Smith was only sixteen when he joined the *Endeavour* as a midshipman. Smith, Mrs Cook's cousin, was reportedly the first to leap ashore at Botany Bay. (Dixson Library, State Library of New South Wales.)

His parting words were: 'During our stay in this Harbour I caused the English Colours to be display'd ashore every day and an inscription to be cut out upon one of the trees near the watering place seting forth the Ships names, date, &c.' (The 'colours' was the red ensign, the flag of exploring and merchant ships in the eighteenth century. The Union Jack in it had the crosses of St George [England] and St Andrew [Scotland]. The cross of St Patrick was included from 1801.)

7 MAY

Port Jackson, the harbour about which Sydney now rises. The chart showed what could be seen between South Head and North Head. The main arm is hidden from the sea. '[A]t Noon we were...about 2 or 3 Miles from the land and abreast of a Bay or Harbour wherein there apperd to be safe anchorage, which I call'd *Port Jackson*.' Jackson (later Sir George) was one of the Lord Commissioners of the Admiralty, and judge advocate of the fleet. Cook had been a stable boy for his sister.

8 MAY

Broken Bay, 40 kilometres north of Port Jackson, is 8 kilometres between heads. The Hawkesbury River flows into it. 'At sunset...some broken land that appear'd to form a Bay...I named [it] *Broken Bay*.'

Actually, Cook saw Narrabeen Lagoon, 11 kilometres from Port Jackson.

Cape Three Points is the northern headland of Broken Bay. 'Some pritty high land which projected out in three bluff points and occasioned my calling it *Cape Three Points*.'

On 11 May Cook noted 'A small round rock or Island' but did not give it a name.

12 MAY

Point Stephens is 40 kilometres north of the present Newcastle. The point is a rock promontory, 3 kilometres southward of the port, which is a kilometre between heads and recedes westward for 17 kilometres.

At 4 PM past at the distance of 1 Mile a low rocky point which I named *Point Stephens* on the north side of this point is an inlet which I call'd *Port Stephens* that appear'd to me from the mast head to be shelterd from all winds. At the entrance lay 3 small Islands [Cabbage, Boondelbah and Little Islands], two of which are of tolerable height and on the Main near the shore are some round hills that make at a distance like Islands, in passing this bay at the distance of 2 or 3 Miles from the shore our soundings were from 33 to 27 fathoms from which I conjector'd that there must be a sufficient depth of water for shipping in the Bay.

Philip Stephens (later Sir Philip) was one of the secretaries of the Admiralty. The first choice for these names was Point Keppel and Keppel Bay.

Black Head is 11 kilometres from Port Stephens. Broughton Island, 1.5 kilometres offshore, was passed in the dusk and, not being distinguishable from the mainland, Cook gave this name to the island's outer point.

Cape Hawke, at Forester: 'we were abreast of a high point of land which made in two hillocks, this point I call'd *Cape Hawke*.' Admiral Sir Edward Hawke was First Lord of the Admiralty. It was first called Cape Morton.

13 MAY

The Three Brothers, 4–13 kilometres inland from Laurieton. 'At sun set...we had in sight...three remarkable large high hills lying contiguous to each other and not far from the shore...As these hills bore some resemblance to each other we call'd them the *Three Brothers*.'

They are now named South Brother, Middle Brother and North Brother.

14 MAY

Smoky Cape, at South West Rocks: 'a point or headland, on which were fires that caused a great quantity of smook...occasioned my giving it the name of *Smooky Cape*'.

16 MAY

Solitary Islands are clusters of scattered islets and rocks 6–9 kilometres offshore, lying between 8 and 43 kilometres northward of Smoky Cape. The editor of *Historical Records of New South Wales* noted: 'Cook does not appear to have seen the southernmost of the islands [Split Solitary]...The complete isolation of these islands, from one another as well as from mainland,was doubtless heightened by the fact that night was fast closing in when they were sighted.'

The one Cook saw was South Solitary Island north of Split Solitary.

Cape Byron, a steep headland at the town of Byron Bay, is the most easterly point on the continent. 'A tolerable high point of land...I named *Cape Byron*. It may be known by a remarkable sharp peaked Mountain lying inland [Mount Warning].' Captain John Byron was one of Cook's predecessors in the exploration of the Pacific. Cook drew a profile of the locality of Cape Byron and Mount Warning.

17 MAY

Mount Warning is a steep and isolated peak 30 kilometres inland and 14 kilometres from Murwillumbah. A well-known landmark by land and sea. 'We now saw the breakers again within us which we past at the distance of 1 League...there situation may always be found by the peaked mountain before mentioned...on this account I have named it *Mount Warning*.' Cook drew its shape on the chart.

Point Danger is the north head of the Tweed River at the boundary of New South Wales and Queensland. 'The point off which these shoals lay I have named *Point Danger*.'

Queensland

18 MAY 1770

Point Lookout is the rocky north-eastern point of North Stradbroke Island, 70 kilometres north of the border. 'The northernmost land...form'd a point which I nam'd *Point Lookout*.' A commemorative plaque was placed there in 1970.

Moreton Bay, formed by South and North Stradbroke Islands and Moreton Island, extends 110 kilometres from the Gold Coast to Caloundra Head, and recedes up to 30 kilometres. The city of Brisbane is on its shores and the Brisbane River flows into it.

'On the north side of this point [Point Lookout] the shore forms a wide open Bay which I have named *Morton bay*, in the bottom of which the land is so low that I could but just see it from the top mast head.' The Earl of Morton was president of the Royal Society which proposed the voyage. Hawkesworth's misspelling of Morton's name in his edition of the journal has been allowed to persist. Redcliffe, a resort town on the shores, has a stone from Whitby Abbey, Yorkshire, in a memorial erected in 1970.

Cape Moreton is the north-east point of an island and northern extremity of Moreton Bay.

> ...Northermost land seen last night...I named *C. Morton* it being the N Point of the Bay of the same name...some on board was of opinion that there is a River there because the Sea lookd paler than usual, upon sounding we found 34 fathom water a fine white sandy bottom, which a lone is sufficeint [to] change the apparant colour of sea water without the assistance of Rivers. The land need only to be as low as here as it is in a thousand other places on the coast to have made it impossible for us to see it at the distance we were off. Be this as it may, it was a point that could not be clear'd up as we had the wind, but should anyone be desirous of doing it that may come after me this place may always be found by three hills [Glass House Mountains] which lay to the northward of it.

Beaglehole comments: 'It [the river] flowed into the south end of the bay and was certainly invisible from Cook's position at sea; nor was it likely to change the colour of the water here.' The island is 38 kilometres long, up to 11 kilometres wide and covers 16 828 hectares. It has immense sandhills, one of 274 metres being claimed to be one of the highest permanent sandhills.

The Glass Houses, Glass House Bay: Eleven steep-sided mountains 72 kilometres north of Brisbane and 20 kilometres inland. The bay which lies under the mountains is no longer shown on charts.

> These hills lay but a little way inland and not far from each other; they are very remarkable on account of there singular form of elivation which very much resembles glass houses which occasioned my giving them that name the northernmost of the three is the highest and largest [Mount Beerwah 556 m]. There are likewise several other peaked hills inland to the northward of these but they are not near so remarkable.

Glass was made in glass houses in Cook's native Yorkshire. He sketched the shapes of these volcanic cones.

19 MAY

Double Island Point is steep and rocky, the south-eastern extremity of Wide Bay, 115 kilometres north of Moreton Bay. 'The land within this Point is of a moderate and pretty equal height but the Point it self is of such an unequal height that it looks like two small Islands laying under the land.'

Wide Bay extends 16 kilometres from Double Island Point to Fraser Island and recedes 6 kilometres. The Mary River flows through the industrial city of Maryborough to the bay.

> Here the land trends to the NW and forms a large open Bay...The land here abouts which is of a moderate height appears more barren than any we have yet seen on this coast and the soil more sandy, there being several large places where nothing else is to be seen; in other places the woods look to be low and shrubby.

The northern end of the bay is the beginning of Fraser or Great Sandy Island, the largest sand island (1590 square km) on the eastern Australian coast. It is 123 kilometres long, 23 kilometres at its widest, 240 metres at the highest point and is now in the register of Australia's National Estate. Great Sandy Strait, between the island and the mainland, is 64 kilometres long.

21 MAY

Indian Head is a steep bluff promontory on the east coast of Fraser Island, 32 kilometres from its northern extremity. 'We pass'd...a black bluf head or point of land on which a number of the natives were assembled which occasioned my nameing it *Indian Head*.'

Sandy Cape is a prominent headland at the northern extremity of Fraser Island. 'I have named it *Sandy Cape* on account of two very large white patches of Sand upon it. It is of a height to be seen 12 Leagues in clear weather.' Cook drew a profile of the locality.

22 MAY

Break Sea Spit: Shoals that extend 25 kilometres northward from Sandy Cape. 'This Shoal I called *Break Sea Spit*, because we now had smooth water whereas up the whole Coast to the Southrd we allways a high Sea or swell from the SE.'

Hervey Bay extends 60 kilometres from Burnett Heads to Fraser Island and recedes 50 kilometres to Pialba. The Burnett River has the port of Bundaberg, a sugar-growing district. Cook described 'the bottom of a deep bay' and named it after Augustus John Hervey, a Lord Commissioner of the Admiralty.

24 MAY

Bustard Bay is Cook's second landing place on the eastern coast and he stayed there for two days. It is 80 kilometres from Hervey Bay. The bay extends 16 kilometres from Round Head, where it recedes 5 kilometres to Bustard Head.

> [at] 5 oClock...we were abreast of the South point of a large open bay where in I intended to anchor...We landed a little within the South point of the Bay...Here is room for a few ships to lay very secure and a small Stream of fresh water...we saw...Bustards such as we have in England one of which we kill'd...which occasioned my giving the place the name of *Bustard Bay*.

The names North and South Head also appear on the chart but are now known as Round Head and Bustard Head. In 1846 Prime Minister W.E. Gladstone proposed to form a new colony. Bustard Bay, Hervey Bay and Port Curtis were explored as possible harbours. Port Curtis was chosen but Gladstone lost office and the project was abandoned. It later became the port of the industrial city of Gladstone.

A tourist centre at the bay was named Seventeen Seventy in 1936 to commemorate Cook's landing. A reserve of 71 hectares was dedicated in 1927 around a commemorative cairn placed in 1926 under the lee of the landing point at Round Hill. In 1970 a more impressive memorial was erected there as the 'birthplace of Queensland'. It is a portico in Classical style inscribed as 'Doorway to Destiny'.

26 MAY

Cape Capricorn, a narrow point, which appears white and barren, is on the tropic at the north east end of the large Curtis Island. 'I found this point to lay directly under the Tropick of *Capricorn* and for that reason call'd it by that Name.'

Cook was entering the tropical thirty-nine per cent of the continent and was now within the Barrier Reef.

28 MAY

Cape Manifold; **Keppel Bay**; **Keppel Islands**: The bay extends 50 kilometres northward from Cape Capricorn and recedes 2 kilometres. The Fitzroy River flows through the central Queensland city of Rockhampton, centre of a beef-producing region, into the bay. Great Keppel Island, the largest in the group, is 16 kilometres south-east of Yeppoon. Cape Manifold is 35 kilometres north of the islands. It is composed of a number of rocky heads, with small beaches between.

At Emu Park, 45 kilometres east of Rockhampton, a 'singing ship' which makes 'music' by wind moving through fluted tubes, overlooks Keppel Bay. It was installed in 1970 and a time capsule was buried to be opened in 2070.

'[T]he northermost point of land we had in sight...I named *Manyfold* from the number of high hills over it...Between them [and Cape Capricorn] the shore forms a large bay which I called *Keppel Bay* and the Islands which lay in off it are known by the same name.'

Augustus, Lord Keppel was a rear admiral, and later First Lord Commissioner of the Admiralty.

29 MAY

The Two Brothers are islands 13 kilometres off Cape Manifold. '[T]he land of this Cape [Manifold] is tolerable high and riseth directly from the Sea; it may be known by three Islands laying off it, one near the shore and the other two 8 Miles out at sea, the one of these is low and flat and the other high and round.'

The chart calls these islands 'the two brothers'. Flinders called them Flat and Peaked Islets, names which have now displaced Cook's.

Northumberland Islands. For the next six days the *Endeavour*'s track for 200 kilometres northward to Hayman Island was through a maze of these islands and the Cumberland Islands from 13 to 56 kilometres offshore. 'Islands...extend out to sea as far as we could see from the Mast head, how much farther will hardly be in my powers to determine, they are as varied both in their height and circuit as they are numerous.' They are named after the Duke of Northumberland, a friend of George III.

Cape Townshend, the northern extremity of Townshend Island, extends 13 kilometres and forms part of the eastern shore of Shoalwater Bay, 55 kilometres from Cape Manifold. '[W]e were abreast of [a] point which I named Cape Townshend; the land of this Cape is of a moderate and pretty even height.' Beaglehole suggests the Townshend honoured is Charles Townshend, who was a Lord Commissioner of the Admiralty, 1765–70. He was an uncle of Lord Sydney, who, as Home Secretary, initiated the settlement in New South Wales and for whom the city of Sydney is named.

Island Head; **Hervey Islands**. The head is 16 kilometres east of the southern extremity of Townshend Island and a sandy ridge connects it to the mainland. The two Hervey Islands (Harvy's Isles in the chart) are 5 kilometres to the east.

Shoalwater Bay extreme extends 40 kilometres north-westward from Townshend Island and recedes for 55 kilometres. '[T]he land...forms a bay in the bottom of which there appeared an inlet or Harbour.' It is so called on the chart from its shallowness.

30–31 MAY

Thirsty Sound, Long Island, 130 kilometres north of Rockhampton was Cook's third landing place. Thirsty Sound, 20 kilometres in extent, is formed by Quail Island, Long Island and other islands and Broad Sound. Cook, Banks and Solander were exploring for two days, mainly at Quail Island and the Bay of Inlets (see June 10). 'This Inlet...I have named *Thirsty Sound* by reason we could find no fresh water.'

In their journals, other officers refer to Labyrinth River and Labyrinth Harbour because of the great number of islands and rocks in the locality of Thirsty Sound.

1 JUNE

Pier Head is a barren round hill on a small island connected with the north-west point of Quail Island. 'The NW point of *Thirsty Sound*...I have named *Peir Head*.' Neither Cook nor his editors explain its meaning. Presumably, it resembled the end of a quay or wharf.

2 JUNE

Broad Sound is geographically similar to Shoalwater Bay, 50 kilometres to the south-east. It is 32 kilometres wide, and it recedes 50 kilometres. 'The western Inlet before mentioned known in the Chart by the name of *Broad Sound* we had now all open. It is at least 9 or 10 Leagues wide at the Entrance with several Islands laying in and before it.'

Cape Palmerston is a bluff, rocky headland, 80 kilometres from Thirsty Sound. 'A Point of Land which forms the NW entrance into Broad Sound...I have named *Cape Palmerston*.' Viscount Palmerston was a Lord Commissioner of the Admiralty.

Bay of Inlets spreads 95 kilometres so as to include Shoalwater Bay, Thirsty Sound and Broad Sound. It is no longer on charts. 'Between this Cape [Palmerston] and C. Townshend lies the *Bay of Inlets*, so named from the number of Inlets, Creeks &c in it.'

Slade Point is a hilly projection on the coast, just north of the city of Mackay, centre of a sugar growing district. Sir Thomas Slade was Surveyor of the Navy and builder of HMS *Victory*.

Cape Hillsborough is a conspicuous, bold headland 24 kilometres from Mackay. 'A pretty high Promontory...I named *Cape Hillsborough*.' Viscount Hillsborough was Secretary of State for the Colonies.

Cumberland Islands extend 95 kilometres north-westward from the north east of Slade Point and form the eastern side of Hillsborough Channel in the south and Whitsunday Passage in the north.

Most of the main islands are off Proserpine and include a number of National Parks and resorts.

> The islands which lay parallel with the Coast and from 5 to 8 or 9 Leagues off are of Various extent both for height and circuit; hardly any exceeds 5 Leagues in circuit and many again are very small, besides this chain of Islands which lay at a distance from the coast there are other small ones laying under the land.

Cook named the island group after the Duke of Cumberland, younger brother of George III.

Cape Conway is a hilly promontory at the southern entrance to Whitsunday Passage. 'This point I have named *Cape Conway* and the Bay Repulse Bay which is form'd by these Two Capes [Conway and Hillsborough].' General Henry Seymour Conway was a cabinet minister, later a field marshal.

Repulse Bay, 65 kilometres north-westward of Mackay, extends 18 kilometres to Cape Conway and recedes 20 kilometres. The editor of *Historical Records of New South Wales* suggests that Cook appears to have been looking for a place to careen the ship, but found this bay unsuitable.

Pentecost Island is 13 kilometres offshore in the Whitsunday Islands group. It resembles a tower and on the eastern side is almost perpendicular. 'Among the many Islands that lay upon this coast there is one more remarkable than the rest being of a small circuit very high and peaked.' Cook drew a profile of 'Pentecost Island at the Southern entrance of Whitsundays Passage'.

Whitsunday Island, the largest island (10 sq. km) among the Cumberland group, is 8 kilometres offshore. 'In the PM steer'd thro the passage [Whitsunday Passage] which we found from 3 to 6 to 7 Miles broad and 8 or 9 Leagues in length.'

Whitsunday Passage, between Cumberland Islands and the coast north of Cape Conway, is 40 kilometres long and a minimum width of 3 kilometres. 'This Passage I have named *Whitsunday's Passage*, as it was discoverd on the Day the Church commemorates that Festival.'

Cape Gloucester, the point of a steep, high island which is now Gloucester Island, a kilometre offshore. The name is now a point on the mainland behind the island. The Duke of Gloucester was a second younger brother of George III. 'A Lofty promontory...I named *Cape Gloucester*; it may be known by an Island [Holbourne Island] which lies out at Sea NBW½W 5 or 6 Leagues from it, this I calld *Holburn Isle*.'

Holbourne Island is 24 kilometres off Gloucester Head. Admiral Francis Holbourne was a Lord Commissioner of the Admiralty.

Edgcumbe Bay, 16 kilometres in length and breadth, contains Port Bowen, which serves the town of Bowen and the Bowen Coal basin. 'On the west side of the Cape [Gloucester] the land...forms a deep bay...without waiting to look into this Bay...I called *Edgcumbe Bay*.' Cook served in the North American fleet under Captain G. Edgcumbe, who later became Earl of Mount Edgcumbe.

6 JUNE

Cape Upstart, a promontory 95 kilometres from Townsville, is now a National Park. '[W]e were abreast of the western point of land (distant from it 3 Miles), which I have named *Cape Upstart* because being surrounded with low land, it starts or riseth singley at the first making of it...and is of a height sufficient to be seen 12 Leagues.' Cook drew its shape on the chart.

7 JUNE

Cape Bowling Green is a low sandy strip between Cape Upstart and Cape Cleveland. Cook gave no reason for the name, though the land is flat and must have been green.

Cleveland Bay contains the port of Townsville, the second city of Queensland and the continent's largest city in the tropics. The bay extends 22 kilometres from Cape Cleveland to Cape Pallarenda and recedes 11 kilometres. 'This bay which I named *Cleveland Bay* appear'd to be about 5 or 6 Miles in extent in every way.'

Cape Cleveland is a narrow hilly point. 'The East point [of the bay] I named *Cape Cleveland*.' The bay and cape were probably named after John Cleveland, a former secretary to the Admiralty.

Magnetic Island, 6 kilometres off Townsville, is now a holiday resort.

> I named [the west point of Cape Cleveland] *Magnetical head* or *Isle* as it had much the appearance of an Island and the Compass would not travis well when near it. They [the cape and the island] are both tolerable high and so is the Mainland within them and the whole appear'd to have the most ruged, rocky and barrenest Surface of any we have yet seen.

Cook first called the island Barren Head. Later navigators disproved this belief that it affected compasses. A commemorative plaque was placed there in 1970.

9 JUNE

Palm Islands are a group of 20 islands 50 kilometres from Townsville and 27 kilometres off Halifax Bay. They were Cook's fourth landing place.

> In the PM...we saw...as we thought Cocoanutt trees upon one of the Islands, and as a few of these nutts would have been very exceptable to us at this time I sent Lieut. Hicks a Shore with whome went Mr Banks and Dr Solander to see what was to be got...At 7 oClock they returnd on board, having met with nothing worth observing, the trees we saw were a small kind of Cabbage Palms; they heard some of the Natives...but saw none.

9 JUNE

Point Hillock, the eastern extremity of Hinchinbrook Island, is formed by a hilly islet. Cook thought it was part of the mainland. Hinchinbrook Island is between Townsville and Innisfail. It is 35 kilometres long, up to 24 kilometres broad, has peaks as high as 1113 metres and is the largest island National Park (35 350 ha). Hinchinbrook Channel is a spectacular passage for small ships.

'This point I have named *Point Hillick* on account of its figure. The land of this Point is tolerable high and may be known by a round hillick or rock that appears to be detached from the Point but I beleive it joins to it.'

Halifax Bay, south of Hinchinbrook Island, extends 75 kilometres from Cape Pallarenda and recedes 22 kilometres.

> Between this Cape [not named] and *Iron Head* [Cape Cleveland] the Shore forms a large Bay which I named [*Halifax Bay*] before it lay the group of Islands [Palm Islands]...and some others nearer the shore...[which] shelter the bay in a manner from all winds, in which is good anchorage.

This was the first of three place names named for the Montagu and Dunk families. (George Montagu Dunk was Earl of Halifax and Sandwich. He was a First Lord of the Admiralty and patron of Cook. His estate was Hinchinbrook but this name was not given until Philip Parker King discovered that it was an island in 1819.)

Cape Sandwich is the north-eastern extremity of Hinchinbrook Island. Two hills rise behind it.

Rockingham Bay extends 27 kilometres northward from Hinchinbrook Island and recedes 13 kilometres.

> From *Cape Sandwich* the Land...forms a fine large Bay which I call'd [*Rockingham Bay*]; it is well shelterd and affords good anchorage, at least so it appear'd to me, for having hitherto met with so little incouragement by going a shore that I would not wait to land or examine it further.

The Marquis of Rockingham was a former Prime Minister.

Family Islands are seven islets 12 kilometres off Tully Heads. '[We] continued rainging along shore to the northward for a parcel of small Islands laying off the northern point of the Bay.'

Dunk Island is a resort island 3 kilometres north of the Family Islands and as far offshore. 'This boundry of the bay [Rockingham] is form'd by a tolerable high Island known in the Chart by the name of *Dunk Isle*.' Author E.J. Banfield lived on the island and wrote about it for 26 years in the early part of this century. His best known book was *Confessions of a Beachcomber*.

Double Point is an isolated hill 25 kilometres north of Dunk Island. Cook named it on his chart, but not in his journal.

10 JUNE

Frankland Islands, 6 kilometres offshore and 32 kilometres south-east of the city of Cairns, are a port for primary exports and a tourist centre. '[W]e were abreast of some small Islands which we call'd *Frankland Isles.*' Sir Thomas Frankland was an admiral.

Fitzroy Island, 3 kilometres offshore and 10 kilometres south-east of Cape Grafton. '[T]his we afterwards found to be an Island tolerable high and about 4 Miles in circuit.' Cook named the island after Augustus Henry Fitzroy, Duke of Grafton, who was prime minister when the *Endeavour* departed England.

Cape Grafton is the point of a sterile rocky ridge at the eastern point of Mission Bay. It appears as three lofty islands. 'The point of land we were now abreast off I call'd *Cape Grafton.*' It was named after the Duke of Grafton.

11 JUNE

Mission Bay is a small shallow bay, 8 kilometres long that recedes 3 kilometres. It was Cook's fifth landing place.

> ...to the Westward of the Cape [Grafton] is a Bay wherein we anchord about 2 Miles from the shore...I went ashore accompaned by Mr Banks and Dr Solander, the first thing I did was to look for fresh water...I found two small streames, which were difficult to get at on account of the surff and rocks upon the shore. We...met with nothing remarkable. My intention was to have stay'd here at least one day to have looked into the Country had we met with fresh water convenient, or any other refreshment.

Cook entered the landing in the log. He did not name the bay, which took its name from an Aboriginal mission, Yarrabah, later established there.

Green Island is a coral cay of 3000 hectares off Grafton and is now a resort. 'This island lies...3 or 4 Legs from *Cape Grafton,* and is known in the Chart by the name *Green Island.*'

Trinity Bay extends 19 kilometres northward from Port Douglas and recedes 6 kilometres. 'The Shore between *Cape Grafton* and the above northern point [Cape Tribulation] forms a large but not very deep Bay which I named *Trinity Bay* after the day on which it was discoverd.'

Cape Tribulation is a grassy hill jutting out from a bold headland and is step-to, 85 kilometres from Cairns. 'I named...the north point *Cape Tribulation* because here began all our troubles.'

Cook gave it the name after the *Endeavour* struck a reef the next day.

12 JUNE

Endeavour Reef is 7 kilometres east and west and 1.5 kilometres broad, 110 kilometres from Cairns, 30 kilometres from Cape Tribulation and 40 kilometres from Endeavour River, Cooktown. It is not named on the chart. On a supplementary chart of the coast from Cape Tribulation to Endeavour Strait at Torres Straits, the reef is marked 'On these Rocks the Ship lay 23 hours'.

In this as well as the whole coast's chart the Cape Tribulation–Endeavour Strait section is marked 'The Labyrinth', an expression of the problems the Barrier Reef caused. In the margin of a copy of Cook's journal the reef is named 'Endeavour Rocks'. It is now Endeavour Reef. The *Endeavour* struck the reef in the night. Coral penetrated four planks and damaged three, causing a leak in the ship's bottom in front of the foremast on the starboard side.

14 JUNE

Hope Islands are two sandy cays 7 kilometres offshore and 8 kilometres from Endeavour Reef. Two days earlier Cook had noted 'two low woody Islands which some took to be rocks above water'.

> we now thought of nothing but...rainging along shore in search of a harbour where we could repair the damages we had susstained...we passed close without two small low Islands ...about 4 Leagues from the Main. I have named them *Hope Islands* because we were always in hopes of being able to reach these Islands.

Beaglehole points out that these islands were a poor hope, being bush-covered sand cays.

15 JUNE

Weary Bay is a shallow indentation extending over 10 kilometres, 19 kilometres WSW from Endeavour Reef. 'At 3 oClock [p.m.] [we] saw an opening that had the appearence of a harbour...the Boats ...found there was not sufficient depth of water for the Ship.'

This expressive name is on the chart. The pinnace was searching for a harbour farther up the coast.

Endeavour River enters the sea 38 kilometres north of Weary Bay. The supplementary chart reads 'Endeavour's River where we repaired the ship'. It was there 47 days from 18 June to 4 August. Cook learnt of the harbour five hours after finding Weary Bay. 'By this time it was almost sun set and seeing many shoals about us we anchord...At 8 oClock [p.m.] the Pinnance in which was one of the Mates return'd on board and reported that they had found a good harbour about 2 Leagues to leeward.' It was his sixth landing.

The next morning a strong wind caused Cook to anchor again. 'I went my self and buoy'd the Channel which I found very narrow [the entrance is half a mile wide] and the harbour much smaller than I had been told but very convenient for our purpose.'

Cook had to wait three more days to get into the harbour. 'we run the Ship a shore twice, the first time she went off without any trouble but the second time She stuck fast, but this was of no concequence any farther than giving us a little trouble and was no more than what I expected as we had the wind'.

Turtle Reef, 8 kilometres offshore. 'In the Evening the Master returnd having been seven Leagues out at sea...he touched upon one of the shoals the same as he was upon the first time he was out, here he saw a great number of turtles three of which he caught.'

The Master probably landed on the reef. As turtles were a source of fresh meat, several visits were made to the reef to take them. Cook marked Turtle Reef on the chart and later commented: 'Altho I speak of this as the Turtle Reef yet It is not to be doubted but that what there are Turtle upon the most of them as well as this one.'

5 AUGUST

Having got under sail again, Cook recorded his impressions of the harbour.

> I shall now give a short description of the harbour or River we have been in which I named after the Ship *Endeavour River* [the only river he named]. It is only a small bar Harbour or Creek which runs winding 3 or 4 Leagues in land, at the head of which is a small fresh water brook as I was told for I was not so high my self; but there is not water for shiping above a Mile within the bar, and this is on the north side where the bank is so steep for nearly a quarter of a mile that ships may lay a float at low water so near the shore as to reach it with a stage, and is extreemly convineint for heaving a ship down [the ship was actually on the south side of the river]; and this is all the River hath to recommend it, especially for large shipping ...Besides this part of the Coast is barricaded with shoals as to make the harbour more difficult of access.

Cook drew three profiles of the 'land about Endeavour River'. One 'was taken when the entrance bore WSW distant 1 Mile'. This shows 'Gores Mount', named for Lieut Gore, one of the crew. It is now known as Mount Cook. He also drew a plan of the entrance of Endeavour River.

Cape Bedford is a range of hills 5 kilometres long, 22 kilometres north of Endeavour River. '[T]he northernmost point of the Mainland we had in sight...I named *Cape Bedford*.' Making slow progress among shoals and with gales, the *Endeavour* had the Cape in view for a week.
The Duke of Bedford was First Lord of the Admiralty, 1774–78.

11 AUGUST

Three Islands are 13 kilometres north-east from Cape Bedford. '[A]fter standing in an hour we edg'd away for 3 small Islands Islands...3 Leagues from *Cape Bedford*, to these Islands the Master had been in the Pinnance when the Ship was in Port.'

The islands are a small cluster surrounded by a reef and they are on the chart. The Master made several searches for a passage out of the reef as far as 32 or more kilometres but it is not known whether he landed on these islands.

Cape Flattery is a bold, well-defined isolated range of hills 50 kilometres from Endeavour River. 'We now judged our selves to be clear of all danger having as we thought a clear open sea before us, but this we soon found otherwise and occasiond my calling the headland above mentioned *Cape Flattery.*'

12 AUGUST

Point Lookout, the eighth landing and second use of this place name, the first being at North Stradbroke Island, Moreton Bay. This point is a bare hill 16 kilometres from Cape Flattery.

> I landed and went upon the point which is pretty high, from which I had a view of the sea-Coast which trended away...8 or 10 Leagues which was as far as I could see, the weather not being very clear...the Point I am now upon...I have named *Point Lookout*...in the evening returnd on board where I came to a resolution to Visit one of the high Islands in the offing in my Boat, as they lay at least 5 Leagues out to sea and seem'd to be of such a hieght that from the top of one of them I hoped to see and find a Passage out to sea clear of the shoals.

Islands of Direction are 24 kilometres north-east of Cape Flattery: South Direction, North Direction and Lizard. After Cook found a passage through the reef from Lizard Island he wrote: 'the three high Islands...I have call'd the *Islands of direction* because by them a safe passage may be found, even by Strangers.'

13 AUGUST

Lizard Island, the ninth landing, is 4 kilometres long and broad. Its vegetation cover consists of grass, brush and trees. It is now a resort.

> I immediatly went upon the highest hill...where to my mortification I discoverd a Reef of Rocks laying about 2 or 3 Leagues without the Island, extending...farther than I could see on which the Sea broke very high. This however gave me great hopes that they were the outermost shoals, as I did not doubt but what should be able to get without them for there appear'd to be several breaks or Partitions in the reef and deep water between it and the Islands.

Cook and Banks spent a night on the island. 'The only Land-animals we saw here were Lizards and these seem'd to be pretty plenty which occasioned my nameing the Island *Lizard Island.*'

14 AUGUST

Eagle Island is 6 kilometres west of Lizard Island.

> After we got on board the Master informed me that he had been down to the Islands I had directed him to go to [to check the depth of water]...He found upon the Islands piles of Turtle shells and some fins that were so fresh that both he and the boats crew eat of them, this shew'd that the Natives must have been lately.

Cook did not give this name to the group.

15 AUGUST

Cook's Passage, 16 kilometres from Lizard Island — 'The Passage or Channel we came out by' — is 1.5 kilometres long and a kilometre broad, and is one of the best passages through the reef. Cook did not give the passage a name.

18 AUGUST

Providential Channel, about 400 metres wide with a rock in the middle, is 250 kilometres from Cook's Passage and is opposite Cape Weymouth. Cook had not charted all the coast between Point Lookout and Cape Weymouth. '[W]ith the help of our boats and a flood tide we soon enter'd the opening and was hurried through in a short time by a rappid tide like a Mill race...The opening we came in by...I have named *Providential Channel.*'

The *Australia Pilot* says the passage is so short that the transition from the heavy ocean seas to smooth water is almost instantaneous.

A twelfth landing was made here on reefs: 'I sent them all out in the morning to the reef to get such refreshments as they could find...the boats return'd from the reef with about 240 of the meat of Shell fish most of cockles.'

Cape Weymouth; **Weymouth Bay**. Providential Channel, opposite the cape, is 35 kilometres away on the outer edge of the reef. The cape is a square-shaped promontory with a double summit; the bay extends 25 kilometres and recedes 6 kilometres. 'On the Main land within us was a pretty high Promontory which I call'd *Cape Weymouth*, on the north side of the Cape is a Bay known by the same name.' Viscount Weymouth was one of the Secretaries of State, 1768–70.

19 AUGUST

'**Sandy Isle**'. Beaglehole points out that as the ship was passing so many 'low small Sandy Isles', this one is difficult to identify. '[W]e passt a low small Sandy Isle...Mr Banks landed upon it and shott several small birds, call'd Nodies.'

20 AUGUST

Forbes Islands are three rocky islets 32 kilometres north of Cape Weymouth. '[T]hese Islands, which are known in the Chart by the name *Forbes's Isles*, lay about 5 Leagues from the Main.' John Forbes was a Lord Commissioner of the Admiralty, 1756–63, and a Commissioner of Longitude, 1768.

Bolt Head is a cliffy inconspicuous point, 50 kilometres from Weymouth, 'a moderately high Point which we call'd *Bolt Head*'. There is a Bolt Head on the coast of Devon, England.

Cape Grenville, a peninsula connected to the mainland by a low sandy isthmus, is 27 kilometres from Bolt Head. 'The Main land within the above Islands [unidentified] forms a point which I call *Cape Granville* [as spelt in the chart].' George Grenville was Prime Minister, 1763–64.

Temple Bay extends 42 kilometres south and recedes 6 kilometres. 'Between this Cape [Grenville] and the Bolt head [south of the cape] is a Bay I named *Temple Bay*.' This was either named for Earl Temple, a brother of Grenville, or more likely for Henry Temple, Viscount Palmerston, a Lord Commissioner of the Admiralty, 1766–77.

Sir Charles Hardy's Island is in fact two islands 22 kilometres east of Cape Grenville. '9 Leagues from Cape Granville lay some tolerable high Islands which I call'd *Sr Charles Hardys Isles*.' Sir Charles Hardy became an admiral in 1770.

Cockburn Islands, 1.5 kilometres off Cape Grenville: 'those [islands] which lay off the Cape I named *Cockburns Isles*'.

The group is now called Home Islands and six of seven islands have names from the *Endeavour*'s complement — Orton (Richard, Cook's clerk), Hicks (Zachary, lieutenant), Perry (William, surgeon), Gore (John, lieutenant), Harvey (William Hicks' servant) and Clerke (Charles, Third Lieutenant). The name Cockburn Islands has been given to another group, which Cook noted but did not name, 13 kilometres north-east of Cape Grenville. They also have names from the *Endeavour* — Bootie (John, midshipman), Manley (Isaac George, midshipman), Magra Islet (James Magra, midshipman) and Buchan Rock (Alexander, artist).

21 AUGUST

Bird Island: three islands 22 kilometres north-west of Cape Grenville. 'On these Isles we saw a good many Birds which occasioned my calling them *Bird Isles*...soundings [which] are best seen upon the Chart as likewise the Islands shoals &c [farther north] which are too numerous to mention singly.'

Shelburne Bay is 16 kilometres north-west of Cape Grenville. It extends 24 kilometres and recedes 8 kilometres. Lord Shelburne was Secretary of State, 1766–68.

Orford Ness is a sandy projection, 48 kilometres north of Shelburne Bay. It was probably named for a resemblance to Orford Ness on the Suffolk coast, England.

22 AUGUST

Cape York is the northern extremity of the continent's east coast and the tip of a peninsula. The land in the immediate vicinity consists of low wooded hills, with small valleys and plains. 'The Point of the Main which forms one side of the Passage [Adolphus Channel] before mentioned and which is the Northern Promontary of this country I have Named in honour of His late Royal Highness the Duke of York.' The Duke of York was a brother of George III.

Adolphus Channel is 6 kilometres broad. It is between Albany and Mount Adolphus Islands and is the main passage into Torres Strait. In 1890 the steamer *Quetta*, bound for India from Brisbane, struck an uncharted rock 2.7 metres below the surface in the channel and sank with the loss of 133 out of a complement of 191.

Newcastle Bay is formed by the eastern coast of Cape York, and extends about 20 kilometres and recedes about 20 kilometres.

> The Shore forms a large open Bay which I call'd *New Castle Bay* wherein are some low Islands and shoals and all the land about it is very low flat and sandy. The Land of the northern part of the Cape is rather more hilly...and the Vallies appear'd to be tolerably well Cloathed with wood.

The Duke of Newcastle had been Lord Privy Seal, 1765–66.

York Island is 11 kilometres north-east of Cape York. 'These Islands [off Cape York] are known in the Chart by the Name of *York Isles*.'

They are now known collectively as the Mount Adolphus Islands, the highest being 147 metres. The name York is for one small and rocky island, a kilometre north of Cape York.

23 AUGUST

Possession Island, 11 kilometres west of Cape York, is the largest of the islands, 3 kilometres long and up to 1.3 kilometres wide at the entrance to Endeavour Strait. It is remarkable for the number of hummocks between which the land is low-wooded and covered with grass.

> ...we could see no land so that we were in great hopes that we had at last found a Passage to the Indian Seas, but in order to be better informd I landed with a party of Men accompan'd by Mr Banks and Dr Solander upon the Island. I went upon the highest hill which however was of no great height, yet not less than twice or thrice the height of the Ships Mast heads, but I could see from it no land...I...took posession of the whole Eastern Coast...by the name of *New South Wales*...about 10 oclock we got under sail...At noon *Posession Island* at the SE entrance of the Passage.

A memorial was placed there in 1925.

Cape Cornwall is the southern extremity of Prince of Wales island in Torres Strait, and the entrance of Prince of Wales channel. 'The SW point of the largest Island on the NW side of the Passage...I named *Cape Cornwell*.' The Prince of Wales, then aged eight years, bore the supplementary title of Duke of Cornwall.

Taking possession at Possession Island. An extract from Captain Cook's journal, Wednesday, 22 August 1770. (National Library of Australia.)

Wallis Islands, in Endeavour Strait, are 16 kilometres south-west of Cape Cornwall. '[S]ome Low Islands laying about the Middle of the Passage I called *Wallice's Isles.*'

Cook presumably named these islands after Captain Samuel Wallis, of the *Dolphin*, the circumnavigator who discovered Tahiti in 1767. The two islands are now known as Red Wallis and Woody Wallis.

24 AUGUST

Booby Island, at the western entrance to Torres Strait, is 19 kilometres from Prince of Wales Island and on the south side of Prince of Wales Channel. It was the fifteenth and last landing. 'Being now near the Island and having but little wind Mr Banks and I landed upon it and found it to be mostly a barren Rock frequented by Birds such as Boobies, a few of which we Shott and occasioned my giving it the Name of *Booby Island.*'

The birds were brown boobies. Satisfied he was through the channel, Cook set more sail but narrowly escaped running on a nearby reef.

Prince of Wales Island, the largest island in Torres Strait, is 17 kilometres long and 16 kilometres broad and 24 kilometres west of Cape York. It is south of the strait and Thursday Island and north of Endeavour Strait.

> The NE entrance of this Passage or Strait [Endeavour Strait]...is form'd by the Main or the Northern extremity of New-Holland on the SE and by a Congeries of Islands to the NW which I Named *Prince of Wales's Islands.* It is...very probable that among these Islands are as good if not better passages than the one we have come thro', although one need hardly wish for a better.

Endeavour Strait is Cook's last place name. It is the most southern of nine channels through Torres Strait from the Coral Sea to the Arafura Sea.

> This Passage, which I have named *Endeavour Straight* after the name of the Ship, is in length NE and SW 10 Leagues and about 5 Leagues broad, except at the NE entrance where it is only 2 Miles broad by reason of several small Islands which lay there, one of which call'd *Posession Island.*.With respect to the Shoals that lay upon this Coast I must observe for the benifit of those who may come after me, that I do not beleive the one 1/2 of them are laid down in my chart, for it would be obsurd to suppose that we could see or find them all, and the same thing may be in some measure be said of the Islands especially between the Latitude of 20° & 22° [Bowen and Thirsty Sound], where we saw Islands out at Sea as far as we could distinguish anything. However take the Chart in general and I beleive it will be found to contain as few errors as most Sea Charts which have not undergone a thorough correction.

Cook was two days in the 50 kilometres between Possession Island and Booby Island. Endeavour Strait is the most extensive of channels through Torres Strait but is difficult to make from the westward and is used only by small ships whose skippers have local knowledge. The most used channel for ships is the Prince of Wales channel, which is 50 kilometres long and from 1 to 4 kilometres broad.

[The Queensland Coast and Torres Strait Pilot Service commenced in 1884 and ceased operation on June 30 1993 when the licensing of Barrier Reef Pilots was transferred from the Queensland Government to the Federal Government's Australian Maritime Safety Authority (AMSA). Since that date two pilotage providers have operated in the area piloting over 2000 ships a year. Ships as large as 230 000 tonnes deadweight have been safely piloted from Booby Island 1600 kilometres to Point Danger on the Queensland-New South Wales border.]

1773–77

Captain Tobias Furneaux, of the *Adventure*, was with Cook in his second voyage and was in Tasmanian waters from 9 to 19 March 1773. By contrast with Cook, Furneaux in his journal gave few reasons for the fifteen place names which Lieutenant James Burney recorded on his chart.

9 MARCH 1773

South West Cape is remarkably bold, with a sharp and rugged outline. It is the western extremity of southern Tasmania. '[W]e saw the Land…moderately high, and uneaven near the Sea…a point much like the Ramhead off Plymouth.'

Mewstone is a lofty islet 30 kilometres from South Cape and the most southerly of the Maatsukyer group. 'The Land from this cape runs directly to the Eastward. About four Leagues alongshore are Three Islands about two miles long and several rocks resembling the Mewstone [at Plymouth] (particularly one which we so named).'

South East Cape is formed by three elevations on the eastern extremity of the coast.

Swilly Islands are another group of islands 30 kilometres south-east of South East Cape. Swilly Islands, near Portsmouth, were Furneaux's birth place. The islands are drawn but not named on the chart. Modern charts retain Tasman's name, Pedra Blanca.

10 MARCH 1773

Friar Rocks are half a mile south of Tasman Head.

> …wewere abreast of the westernmost point of a very deep Bay called by Tasman, Stormy bay. [Actually, he was sailing across the southern entrance to D'Entrecasteaux Channel. Storm Bay is farther north.] From the West to the East point of this bay there were several small Islands and black rocks which we called the Friars. [The Dominican friars wore black clothes.]

Fluted Cape is the southern extremity of Adventure Bay. Its cliffs are composed of basaltic columns. '[W]e hauled around a high bluff point, the Rocks whereof were like so many fluted pillars.' Fluted Head is on the chart.

11 MARCH 1773

Penguin Island is 1.5 kilometres north of Fluted Cape. '[W]e named Penguin Island from a curious one we caught there [the rockhopper penguin.]'

Adventure Bay is on the eastern side of South Bruny Island, 32 kilometres south-east from Hobart; it extends 11 kilometres northward and recedes 5 kilometres. It is on the chart. The *Adventure* remained there five days. Tasman tried to enter the bay in 1642 but was driven off by the wind. As well as landing at Adventure Bay and Penguin Island, the cutter landed on 10 March at an unidentified place in a search for a harbour or a bay.

Cape Frederick Henry is on the south eastern point of North Bay where Tasman anchored in 1642. Furneaux misplaced it at the northern point of Adventure Bay, and D'Entrecasteaux corrected its position.

17 MARCH 1773

St Patricks Head consists of several remarkable summits rising to 233 metres. It is 150 kilometres north of Adventure Bay and is on the chart. One of the crew, John Wilby, wrote in his journal: 'at noon gave name to a Bluff Point call'd it St Patricks Head in Honour to the Day, have a great number of his Country on Board'.

18 MARCH 1773

St Helen's Point is a narrow tongue of land with a continuous ridge of hills, which forms the south point of the Bay of Fires. It is 25 kilometres north of St Patrick's Head and is on the chart. No reason was given for the naming. It may have been for St Helens on the Isle of Wight, England.

Bay of Fires extends 30 kilometres and recedes 6 kilometres. 'At midnight saw many large fires along shore.' Furneaux had described the countryside as populous.

Eddystone Point, the north-eastern extremity of the Bay of Fires, is on the chart.

Cape Barren is a rounded rocky point, the eastern point of Barren Island, which is 32 kilometres north of the north-east tip of Tasmania. On his chart Burney noted: 'Barren and uninhabited'.

19 MARCH 1773

Bay of Shoals, on the eastern coast of Cape Barren Island, is on the chart but no longer on maps.

OCTOBER 1774

Norfolk Island is a volcanic island of 3455 hectares lying 1700 kilometres east-north-east of Sydney.

> At Day-break as we were standing to the West, an Island was discovered bearing SWBS...At Noon the isle extended from S 37°E to S 20°W. A Hill nearly in the middle of the Isle bore south 3 miles distant...I took posission of this Isle as I had done of all the others we had discovered, and named it *Norfolk Isle*, in honour of that noble family.

There were penal colonies on Norfolk Island from 1788–1814, and 1825–55. Descendants of the *Bounty* mutineers and the Polynesians who accompanied them were relocated there in 1856 from Pitcairn Island. It is now a dependency of the Commonwealth of Australia, and its main business is tourism.

1777 (exact date unknown)

Furneaux Group. Cook named the group of islands which Furneaux discovered and gave some names to. They consist of islands, rocks and shoals at the eastern end of Bass Strait and extend 100 kilometres south-south-east. Flinders Island, the largest, is 84 kilometres long and 28 kilometres broad. Other large islands are Cape Barren and Clarke. Activities of the inhabitants are stock raising, dairying, sheep farming and mutton-birding.

Sisters are two remarkable round hills. West Sister is 1.5 kilometres and East Sister 5 kilometres off the north-eastern point of Flinders Island. They are now called Inner and Outer Sisters.

Cook was in Tasmanian waters from 24 January to 10 February in 1777. He bestowed only two place names.

24 JANUARY 1777

Eddystone is 2 kilometres off Pedra Branca.

> About a league to the Eastward of Swilly [isle or rock] is another elevated rock that is not taken notice of by Captain Furneaux; I called it the Eddystone from its very great resemblance to that light house. Nature seems to have left these two rocks for the same purpose that the Eddystone light house was built by man, viz to give navigators notice of the dangers around them, for they are the elevated summits of a ledge of rocks under water on which the sea in many places breakes very high.

Tasman Head is high and abrupt and is composed of basaltic pillars. It is the southern extremity of South Bruny Island, 16 kilometres south of Adventure Bay, where Cook landed and remained six days:

> On the NE side of Storm bay [i.e. D'Entrecasteaux Channel], which lies between the SE Cape and Tasmans head, there are some Coves or Creeks that seemed to be sheltered from the sea winds, and I am of opinion that was this Coast examined, there would be found some good harbours.

Charles Clerke, commander of the *Discovery*, Cook's accompanying ship on his third voyage, was with Cook at Adventure Bay in 1777. He wrote in his journal:

> This Bay...is a prodigious fine, spacious place, having very good room for the Navy of England to moor about it...I know no place so compleatly furnish'd by Nature for the general general Supply of a Ship than this good Bay, and I believe there are few to be found so compleat.

References

Banks, J., *The Endeavour Journal of Joseph Banks*, 1768–1771, ed. J.C. Beaglehole. 2 vols, Trustees of the Public Library of New South Wales in association with Angus and Robertson, Sydney, 1962.

Bougainville, Louis de, *A Voyage Round the World*, trans. J.R. Forster. London, 1772.

Cook, J., *The Journals of Captain James Cook*, ed. J.C. Beaglehole. 4 vols, Hakluyt Society, Cambridge, 1955–67.

Dampier, W., *A New Voyage Round the World*, ed. A. Gray. Dover, New York, 1968.

Dampier, W., *The Voyages of Captain William Dampier*, ed. J. Masefield. 2 vols, E. Grant Richards, London, 1906.

Duyker, E., ed., *The Discovery of Tasmania.* St David's Park Publishing, Hobart, 1992.

Duyker, E., *An Officer of the Blue: Marc-Joseph Marion du Fresne, South Sea Explorer, 1724–1772.* Melbourne University Press, Melbourne, 1994.

Heeres, J.E., *The Part Borne by the Dutch in the Discovery of Australia, 1606–1765.* Amsterdam, 1897.

Linnaeus, C., *A Selection of the Correspondence of Linnaeus*, ed. J.E. Smith. London, 1821.

Major, R.H., ed., *Early Voyages to Terra Australis, now called Australia.* London, 1859.

Parkinson, S., *A Journal of a Voyage to the South Seas.* London, 1773.

Purry, J.P., *A Method for determining the Best Climate of the Earth.* London, 1744.

Schilder, G., ed., *Voyage to the Great South Land: Willem de Vlamingh, 1696–1697*, trans. C. de Heer. Royal Australian Historical Society in association with the Australian Bank, Sydney, 1985.

Sharp, A., *The Discovery of Australia.* Clarendon Press, Oxford, 1963.

Tasman, A.J., *The Voyages of Abel Janszoon Tasman*, ed. A. Sharp. Clarendon Press, Oxford, 1968.

Wharton, W.J.L., ed., *Captain Cook's Journal during his First Voyage Round the World.* London, 1893.

White, J., *Journal of a Voyage to New South Wales*, ed. A.H. Chisholm. Angus and Robertson in association with the Royal Australian Historical Society, Sydney, 1962.

Bibliography

Adams, B., *The Flowering of the Pacific: Being an account of Joseph Banks' travels in the South Seas and the story of his Florilegium.* Collins and British Museum (Natural History), London, 1986.

Beddie, M.K., *Bibliography of Captain James Cook, R.N., F.R.S., Circumnavigator.* Trustees of the Public Library of New South Wales, Sydney, 1970.

Carr, D.J., ed., *Sydney Parkinson, Artist of Cook's Endeavour Voyage.* British Museum (Natural History) in association with Australian National University Press, Canberra, 1983.

Carter, H. B., *Sir Joseph Banks, 1743-1820.* British Museum (Natural History), London, 1988.

Coote, C.H., ed., *Remarkable Maps.* Department of Printed Books, Geographical Section, British Museum, Frederick Muller, Amsterdam, 1895.

Clarke, J., *The Aboriginal People of Tasmania.* Tasmanian Museum and Art Gallery, Hobart, 1986.

Crozet, J., *Nouveau Voyage à la Mer du Sud.* ed. A. Rochon, Barrois, Paris, 1783.

Dalrymple, A., *An Historical Collection of the Several Voyages and Discoveries in the South Pacifick Ocean.* 2 vols. Nourse, London, 1770.

de Bruin, C., *Reizen over Moscovie door Persie en Indie*, Amsterdam, 1714.

Drake-Brockman, H., *Voyage to Disaster: the life of Francisco Pelsaert.* Angus and Robertson, Sydney, 1963.

Dunmore, J., *French Explorers in the Pacific.* 2 vols. Oxford University Press, London, 1965-1969.

Edwards, H., *Island of Angry Ghosts.* Angus and Robertson, Arkon edition, Sydney, 1979.

Eisler, W., and Smith, B., *Terra Australia—the Furthest Shore.* Art Gallery of New South Wales, Sydney, 1988.

Finney, C.M., *To Sail Beyond the Sunset—Natural History in Australia, 1699-1829.* Rigby, Adelaide, 1984.

Forsyth, W.D., *Captain Cook's Australian Landfalls: eye-witness accounts by members of the ship's company of H.M.S. Endeavour, 1770.* Canberra National Printers, Roebuck Society Publication No. 2. Canberra, 1970.

Fowler, R.M., *The Furneaux Group Bass Strait—A History.* Roebuck Society Publication No. 28, Canberra, 1980.

Godard, P., *The First and Last Voyage of the Batavia.* Abrolhos Publishing, Perth, 1993.

Government Publications and Maps, State Reference Library of Western Australia, *Terra Australia Percepta. The Discovery and settlement of Australia as seen through maps 1542 to 1900*, catalogue of exhibition at the Art Gallery of Western Australia, in association with the International Cartographic Association, Perth, August, 1984, I.C.A. Committee, 1984.

Heeres, J.E., *The Part Borne by the Dutch in the Discovery of Australia, 1606-1765*. Luzac, London, 1899.

Heeres, J.E., *Abel Janszoon Tasman's Journal*. Frederick Muller & Co., Amsterdam, 1898.

Henderson, J. A., *Phantoms of the Tryall—Australia's First Shipwreck—1622*. St. George Books, Perth, 1993.

Heuken, A.S.J., *Historical Sites of Jakarta*, Foundation Cipta Loka Caraka, Jakarta, 1982.

Hilder, B., *The Voyage of Torres*. University of Queensland Press, St Lucia, 1980.

Ingleton, Geoffrey C., illus., *The Explorations of Captain James Cook in the Pacific as told by selections of his own journals, 1768-1799*, ed. A. Grenfell Price.

Georgian House, Melbourne, by arrangement with the Heritage Press, New York, 1958.

Jack, R.L., *Northmost Australia: three centuries of exploration*, G. Robertson and Co., Melbourne, 1922.

Joppien, R. and Smith B., *The Art of Captain Cook's Voyages*. 4 vols. Volume One—*The Voyage of the Endeavour 1768-1771*, Volume Two—*The Voyage of the Resolution and Adventure 1772-1775*, Volume Three Text—*The Voyage of the Resolution and Discovery 1776-1780*, Volume Three Catalogue—*The Voyage of the Resolution and Discovery 1776-1780*. Oxford University Press in association with the Australian Academy of the Humanities, Melbourne, 1985, 1987.

Kunz, E. and E., *A Continent Takes Shape*. Collins, Sydney, 1971.

Lysaght, A.M., 'Banks' Artists and his Endeavour collections', in *Captain Cook and the South Pacific*, ed., T.C. Mitchell, Australian National University, Canberra, 1979.

Major, R.H., *Early Voyages to Terra Australis now called Australia... a collection of documents from the beginning of the sixteenth century to the time of Captain Cook*. Hakluyt Society, London, 1859.

Marchant, L., *France Australe*. Artlook Books, Perth, 1982.

Macknight, C.C., ed., *The farthest coast: a selection of writings relating to the history of the northern coast of Australia*. Melbourne University Press, Melbourne, 1969.

McBryde, I. 'The contribution to Australian ethno-graphy', in H.T. Fry, J.M. Thomson and I. McBryde, *The Significance of Cook's Endeavour Voyage: three bicentennial lectures*, James Cook University of North Queensland, Townsville, 1970.

Megaw, John V.S., ed., *Employ'd as a discoverer: papers presented at the Captain Cook bicentenary Symposium*, Sutherland Shire, 1–3 May, Sydney, 1970.

Nisbet, A., *French Navigators and the Discovery of Australia. Les navigateurs francais et la decouverte de l'Australie*. School of French, University of N.S.W. as part of 'Our French Connections', a project of the Education Department of Western Australia, Audio-Visual Branch, developed in conjunction with Centre d'Etudes et d'Echanges Francophones en Australie, Services Culturels Ambassade de France, 1985.

Pelsaert, F., *The Voyage of the Batavia*. Hordern House, Australian National Maritime Museum, Sydney, 1994.

Reader's Digest, Atlas of Australia. Reader's Digest, Sydney, 1977.

Reed A.W., *Place Names of Australia*. Reed, Wellington, 1979.

Rienits, R. & T., *Early Artists of Australia*, Angus and Robertson, 1963.

Roberts, W.C.H., *The Explorations 1696-1697 of Australia by Willem de Vlamingh*.

Original Dutch texts, edited with English translations. Philo Press, Amsterdam, 1972.

Robson, L. *A History of Tasmania—Van Diemen's Land from the Earliest Times to 1855*. Oxford University Press, 1983.

Schilder, G., *Australia Unveiled: The Share of the Dutch Navigators in the Discovery of Australia*, translated from the German by Olaf Richter, Theatrum Orbis Terrarum, Amsterdam, 1976.

Sigmond, J.P. and Zuiderbaan, L.H., *Dutch Discoveries of Australia—Shipwrecks, treasures and early voyages off the West Coast*. Rigby, Adelaide, 1979.

Smith, B., *European Vision and the South Pacific*. Harper and Row, Sydney, 1984.

Tasman, A.J., *The Discovery of Tasmania, 1642*. Extracts from the Journal of Extracts, from translation of the original manuscript in the Colonial Archives at the Hague by J.E. Heeres, and facsimiles of original maps, A.D. Caudell, Government Printer, Hobart, 1985.

Tasman, A.J., *Journal, 1642, with documents relating to his exploration of Australia in 1644*, ed. G.H. Kenihan, Heritage Press, Adelaide, 1964.

Weidenhofer, M., *Maria Island—A Tasmanian Eden*. Darlington Press, Melbourne, 1977.

Whitley, G. P., *Early History of Australian Zoology*. Published by the Royal Zoological Society of New South Wales to commemorate the Captain Cook Bicentenary, 1770–1970.

Williams, G. and Frost, A., *Terra Australis to Australia*. Oxford University Press in association with the Australian Academy of the Humanities, Melbourne, 1988.

Journals

Alexander, W.B., 'The History of Zoology in Western Australia, Part 1—Discoveries in the17th Century'. *Journal of the Naural History and Science Society of Western Australia*, vol. 5, 1914.

Alexander, W.B., 'The History of Zoology in Western Australia. Part 2: 1791–1829'. *Journal and Proceedings of the Royal Society of Western Australia*, vol. 1, 1915 pp. 83-142.

Beale, E. 'Cook: Landfall and the Next Eight Days'. *Journal of the Royal Australian Historical Society*, vol. 57, pt 4, Dec. 1971.

'Captain Cook Bicentenary Celebrations in Victoria in 1970'. Extract from the *Victorian Historical Magazine*, vol. 41, no. 2, May, 1970.

Drake-Brockman, H., 'The reports of Francisco Pelsaert'. *Journal and Proceedings of the Western Australian Historical Society*, , vol. 5 pt 2, 1956, pp. 1-18.

Dunbabin, T., 'France and Australia, the *prise de possession*'. originally written for the Hobart-Melbourne Meeting of the Australasian Association for the Advancement of Science, January 1921, read before the Royal Society of Tasmania, 8 August, 1921.

Edwards, P. I., 'Sir Joseph Banks and the botany of Captain Cook's three voyages of exploration'. *Pacific Studies*, vol. 2, no. 1, 1978, pp. 20–43, bibl.

Frost, A., 'New South Wales as *terra nullius*: the British Denial of Aboriginal Land Rights'. *Australian Historical Studies*. vol. 19, 1981, pp. 513–23.

George, A.S., 'The Plants seen and collected in North-Western Australia by William Dampier'. *Western Australian Naturalist*, Feb, 1971.

Gilbert, L. A., 'Plants, politics and personalities in Colonial New South Wales'. *Journal of the Royal Australian Historical Society*, vol. 56 pt.1, 1970, pp. 15–35.

Groves, E.W., 'Notes on the botanical specimens by Banks and Solander on Cook's first voyage, together with an itinerary of landing localities'. *Journal of the Society for the Bibliography of Natural History*, 4 (1), January, 1962.

Henn, P.U., 'French Exploration on the Western Australian Coast'. *Journal of the Western Australian Historical Society*, vol. II, pt XV, pp. 1-22, Perth, 1934

Howse, D., 'The principal scientific instruments taken on Captain Cook's voyages of exploration, 1768-80'. *Mariner's Mirror*, vol. 65 no. 2, May 1979, pp.119–135.

Hull, B.A.F., 'Birds of Lord Howe and Norfolk Islands'. Proceedings Linnean Society of NSW', 1910-11.

Loos, N.A., 'Aboriginal-Dutch relations in north Queensland 1606-1756'. *Queensland Heritage*, vol. 3, no. 1, Nov 1974.

Lysaght, A.M., 'Why did Sonnerat record the kookaburra?' *Emu*, vol. 56, pp. 224-25, August 1956.

Mault, A., Notes on the charts of the coast of Tasmania, obtained from the Hydrographical Department, Paris, and copies by permission of the French Government, in Papers and Proceedings of the Royal Society of Tasmania, 1889, pp. 107-120.

McGillivray, D.J., 'A checklist for the illustrations of the botany of Cook's first voyage'. *Contributions from NSW National Herbarium*, vol. 4, no. 3, 1970, pp. 112–25.

Meagher, S.J., The Food Resources of the Aborigines of the South-West of Western Australia, reprinted with original page numbers from the records of the Western Australian Museum, vol 3, pt 1, 1974.

Megaw, J.V.S., ed., 'Captain Cook and the Australian Aborigine'. *Australian Natural History*, vol. 16, no. 8, 1969.

Nelson, E. C., 'Australian plants cultivated in England before 1788'. *Telopea*, vol. 2, no. 4 1983, pp. 347-353.

Nelson, E.C., Botanical Exploration in Australia, 1606-1788. Food plants and antiscorbutics. Paper prepared for the Second International Conference on Indian Ocean Studies held in Perth, Western Australia, December, 1984.

Pen, L.J. and Green, J.W., 'Botanical exploration and vegetational changes on Rottnest Island'. *Journal of the Royal Society of Western Australia*, vol. 66, pts 1 and 2, 1983.

Plomley, N.J.B., Pre-settlement exploration of Tasmania and the natural sciences: the Clive Lord Memorial Lecture, 1983, from papers and proceedings of the Royal Society of Tasmania, vol. 118, 1984, pp. 69–78.

Powell, A., 'Culture contact and changes in land occupation on the Cobourg Peninsula', in A.J. Heatley and P. Loveday, eds, *Aborigines, land and mining: three historical essays*, Australian National University, North Australia Research Unit, Darwin, 1982.

Stearn, W.T., 'The botanical results of Captain Cook's three voyages and their later influence'. *Pacific Studies*, vol. 1, 1978, pp. 147–62.

Whitehead, P.J.P., 'Zoological Specimens from Captain Cook's Voyages'. *Journal of the Society for the Bibliography of Natural History*, vol. 5 no.3, 1969, pp. 161-201.

Williams, G., 'Far more happier than we: Europeans' reactions to the Australian Aborigines on Cook's voyage'. *Australian Historical Studies*, vol. 19, 1981, pp. 499–512.

Woolston, F.P., 'The Gogo-Yimidja people and the *Endeavour*'. *Queensland Heritage*, vol. 2, no. 2., 1970.

Manuscripts

Australia—Early Voyages (1696-1807). Copies of MSS in Service Hydrographique, Paris, relating to Australasia. (Mitchell Library, B1190).

Banks, Sir Joseph. A guide to his papers, in the National Library of Australia, MS9 etc.

Memoire sur l'etablissement d'une coloure dans la France australe, 1772. Copies of MSS. in Bibliotheque Nationale, Vol. 2. (Mitchell Library, B1192).

Plomley, N.J.B., French MS referring to Tasmanian Aborigines. (Queen Victoria Museum records, no. 23, 1966).

Saint Allouarn, François Alesne de Comte, Journal du voyage de la Flute du Roy, Le Gros Ventre, commandé par M. Le Comte de St. Allouarn, 1772, Y.J. de Kerguelen Tremarec, Voyage dans l'Inde et aux Terres Australes, 1771-2. vol. 2. (Mitchell Library, B1204).

Index

LUNA
MERCURIUS
VENUS
S E P
P L A N
QUATUOR ELEMENTAE
IGNIS
AER
AQUA
TERRA
ZONA FRIGIDA
ZONA TEMPERATA
ZONA TORRIDA
ZONA TEMPERATA
FRIGIDA ZONA
NOVA TOTIUS TERRARUM ORBIS GEOG
Ulterius Septentrionem versus America omninò est incognita sitne aqua vel terra hoc loco incertum est. plurimi tam ex rerum circumstantijs, conjectant Americam ab hac parte Septentrionali mari succinctam.
AMERICA
Anno Domini 1492 a Christophoro Columbo nomine Regis Castellæ primum detecta, et ab Americo Vespucio nomen sortita 1499.
AMERICA SEPTENTRIONALIS
NOVA FRANCIA
Ilhas de Ladrones
MAR DEL ZUR
Linea Aequinoctialis
Tropicus Cancri
Tropicus Capricorni
PACIFICUM MARE
Fretum Magelanicum
MA
TERRA AUSTRALIS
Cum ob terrestrem sphæram hoc modo in planum redactam situm pro pe polos animadvertere non possimus Borealiorum et Australiorem partem a quinquagesimo parallelo duobus circulis hic delineatis: conclusimus vale et fruere.
MURUS BABYLONIÆ
COLOSSUS
PYRAMIDES
MAUSO
S E P